21世纪内容语言融合（CLI）系列英语教材

Intercultural Communication
(Second Edition)

跨文化交际

（第2版）

常俊跃　吕春媚　赵永青　主编

北京大学出版社
PEKING UNIVERSITY PRESS

图书在版编目 (CIP) 数据

跨文化交际 / 常俊跃，吕春媚，赵永青主编 . —2 版 . —北京：北京大学出版社，2021.10
21 世纪内容语言融合（CLI）系列英语教材
ISBN 978-7-301-32601-5

Ⅰ. ①跨… Ⅱ. ①常… ②吕… ③赵… Ⅲ. ①英语 – 阅读教学 – 高等学校 – 教材②文化交流 Ⅳ. ① H319.37 ② G115

中国版本图书馆 CIP 数据核字 (2021) 第 202410 号

书　　名	跨文化交际（第2版） KUAWENHUA JIAOJI（DI-ER BAN）
著作责任者	常俊跃　吕春媚　赵永青　主编
责任编辑	刘文静　吴宇森
标准书号	ISBN 978-7-301-32601-5
出版发行	北京大学出版社
地　　址	北京市海淀区成府路 205 号　100871
网　　址	http://www.pup.cn　　新浪微博：@ 北京大学出版社
电子邮箱	编辑部　pupwaiwen@pup.cn　　总编室　zpup@pup.cn
电　　话	邮购部 010-62752015　发行部 010-62750672　编辑部 010-62759634
印 刷 者	北京圣夫亚美印刷有限公司
经 销 者	新华书店
	787 毫米 ×1092 毫米　16 开本　13 印张　324 千字 2011 年 9 月第 1 版 2021 年 10 月第 2 版　2025 年 1 月第 6 次印刷
定　　价	49.00 元

未经许可，不得以任何方式复制或抄袭本书之部分或全部内容。
版权所有，侵权必究
举报电话：010-62752024　电子信箱：fd@pup.pku.edu.cn
图书如有印装质量问题，请与出版部联系，电话：010-62756370

第 2 版前言

长期以来,"以语言技能训练为导向"(Skill-Oriented Instruction,SOI)的教学理念主导了我国高校外语专业教育,即通过开设语音、语法、基础外语、高级外语、听力、口语、阅读、写作、翻译等语言课程开展语言教学,帮助学生提高语言技能。该理念对强化学生的语言技能具有一定的积极作用,但也导致了学生知识面偏窄、思辨能力偏弱、综合素质偏低等问题。

为了探寻我国外语专业教育的新道路,大连外国语大学英语专业教研团队在北美内容依托教学理念(Content-Based Instruction,CBI)的启发下,于 2006 年开展了校级和省级"内容本位教学"改革项目,还于 2007 年、2012 年和 2017 年开展了 3 次国家社会科学基金项目推进课程体系改革,为推出内容语言融合教育理念(Content and Language Integration,CLI)奠定了实践基础。

CLI 批判性地吸收了国外 CBI、内容语言融合学习(Content and Language Integrated Learning,CLIL)、以英语为媒介的教学(English as a Medium of Instruction,EMI)、沉浸式教学(Immersion)等理念关注内容的优点,以我国外语教学背景下十几年的课程改革实践为依托,提出了具有中国特色的内容语言融合教育理念,将目标语用于内容和语言的教与学,培养学生的多种能力和综合素质。其特点如下:

1. **教育目标**　有别于诸多外语教学理念,CLI 不局限于语言,而是包含知识、能力和素质培养三个方面的目标。知识目标包含专业知识、相关专业知识、跨学科知识;能力目标包含语言能力、认知能力、交际能力、思辨能力等;素质目标包含人生观、价值观、世界观、人文修养、国际视野、中国情怀、责任感、团队意识等。

2. **教学特点**　有别于单纯训练语言的教学,CLI 主要特点体现在:语言训练依托内容,内容教学依靠语言;语言内容融合教学,二者不再人为割裂。

3. **师生角色**　有别于传统教学和学生中心理念对师生角色的期待,CLI 是在充分发挥教师主导作用的同时发挥学生的主体作用。教师可以扮演讲授者、评估者、建议者、资源提供者、组织者、帮助者、咨询者,同时也不排斥教师的权威角色、控制者等角色。学生角色也更加多元,包括学习者、参与者、发起者、创新者、研究者、问题解决者,乃至追随者。

4. **教学材料**　有别于我国传统的外语教科书,它具有多类型、多样化的特点,包括课本、音频资料、视频资料、网站资料、教学课件、学生作品等。整个教材内容具有连续性和系统性;每个单元的内容都围绕主题展开。

5. **教学侧重**　教学过程中,教师根据教学阶段或教学内容的特点确定教学重点,或侧重语言知识教学,或侧重语言技能教学,或侧重专业知识教学,或在语言教学和内容教学中达成某种平衡。

6. **教学活动**　教学活动不拘泥于某一种教法所规定的某几种技巧,倡导充分吸收各种教法促进语言学习、内容学习、素质培养,运用多种教学手段,通过问题驱动、输出驱动等方法调动学生主动学习;运用启发式、任务式、讨论式、结对子、小组活动、课堂展示、项目依托教学等行之有效的方法、活动与学科内容教学有机结合,提高学生的语言技能,激发学生的学习兴趣,培养学生的自主性和创造性,提升学生的思辨能力和综合素质。

7. 教学测评　其测评吸收测试研究和评价研究的成果,包括形成性评价和终结性评价。形成性评价可以有小测验、课堂报告、角色扮演、小组活动、双人活动、项目、撰写论文、撰写研究报告、创意写作、创意改写、反馈性写作、制作张贴作品等;终结性评价可以包括传统的选择题等各种题型。

8. 互动性质　它有别于传统教学中信息从教师向学生的单向传送,其课堂互动是在师生互动基础上的生生互动、生师互动乃至师生与其他人员的互动。

9. 情感处理　它重视对学生的人文关怀,主张教师关注学生的情感反应,教学中有必要有效处理影响学生学习的各种情感因素。

10. 母语作用　它尊重外语环境下师生的母语优势并加以利用。不绝对禁止母语的使用。母语的使用取决于教学的需要,母语用于有效支持教育目标的达成。

11. 应对失误　它认可失误是学生获得语言或知识内容不可避免的现象,对学生失误采取包容的态度。针对具体情况应对学生的失误,或不去干预,允许学生自我纠正,或有针对性地适时给予纠正。

12. 理论支撑　它的语言学理论支撑包括:语言是以文本或话语为基础的;语言的运用凭借各种技能的融合;语言具有目的性。它的学习理论支撑包括:当人们把语言当成获取信息的工具而不是目的时学习语言更成功,作为语言学习基础的一些内容比另外一些内容更有用;当教学关注学生的需求时学生的学习效果会更好;教学应该以学生以前的学习经历为基础。

在 CLI 教育理念指导下,依托 3 个国家社会科学基金项目,我们将教育部外语专业教育指导文件规定的语音、语法、听力、口语、阅读、写作、笔译、口译等语言技能课程和国家概况、文学、语言学、学术论文写作等专业知识课程进行了系统改革,逐步构建了全新的专业课程体系,包括八个系列的核心课程:

1. 综合英语课: 美国文学经典作品、英国文学经典作品、世界文学经典作品、西方思想经典。依托美国、英国及其他国家的英语文学经典作品和西方思想经典的内容,提高学生综合运用英语的能力,丰富对英语文学及西方思想的认知,提高综合能力和综合素养。

2. 英语视听说: 美国社会文化经典电影、英国社会文化经典电影、环球资讯、专题资讯。依托美、英社会文化经典电影、环球资讯、专题资讯内容,提高学生的英语听说能力,同时增加学生对相关国家社会文化的了解。

3. 英语口语课: 功能英语交际、情景英语交际、英语演讲、英语辩论。依托人际交往的知识内容,提高学生的英语口语交际能力,增进对人际沟通的了解。

4. 英语写作课: 段落写作、篇章写作、创意写作、学术英语写作。依托笔头交际的知识内容,提高学生的英语笔头表达能力。

5. 英汉互译课: 英汉笔译、汉英笔译、交替传译、同声传译、专题口译。依托相关学科领域的知识内容,提高学生的英汉笔译、交传、同传、专题口译技能,增加学生对相关领域的了解。

6. 社会文化课：美国社会与文化、美国自然人文地理、美国历史文化、英国社会与文化、英国自然人文地理、英国历史文化、澳新加社会与文化、欧洲文化、中国文化、古希腊罗马神话、《圣经》与文化、跨文化交际。依托相关国家或区域的社会、文化、史地等知识，扩展学生的社会文化知识，增加学生专业知识的系统性，拓宽学生的国际视野，同时提高学生的英语能力。

7. 英语文学课：英语短篇小说、英语长篇小说、英语散文、英语戏剧、英语诗歌。依托各种体裁的优秀文学作品内容，强化学生对英语文学文本的阅读，提高学生的文学欣赏能力及语言表达能力，提升学生的文学素养。

8. 语言学课程：英语语言学、英语词汇学、语言与社会、语言与文化、语言与语用。依托英语语言学知识内容，帮助学生深入了解英语语言，增加对语言与社会、文化、语用关系的认识，同时提升学生的专业表达能力。

此外，每门课程均通过开展多种教学活动，服务于学生的综合能力和综合素质培养目标。

研究表明，CLI 指导下的课程改革在学生的语音、词汇、语法、听力、口语、写作、交际、思辨、情感、专业知识等诸多方面产生了积极的教学效果，对学生的文学作品分析能力、创新能力、思辨能力及逻辑思维能力发展也大有裨益。CLI 教育理念在国际、全国、区域研讨会及我国高校广泛交流，产生了广泛的积极影响。

1. CLI 教育理念影响了教师的教育理念。 随着教学研究成果的不断出现，越来越多的英语教师开始关注 CLI 教育理念及其指导下的改革，数以百计的教师积极参与 CLI 教育教学研讨与交流，国际关系学院、华中农业大学、黑龙江大学等高校领导积极与团队成员交流理念及课程建设经验，两百多所高校引介了改革的理念、课程建设理念及开发的课程，而且还结合本校实际开展了课程改革，取得了积极成果。

2. CLI 教育教学研究成果影响数万学生。 在 CLI 教育理念指导下开发了系列课程和教材，在北京大学出版社、上海外语教育出版社等出版社出版；推出的校级、省级和国家级教学研究成果开始发挥辐射作用，通过《外语教学与研究》《中国外语》等期刊发表的研究论文向同行汇报了改革遇到的问题及取得的进展；数以万计的师生使用了我们开发的教材，在提高语言技能的同时扩展专业知识，提高综合素质。改革成果在我国的英语专业教育中发挥着积极的作用。

该理念不仅得到一线教师的广泛支持，也得到了戴炜栋、王守仁、文秋芳等知名专家的高度肯定。蔡基刚教授认为其具有"导向性"作用。孙有中教授认为，该理念指导的教学改革"走在了全国的前列"。教育部高等学校外语专业教学指导委员会前主任委员戴炜栋曾表示，开发的课程值得推广。此外，该理念被作为教学要求写入《外国语言文学类教学质量国家标准》及《普通高等学校本科外国语言文学类专业教学指南（上）：英语类专业教学指南》，用于指导全国的外语专业教育，对我国的外语教育及教育教学改革必将产生深远的影响。

《跨文化交际（第 2 版）》是 CLI 教育理念指导下英语专业知识课程体系中"跨文化交际"课程所使用的教材。教材针对的学生群体是具有中学英语基础的大学生，适用于英语专业一、二年级学生，也适用于具有中学英语基础的非英语专业学生和英语爱好者。总体看来，本教材具备以下主要特色：

1. 打破了传统的教学理念。 本教材改变了"为学语言而学语言"的传统教材建设理念，在具有时代特色且被证明行之有效的内容语言融合教育理念指导下，改变了片面关注语言知识和语言技能而忽视内容学习的做法。教材依托学生密切关注的跨文化交际内容，结合跨文化交际知识组织学生进行语言交际活动，在语言交流中学习有意义的知识内容，训练语言技能，丰富相关知识，提高综合素质，起到的是一箭多雕的作用。

2. 涉及了丰富的教学内容。《跨文化交际（第2版）》共设计十五个单元。第一单元为绪论，总体介绍跨文化交际学的基本知识。第二到第七单元主要以交际为内容，包括如何理解交际、言语交际、非言语交际以及跨性别交际。第八到第十一单元主要以文化为内容，包括如何理解文化、文化的多样性、文化对认知的影响和文化冲突。第十二到第十四单元讨论教育、礼仪和商业谈判语境下的跨文化交际。第十五单元为如何提高跨文化交际提出了一些具体的建议和意见。

3. 引进了真实的教学材料。 英语教材是英语学习者英语语言输入和相关知识输入的重要渠道。本教材大量使用真实、地道的语言材料，为学生提供了高质量的语言输入。此外，为了使课文内容更加充实生动，易于学生理解接受，编者在课文中穿插了大量的插图、表格、照片等真实的视觉材料，表现手法活泼，形式多种多样，效果生动直观。

4. 设计了新颖的教材板块。 本教材每一单元的主体内容均包括 Before You Read，Start to Read，After You Read 和 Read More 四大板块，不仅在结构上确立了学生的主体地位，而且系统的安排也方便教师借助教材有条不紊地开展教学活动。它改变了教师单纯灌输、学生被动接受的教学方式，促使学生积极思考、提问、探索、发现、批判，培养自主获得知识、发现问题和解决问题的能力。

5. 提供了有趣的训练活动。 为了培养学生的语言技能和综合素质，本教材在关注英语语言知识训练和相关知识内容传授的基础上精心设计了生动多样的综合训练活动，例如头脑风暴、话题辩论、角色表演、主题陈述、故事编述等。多样化的活动打破了传统教材单调的训练程式，帮助教师设置真实的语言运用情境，组织富于挑战性的、具有意义的语言实践活动，培养学生的语言综合运用能力。

6. 推荐了经典的学习材料。 教材的另一特色在于它对教学内容的延伸和拓展。在每章的最后，编者向学生推荐经典的图书、电影、诗歌、歌曲等学习资料，这不仅有益于学生开阔视野，也使教材具有了弹性和开放性，方便不同院校、不同水平的学生使用。

本教材是我国英语专业综合课程改革的一项探索，凝聚了全体编写人员的艰苦努力。然而由于水平有限，本教材还存在疏漏和不足，希望老师和同学们能为我们提出宝贵的意见和建议。您的指导和建议将是我们提高的动力。

编者

2020 年 5 月 30 日

于大连外国语大学

Unit 1 An Introduction to Intercultural Communication / 1
  Text A Intercultural Communication / 2
  Text B The Importance of Training Intercultural Communication Awareness / 3
  Text C The Era of Intercultural Communication / 8
  Text D Stereotypes: An Intercultural No-No / 10
  Text E Chinese and American Understandings on Friendship / 12

Unit 2 Understanding Communication / 16
  Text A Components of Communication / 17
  Text B Features of Communication / 18
  Text C How Long Does It Take to Say I'm Getting Married (I) / 24

Unit 3 Verbal Communication (I) / 28
  Text A Cultural Differences on Lexical Level / 29
  Text B Translation and Cultures / 35
  Text C How to Improve Verbal Communication / 37

Unit 4 Verbal Communication (II) / 40
  Text A Compliments in Chinese and American English (I) / 41
  Text B Compliments in Chinese and American English (II) / 43
  Text C How to Address People? / 48
  Text D Conversation and Culture / 49

Unit 5 Nonverbal Communication (I) / 52
  Text A Nonverbal Communication / 53
  Text B Making a Gesture / 54
  Text C Every Body's Talking / 60
  Text D Top 10 Nonverbal Communication Tips / 63

Unit 6 Nonverbal Communication (II) / 67
  Text A How Big Is Your Space Bubble / 68
  Text B Time Sense: Polychronicity and Monochronicity / 69
  Text C Eye Contact / 76

Unit 7 Cross-gender Communication / 79
  Text A Gender Differences in Communication / 80

Text B　Six Principles for Effective Cross-gender Communication / 83
　　Text C　Gender Issues / 88
　　Text D　Rapport-Talk and Report-Talk / 91

Unit 8　Understanding Culture / 94
　　Text A　What Is Culture? / 95
　　Text B　Features of Culture / 101
　　Text C　How Long Does It Take to Say I'm Getting Married (II) / 102

Unit 9　Cultural Diversity / 106
　　Text A　The Basic Unit of Society: The Individual or the Collective? / 108
　　Text B　Create an Asian Community of Shared Future Through Mutual Learning / 114
　　Text C　Family Structure / 116
　　Text D　Friendship of American Style / 118

Unit 10　Cultural Influence on Perception / 121
　　Text A　Shakespeare in the Bush / 122
　　Text B　Generalizations and Stereotypes / 129
　　Text C　American Stereotypes of China / 131

Unit 11　Culture Shock / 135
　　Text A　Culture Shock / 136
　　Text B　How to Survive Culture Shock / 142
　　Text C　Can You Survive Reverse Culture Shock? / 143

Unit 12　Cultural Differences in Education / 146
　　Text A　Classroom Expectations / 148
　　Text B　15 Important Cultural Differences in the Classroom / 154
　　Text C　Classroom Culture / 157

Unit 13　Cultural Differences in Etiquette and Protocol / 160
　　Text A　International Gift-giving Etiquette / 161
　　Text B　Business Card Etiquette / 166
　　Text C　How Tipping Works / 168

Unit 14　Cultural Differences in Business Negotiation / 171
　　Text A　Cross-cultural Negotiation / 173
　　Text B　How to Steer Clear of Pitfalls in Cross-cultural Negotiation / 179
　　Text C　The Top Ten Ways Culture Affects Negotiating Style / 181

Unit 15　Developing Intercultural Competence / 187
　　Text A　A Four-step Approach to Intercultural Communication Training / 188
　　Text B　Developing Intercultural Communication Competence / 193
　　Text C　Cultural Awareness / 195

主要参考文献 / 198

Unit 1
An Introduction to Intercultural Communication

> To know another's language and not his culture is a very good way to make a fluent fool of one's self.
> —— Winston Brembeck
>
> Our most basic common link is that we all inhabit this planet.
> —— John F. Kennedy

Unit Goals

- To understand the definition of intercultural communication
- To learn to describe the development of intercultural communication
- To comprehend the importance of intercultural communication
- To learn useful words and expressions about intercultural communication and improve language skills

Before You Read

1. Please find a Chinese equivalent for the English phrase "intercultural communication." Tick the item that you think can be a candidate.

    ☐ 跨文化交际   ☐ 跨文化沟通
    ☐ 跨文化传播   ☐ 跨文化传理
    ☐ 跨文化交流   ☐ 文化差异交流

2. You are invited to discover the scope of intercultural communication by yourself. Please label the following situations that you think are instances of intercultural communication.

SITUATIONS	YES	NO
☞ Chinese Premier met with British Prime Minister in London.	☐	☐
☞ Two blind people exchange ideas in Braille.	☐	☐
☞ A Chinese of Han nationality converses with a Chinese Mongolian.	☐	☐
☞ A white American communicates with an Afro-American.	☐	☐

(continued)

SITUATIONS	YES	NO
☞ Mike talks to himself while playing computer games.	☐	☐
☞ You call your British instructor to ask for sick leave.	☐	☐
☞ A businessman from Shenyang negotiates with his counterpart from Chengdu.	☐	☐
☞ A programmer issues commands to a computer.	☐	☐
☞ You chat with your American friends via Skype.	☐	☐
☞ You watch your favorite American sitcom *Friends*.	☐	☐

3. **Study the following Chinese poem by Su Shi and try to tell the messages you can find from an intercultural communication perspective.**

题西林壁
苏轼
横看成岭侧成峰，
远近高低各不同。
不识庐山真面目，
只缘身在此山中。

Start to Read

Text A　Intercultural Communication

The term "intercultural communication" (ICC) is first used by Edward T. Hall in 1959 and is simply defined as interpersonal communication between people from different cultural backgrounds. It occurs when a member of one culture produces a message for consumption by a member of another culture. It consists of international, interethnic, interracial and interregional communication.

International Communication

International communication takes place between nations and governments as well as individuals; it is quite formal and ritualized. A dialogue at the United Nations, for example, would be termed international communication. If a talk with Mexican President is held, this is the communication between two nations or countries.

Interethnic Communication

Ethnic groups usually form their own communities in a country or culture. Interethnic communication refers to communication between people of the same race but different ethnic backgrounds. For example, in America, if an Alaska native communicates with a non-native American, this is interethnic communication because they are from different ethnic groups.

Interracial Communication

Interracial communication occurs when the source and the receiver exchanging messages are from different races which are related to physical characteristics. For example, if a white American student discusses issues with an Afro-American student, it is interracial communication. Interracial communication may or may not be intercultural.

Interregional Communication

Interregional communication refers to the exchange of messages between members of the dominant culture within a country. If an American from Boston interacts with an American from New Orleans, we have interregional communication. They are members of a culture who share common messages and experiences over a long period of time. However, they live in different regions of the same country.

Intercultural communication is a universal phenomenon. It occurs everywhere in the world. When you talk with an American teacher, or send an email to a foreigner, or even when you watch a foreign film or read an English novel, you are engaged in intercultural communication.

Communication between cultures has been going on for thousands of years. The history of intercultural communication is almost as long as human history itself. It dates back to when primitive nomadic tribes started mingling with each other and needed to communicate with each other. It became even more necessary when sailors visited alien lands; and when thousands of gold-diggers from Asia and different European countries migrated to North America in search of wealth, there was intercultural communication. During the Tang Dynasty in China, there was the example of the famous "Silk Road" in which people of Asia, Africa and Europe interacted and communicated with each other in order to conduct their business transactions.

Intercultural communication is a common daily occurrence. The communication between cultures today is happening continuously, taking place almost every day. Today, thousands of Chinese students going abroad to study, millions of foreign travelers coming to China, foreign artists coming to China to give performances and many joint venture enterprises doing business in many cities in China. These are all examples showing how prevalent intercultural communication is today.

Text B The Importance of Training Intercultural Communication Awareness

Modern society has made intercultural communication a necessity. With the development of science and technology, the world seems to be shrinking. Modern transportation and communication, electronic media and international organizations have brought near the people in the other hemisphere as if they were our next-door neighbors. The mobility of people and contact between countries have greatly increased intercultural communication. In today's world,

intercultural awareness has become a prerequisite for successful intercultural communication.

English, as an international language, has called for Chinese learners' intercultural awareness. People used to assume that learning the rules of English grammar and a large amount of vocabulary was sufficient in learning English. The more grammar and words a learner had learned, the higher his level of proficiency was. Experience has shown, however, that many learners, while knowing a lot about the target language, were, in fact, unable to communicate effectively in it. Intercultural awareness is required if the learner is to achieve communicative competence, which is now considered as the goal of language learning universally.

Intercultural awareness becomes especially important when a learner reaches the advanced stage and reads authentic English texts. Very often, familiarity with the dictionary definitions of lexical items and the mastery of sentence structures do not seem to be enough for the learner to understand the information. Lack of cultural knowledge affects his comprehension.

Moreover, intercultural awareness cannot grow naturally. It has to be trained. For example, when a child from the Anglo-American world learns the word "dog," he will normally learn the cultural meaning of the word: the dog is "man's best friend." A child brought up in some regions in China would be taught that the dog is a dangerous animal. People, who have thus been initiated into the culture associated with their mother tongue, are naturally inclined to interpret things with their own cultural references. This natural inclination is called "intuitive competence." When people from different cultures communicate, their respective "intuitive competence" may cause miscommunication. "Intuitive competence" is something native speakers possess, but foreign learners have to be trained in. Therefore, it becomes necessary for Chinese students to increase intercultural awareness in English language learning.

After You Read

Knowledge Focus

1. **Pair Work: Discuss the following questions with your partner.**
   1) What does intercultural communication mean to you?
   2) Give examples to illustrate different types of intercultural communication.
   3) What features does intercultural communication have?
   4) Why does intercultural awareness play a crucial role in the process of intercultural communication?
   5) What is intuitive competence? How does it affect intercultural communication?

2. **Solo Work: Tell whether the following statements are true or false according to the knowledge you learned and explain why.**
   1) The terms "intercultural" and "international" can be used interchangeably. (　)
   2) International communication takes place between groups like African Americans and Latin Americans. (　)
   3) As a phenomenon, intercultural communication has existed for thousands of years. (　)
   4) All people of the same nationality will have the same culture. (　)
   5) Intercultural communication happens only when we meet face-to-face with foreigners. (　)

6) Due to the improvements in transportation and communication technology, intercultural communication has increased rapidly. (　)
7) Cultural mistakes are more serious than linguistic mistakes. (　)
8) Language competence is not enough for successful intercultural communication. (　)
9) One's actions are totally independent of his/her culture. (　)
10) In intercultural communication, one's intuitive competence may lead to miscommunication. (　)

Language Focus

1. Fill in the blanks with the following words or expressions you have learned in Text A and Text B.

incline	relate	conduct	involve	call for
interact	mingle	associate with	take place	initiate

1) Lengthy negotiation must _____ before any agreement can be reached.
2) It is difficult to _____ cause and effect in this case.
3) A lot of researches have proved that mother and baby _____ in a very complex way.
4) How could we _____ ourselves in school life?
5) He _____ in the crowd and lost in sight immediately.
6) I think he _____ himself admirably, considering the difficult circumstances.
7) — "You know what? I've been promoted!"
   — "This _____ a celebration!"
8) In the first Spanish class, the professor _____ students into the principles of grammar.
9) We do not want to _____ him because he always brings humiliation to our team.
10) Having known him for a long time, I am _____ to believe him innocent.

2. Fill in the blanks with the proper form of the words in the brackets.
1) You need to take fuel _____ (consume) into consideration when buying a car.
2) The growing up of children has become _____ (ritual) in many cultures.
3) Television plays a _____ (dominate) role in molding public opinion.
4) Globalization of the world economy is crucial to the rapid increase of _____ (culture) communication.
5) Dance inspires him _____ (continue) to strive higher and higher toward the shining pinnacle of perfection.
6) A private car gives a much greater degree of comfort and _____ (mobile).
7) The government is working on improving the ecological _____ (aware) of the citizens.
8) Are women more _____ (intuition) than men?

3. Find the appropriate prepositions or adverbs that collocate with the words in bold letters.
1) Matters **consist** _____ molecules, and molecules _____ atoms.
2) For more information, you have to **refer** _____ the authority.
3) Some training drills should **be** closely **related** _____ actual badminton playing skills.

4) He was really exhausted _____ **a result of** long-time stress.
5) You would be well-advised not to **get involved** _____ their quarrel.
6) If we **mingle** _____ the crowd we shall not be noticed.
7) I did not want to **be engaged** _____ boxing last year.
8) I cannot play the piano like I used to — my fingers have gone stiff from **lack** _____ practice.

4. **Error Correction**: Each of the following sentences has at least one grammatical error. Identify the errors and make corrections.

   1) Interracial communication occurs when the source and the receiver exchanging messages are from different race which are related to physical characteristics.
   2) Intercultural communication is an universal phenomenon.
   3) Communication between cultures have been going on for thousands of years.
   4) It became even more necessary when thousand of gold-diggers from Asia and different European countries migrated to North America in search of wealth.
   5) There is the example of the famous "Silk Road" in which people of Asia, Africa and Europe interacted and communicated with each other in order to conduct their business transactions.
   6) Intercultural communication is common daily occurrence.
   7) Today, thousands of Chinese students going abroad to study, millions of foreign travelers come to China, foreign artists come to China to give performances and many joint venture enterprises do business in many cities in China.
   8) These are all examples shown how prevalent intercultural communication is today.
   9) Modern transportation and communication, electronic media and international organizations have brought near the people in the other hemisphere as if they are our next-door neighbors.
   10) The mobility of people and contact between countries has greatly increased intercultural communication.
   11) People is used to assume that learning the rules of English grammar and a large amount of vocabulary was sufficient in learning English.
   12) The more grammar and words a learner had learned, the high his level of proficiency was.
   13) Experience has shown that many learners, while knows a lot about the target language, were, in fact, unable to communicate effectively in it.
   14) A child bringing up in some regions in China would be taught that the dog is a dangerous animal.
   15) People, who have thus been initiated into the culture associated with their mother tongue, is naturally inclined to interpret things with their own cultural references.
   16) "Intuitive competence" is something which native speakers possess, but foreign learners have to be trained in.

Comprehensive Work

1. Pair Work: Analyze the following cases with your partner.

Case Study 1

The following is a conversation between a Chinese tourist guide Xiao Lin and a British visitor Peter.

Xiao Lin: You must be very tired. You're old...
Peter: Oh, I'm NOT old, and I'm NOT tired.

Case Study 2

The following is an email written by Chinese students to their Australian professor.

Dear Teacher,
    It is our honor to be with you for the whole semester. We have learned a lot from you. We are deeply impressed by your knowledge and kindness. Thank you for your hard work. We will remember you forever.

Your students

2. Group Work

1) **Form groups of three or four. First share with your group members whatever you have had in communication events that can be considered as intercultural. Then discuss the following cases of communication and decide to what extent they are intercultural.**

Communication between...
a Chinese and an American 
a Canadian and a South African 
a male and a female 

Intercultural Communication (Second Edition)

a father and a son

a first-generation Chinese American
and a third-generation one

2) **In groups, discuss the question: Why would intercultural communication be more difficult than communication between people from the same culture? List as many reasons as you can think of, stating each as an answer to the question.**

_____
_____
_____
_____
_____
_____

3. Writing

As people are becoming more and more mobile, communication in our life tends to be more and more intercultural. Conduct a small-scale survey in everyday life to see what cases of communication can be considered as somewhat intercultural. Write a short essay to report the results of your survey and try to explain to what extent each case can be intercultural and what makes it so.

Text C   The Era of Intercultural Communication

On April 8, 1960, the world entered a new era. On this date, the first attempt was made to communicate with extraterrestrial life as part of Project Ozma, organized by Frank Drake of the National Radio Astronomy Observatory in Green Bank, West Virginia. Pioneer 10—launched on March 3, 1973—included a six-by-nine inch gold-plated aluminum plaque with a message for any extraterrestrial being coming across it. The plaque on Pioneer 10 was designed by the astronomer Carl Sagan. The left side of the plaque contained a representation of the periods of pulsars to indicate the solar system of origin, while across the bottom the planets of the solar system were drawn with an indication that Pioneer 10 originated on the third planet. The right side of the plaque contained drawings of unclothed male and female figures, the man having his right arm raised with the palm extending outward. Pictures of the plaque appeared in newspapers around the world when Pioneer 10 was launched.

What does the plaque on Pioneer 10 have to do with intercultural communication? Think about it for a moment. Does the plaque have anything in common with your attempts to communicate with people from other cultures? The plaque illustrates what often happens when two people who do not share a common language try to communicate: they try to get their ideas across nonverbally. Reactions to the plaque when it appeared in newspapers around the world further illustrate what can happen when we use this method in our everyday encounters with people from other cultures. People in some cultures interpreted the man's gesture to be a universal gesture of friendliness, while people in other cultures interpreted it as one of hostility. The point is that gestures used by people in one culture often do not mean the same thing in another culture. Trying to communicate through nonverbal means as well as through verbal means may, therefore, lead to misunderstandings.

In order to minimize misunderstandings when we communicate with people from other cultures, we need to understand the process of intercultural communication, and we need to understand people of other cultures and their patterns of communication. This is important not only to decrease misunderstandings but also to make the world a safer place for all of us to live.

In the past, most human beings were born, lived, and died within a limited geographical area, never encountering people of other cultural backgrounds. Such an existence, however, no longer prevails in the world. The international and domestic changes in the past few decades have brought us into direct and indirect contact with people who, because of their cultural diversity, often behave in ways that we do not understand. It is no longer difficult to find social and professional situations in which members of once isolated groups of people communicate with members of other cultural groups. Now these people may live thousands of miles away or right next door to each other.

McLuhan characterized today's world as a "global village" because of the rapid expansion of worldwide transportation and communication networks. We can now board a plane and fly anywhere in the world in a matter of hours. Communication satellites, sophisticated television transmission equipment, and the World Wide Web now allow people throughout the world to share information and ideas at the same time. It is now possible for a person in one country to communicate with a person in another country within seconds.

In a world of international interdependence, the ability to understand and communicate effectively with people from other cultures takes on extreme urgency. However, we may find intercultural communication different from communication within our own cultural group. Even if we overcome the natural barriers of language difference, we may fail to understand and to be understood. Misunderstanding may even become the rule rather than the exception. And, if we are unaware of the significant role culture plays in communication, we may place the blame for communication failure on those other people. This is unfortunate because our problem is really culture and the difficulty of communicating across cultural boundaries.

It is recognized widely that one of the characteristics separating humans from other animals is our development of culture. The development of human culture is made possible through communication, and it is through communication that culture is transmitted from one generation to another. Culture and communication are intertwined so closely that Hall maintains that "culture is communication" and "communication is culture." In other words, we communicate the way we do because we are raised in a particular culture and learn its language, rules, and norms. Because we learn the language, rules, and norms of our culture at a very early age, however, we generally are unaware of how culture influences our behavior in general and our communication in particular.

When we communicate with people from other cultures, we are often confronted with languages, rules, and norms different from our own. Confronting these differences can be a source of insight into the rules and norms of our own culture, as well as being a source of frustration or gratification. Therefore, what we have to learn is to understand the culture, communication, how culture influences communication, and the process of communication between people from different cultures. Such knowledge is extremely important. In fact, it is necessary if we are to comprehend fully the daily events of today's multicultural world. It will help us not only analyze our intercultural encounters in order to determine where misunderstandings occur, but also determine how these misunderstandings can be minimized in future interactions.

Questions for Discussion or Reflection

1. In what way is the plaque on Pioneer 10 related to intercultural communication?
2. How does intercultural communication differ from communication within the same culture?
3. Why does Hall maintain that "culture is communication" and "communication is culture"? Can you give some examples to illustrate this?
4. For what reasons is intercultural communication important to people living in the global village?

Notes

1. **McLuhan, H. M.** (1911—1980): Herbert Marshall McLuhan, Canadian scholar and literary critic, theorist of literature, media and communication.
2. **Hall, E.** (1914—2009): Edward T. Hall, a respected American anthropologist and cross-cultural researcher.

Text D Stereotypes: An Intercultural No-No

As more or more people from different backgrounds, countries, cultures and religions immigrate to foreign lands, those countries become an intercultural melting pot. In order for the native people and the immigrant population to blend and create a thriving and successful atmosphere both sides need to develop some sort of intercultural tolerance and understanding of the differences that may exist between them. An example of poor intercultural understanding, or one based simply on stereotypes, is offered by the town of Herouxville in Quebec, Canada.

A declaration issued by the town in January 2007, which was designed to inform immigrants, "that the way of life which they abandoned when they left their countries of origin cannot be recreated here, (i. e. Herouxville)." It then went on to state that the immigrant population would therefore have to refrain from their cultural norms and activities such as to "kill women by stoning them in public, burning them alive, burning them with acid, circumcising them, etc."

The declaration paints a rather sad picture of the officials that administer the town and highlights not only their rather insular outlook but a world view of "others" based on crass and frankly incorrect stereotypes. To simply consider that anyone from another country (in this case more than likely a Middle Eastern or Asian one) regards the stoning of women and burning them alive as part of daily life derives from crude, and media led, stereotypes of other peoples.

Stereotypes are at their most basic level a set of assumed characteristics about a certain group of people whose actual beliefs, habits and realities more often than not disagree with the imposed assumptions. Stereotypes are usually based on factors such as exaggeration, distortion, ignorance, racism, cultural factors or even historical experiences. Stereotyping is therefore rightly seen as a negative way of seeing people. This is even true of what are called "positive stereotypes." A positive stereotype is where we use a blanket expression for a whole people, i. e. all the Chinese are great at maths, all Germans are well organized or all English people are well mannered. Although the intent behind the statement is positive, it still does not reflect the truth.

What we have witnessed in Herouxville should not be seen as an isolated incident. Such assumptions about foreigners exist all over the planet. However, this does not make it right or excusable. The message it does give is that there is a lot of work to be done in order to educate people to become more culturally competent.

Cultural competency is a term used to describe the ability to work, communicate and live across cultures and cultural boundaries. One achieves this through an instilled understanding of cultures on a general level as well as an informed one about specific cultures on a more detailed level. As well as knowledge it has to work in tandem with behavioral and attitudinal changes.

Cultural competency is important in this day and age for exactly the reasons cited in this article. We, as citizens of planet earth, are no longer confined to our national and cultural borders. We mix with people from different cultures, ethnicities, religions and colors on a daily basis. In order to make this intercultural experience work on all levels from education to business to government, people have to develop basic skills in intercultural communication and understanding.

Questions for Discussion or Reflection

1. What can you learn from the example of Herouxville in terms of intercultural communication?
2. What does the term "stereotype" mean? What kind of impact can stereotypes have on individuals?
3. How can we break negative stereotypes?

Herouxville: It is 160km (100 miles) north-east of Montreal with a population of about 1,300. In January 2007, its council published the new rules on the town's website: "We wish to inform these new arrivals that the way of life which they abandoned when they left their countries of origin cannot be recreated here." "We consider it completely outside norms to... kill women by stoning them in public, burning them alive, burning them with acid, circumcising them, etc." This declaration put Quebec into a huge debate on integrating immigrant cultures.

Text E Chinese and American Understandings on Friendship

A Friendship Quiz

Where do you sit on the scale of friendship? Are you a good friend or something else? Before reading Text E, take the following quiz and find out your understanding of friendship!

1. You are working on your mid-term project. Your friend drops in and expects you to go to the mall with her. You will _____.
   A. go with her immediately
   B. explain you are working on the project and ask her to go with someone else

2. What do you think of friendship?
   A. True friendship is a relationship that endures through life changes.
   B. Friends will change over life changes. One may have different friends in different periods of his/her life.

3. When your friend is struggling with some difficult issue, you would _____.
   A. give him/her some concrete help
   B. give him/her emotional support

4. If your friend tells you something about himself/herself that was quite shameful, you would _____.
   A. tell him/her that you understand and try to help him/her figure out how to get past it
   B. listen in a non-judgmental way

5. Your friend's new boyfriend is a total fool. What would you say when she asks what you think of him?
   A. Tell her the truth, even if it is mean.
   B. Give no comment and tell her to get to him better.

6. Do you make apologies to your good friend when you ask him/her to give you a ride?
   A. No. Since we are buddies, it is unnecessary.

B. Yes. Even if we are buddies, I need to be polite with him/her.

If you have chosen a lot of A's, it is likely you have a traditional Chinese understanding of friendship. If you have chosen many B's, then you have an American view on friendship. Want to know why? Continue to read the following text, and you will figure out the reasons by yourself.

In writing assignments in English classes, my students frequently raise the topic of friendship. Reading what they write, I start to understand Chinese friendship obligation. For instance, once a student wrote that she understood that her friend wanted to go shopping. My student was busy and really had no time to do that, but she kept silent, put her work aside and went shopping with her friend. Sometimes they write about middle school friends and describe the closeness they feel when they are together. Sometimes they write with great sadness when they feel they are no longer close to someone they considered a friend. All this is quite different from what American young people would say about friendship.

In the Untied States you can certainly ask a friend to do something with you, but you would not expect a friend to recognize and respond to your wishes without stating them. Nor would you expect a friend to drop everything to respond to a non-urgent need such as going shopping. In fact, an American friend would feel that they had imposed too much if the friend gave up a real need study to go shopping. There are limits to what you can expect from a friend. In the U.S. you feel free to ask your friend for help, but you recognize that the friend may say no, if they give you a reason. A friend in China is someone who, sensing that you are in need in some way, offers to assist you without waiting to be asked. In China, there are few limits on what you can ask or expect of a friend. You can feel free to tell your friend what he or she can or should do to help you or please you.

Another difference is that my Chinese students seem to expect their friendships to stay the same over a long period of time, maybe for a lifetime. True friendship is a relationship that endures through changes in the lives of the friends. In the United States, a person is likely to change even "best friends" several times over the years. Even this relationship in which people feel close emotionally and tell each other their secrets and personal problems may not survive life changes such as move to another city, graduation from a university, a significant change in economic circumstances, or the marriage of one of the friends. I think the reason is that friendship, like so many other relationships in the United States including marriage, depends on frequent interaction with the other person. If the people involved do not see each other and interact regularly, the relationship is likely to wither and die.

In the West, people often have many friends at one time, but the friendships are usually tied to specific circumstances or activities. When a person changes circumstances and activities, he or she changes friends. A person may have work friends, leisure activity friends and neighborhood friends. Also, two people who are friends usually have similar financial circumstances. This is because friendships in the West are based on equality. Friends should exchange similar activities and give similar things to one another. If one can afford to treat the other to a meal at an expensive restaurant and the other does not have enough money to do the same, it will cause a problem in the relationship.

As with so many other things in the West, people prefer to be independent rather than dependent, so they do not feel comfortable in a relationship in which one person is giving more and the other person is dependent on what is being given. For Westerners' friendship is mostly a matter of providing emotional support and spending time together. Chinese friends give each other much more concrete help and assistance than Western friends do. A Chinese friend will use personal connections to help a friend get something hard to obtain such as job, an appointment with a good doctor, an easier path through an official procedure or an introduction to another person who might also be able to give concrete help. Chinese friends give each other money and might help each other out financially over a long period of time. This is rarely part of Western friendships, because it creates dependence of one person on the other and it goes against the principle of equality.

American friends like Chinese friends give each other emotional support in times of trouble, but they do it differently. A Westerner will respond to a friend's trouble by asking, "What do you want to do?" The idea is to help the friend think out the problem and discover the solution he or she really prefers and then to support that solution. A Chinese friend is more likely to give specific advice to a friend. For instance, if in a friendship between two Chinese women, one woman is arguing with her husband, the friend might advise and she says so directly. An American friend in a similar situation may want her friend to choose wise actions too, but she will be very cautious about giving direct advice. Instead, she may raise questions to encourage her friend to consider carefully what may happen if she does one thing instead of another.

We have noted that Chinese people often communicate indirectly while Westerners tend to be more direct. In close personal relationships as friendship, the opposite is often the case. Talk between Chinese friends would probably sound too direct to Western ears. As we have seen, Chinese interactions with strangers or guests are more formal and polite than is typical in the west, but in China relationships with friends are much more informal than similar Western relationships.

Americans apologize to their friends for minor inconveniences such as telephoning late at night or asking for some specific help. Even in close friendships, Americans use polite forms such as "could you ..." and "would you mind ..." Because Chinese do not use these polite forms in their close relationships, they probably do not use them when speaking English with Westerners they know well. As a result, they may seem to be too direct or demanding to their Western friends. At the same time, a Chinese person who is friends with an American continues to be formally polite after the two have established their relationship.

Books to Read

1. Hu, Wenzhong and Cornelius Lee Grove. *Encountering the Chinese: A Guide for Americans*. Yarmouth: Intercultural Press, 1999.
   - The book takes the two perspectives of the authors, one American and one Chinese, to help explain the ways of the Chinese people, so that they can be better understood from an American perspective. Merely explaining the customs of the Chinese to an outsider would be superficial. To really understand where the Chinese are coming from and how it

affects their beliefs and rituals in everyday life, one must be able to relate and understand why they do what they do. This book does a beautiful job at detailing every aspect of Chinese life and creating a way to help the outside reader grasp Chinese culture.
2. Gudykunst, William B. and Young Yun Kim. *Communicating with Strangers: An Approach to Intercultural Communication*. New York: Mcgraw-Hill, 1997.
- This highly successful intercultural communication book provides a comprehensive overview of important theory and research in intercultural communications. *Communicating with Strangers* looks at the basic processes of intercultural communication and then ties those processes to the practical task of creating understanding between people with different cultures, backgrounds and communication patterns.

Movie to Watch

A Passage to India is a 1984 adventure-drama film directed by David Lean, based on the novel of the same name by E. M. Forster. It is a masterpiece of cultural misunderstandings. Cultural mistrust and false accusations doom a friendship in British colonial India between an Indian doctor, an Englishwoman engaged to marry a city magistrate, and an English educator.

Unit 2
Understanding Communication

> Every tale can be told in a different way.
> —— Greek proverb
>
> Good communication is as stimulating as black coffee, and just as hard to sleep after.
> —— Anne Morrow Lindbergh

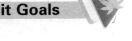
Unit Goals

- To understand the term of communication
- To learn to explain the process of communication
- To understand the features of communication
- To learn some useful words and expressions about communication and improve language skills

Before You Read

Study the following case with your partner and work out the following questions.

A Turkish university student in the United States shared a room with an American. One day his American roommate went into the bathroom and completely shaved his head. When the Turkish student visited the bathroom, he saw the hair everywhere and was very uncomfortable with the mess his roommate had made. He returned to their room and said to his roommate ...

If you were the Turkish student, what would you say to your roommate?

The Turkish student said to his roommate, "You've shaved your head." The American replied, "Yeah, I have."

What did the Turkish student mean by saying "You've shaved your head"?

The Turkish student waited a little and then said, "I discovered you'd shaved your head when I went into the bathroom and saw the hair." "Yeah,"

the American confirmed. **What did the Turkish student expect from the American?**

_____

The Turk was at a loss. He believed he had communicated in the strongest possible language his wish that the American would clean up the mess he has made in the bathroom.

What is wrong in the communication between the Turkish student and the American? What elements are necessary for a successful communication event to take place?

_____

_____

Start to Read

Text A — Components of Communication

Communication is related to both "communion" and "community." It comes from the Latin "communicare," which means, "to make common" or "to share." The basic assumption is: communication is a form of human behavior derived from a need to connect and interact with other human beings. Therefore, communication can simply refer to the act and process of sending and receiving messages among people.

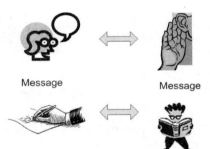

Communication can take place on different levels and can be classified into several types. It is the process of understanding and sharing of meaning in pairs or in small groups. What, then, constitutes such interaction? The following short dialogue can be used to illustrate the components of interpersonal interaction:

A and B are two students in the classroom a couple of minutes before the class begins:

A: Hi, Bob, are you doing anything tonight?
B: No, why?
A: I've got two tickets for *The Butterfly Effect* . Like to go with me?
B: Sure. (The instructor came in the classroom, so B lowers his voice) When?
A: Shh, let's talk after class.

In this dialogue, A wants to invite B to go to see the movie with him. A starts the dialogue and he is the **source** — the point at which information or interaction originates. A organized his idea and puts it into words — verbal **code**, such a process is called **encoding**. A expresses his idea — the **message** by way of talking, i. e. the verbal **channel**. B, the **receiver** of the message, after interpreting the message through the process of **decoding**, gives his **response** to the coming information. The entrance of the teacher interferes with the talk and is considered "**noise**" of the interaction. A knows that his invitation has been accepted and decides to talk about it later. Here the receiver B's response to the message enables the source or sender A to understand how his message has been taken, such information is called **feedback**.

Feedback in fact makes it possible for the source or sender to adjust himself so as to proceed with the interaction. Feedback and response are related because the receiver's response is a normal source of the sender's feedback. And the dialogue between A and B takes place in the setting or context of the classroom. The context could be as small as a classroom or a dinner table, and at the same time it could be as big as the entire cultural environment. Different context often calls for different communicative behavior. Intercultural communication and intracultural communication consist of the same components, but in the former the sender and the receiver of the message come from different cultures and each of them may have very different ways of encoding and decoding as well as reactions to the environment or situation of the communication event. The following diagram shows the components and the process of a communication event.

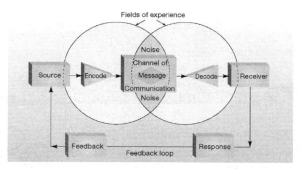

Text B   Features of Communication

Interpersonal communication is a complex process. The following are some of the most distinctive features of communication.

Communication is dynamic

Communication is an on-going activity. In any communication event, the sender and the receiver of messages constantly shift from being encoders to decoders and the messages also change in each turn of interaction.

Communication is interactive

Communication is always done in two ways: the source sends messages to the receiver and the receiver responds to the message received and sends his message or response to the source. Thus the source and receiver are in a reciprocal situation attempting to influence one another in the process. What the influences are and how the influences function are among the major concerns of intercultural communicators.

Communication is both verbal and non-verbal

Speech is only one of the channels that messages are transmitted. We do not have to say everything we intend to communicate in words. We use our body, signs and even clothing to show others what we have in our minds. According to statistics, most part of our communication is done by non-verbal means.

Communication can be either intentional or unintentional

Intention is not a necessary condition for communication to take place. A sigh or frown accompanying speech, if noticed by the receiver, may also carry unintended messages to the receiver. For the two parties involved in the communication process, any behavior of one interlocutor, intentional or unintentional, can produce certain effects and generate certain meanings to the other. To complicate the matter, very often we are unconscious of the message sent and the effect it has produced. Therefore, unexpected results may arise.

Communication is rule-governed

Though communication is a complex process, there are still rules for speakers to follow as to how messages are constructed and interpreted. The patterns, however, are culturally defined. To study communication and intercultural communication in particular is, to a large extent, to discover the patterns that regulate the communicative behavior of the interlocutors. If the patterns are shared and understood, any communication will become easy and effective.

Communication depends on the use of symbols

Symbols or codes are the basic ingredients of communication. Symbols may take the form of written or spoken words, body signs, Braille, an object like a picture or a dress, color, and many other symbols that represent certain meanings to whoever recognizes them and make sense of them. All cultures use symbols, but they usually attribute different meanings to the same symbol and may use different
symbols to mean the same. Competent intercultural communicators, therefore, must learn to "read" the symbols used by their interlocutors and understand the exact message.

Communication is irreversible

Communication cannot be retrieved — the message delivered and interpreted by the receiver can never be taken back. Though we can modify our message, the effect produced by the original message remains. The implication is that improper communicative behavior may have serious consequences.

Communication takes place in both a physical and a social context

Communication does not take place in a vacuum. We interact with other people within specific physical surroundings and under a set of specific social factors. The physical surroundings serve as the background of our interaction and, to a large extent, define what we communicate and how we do it. In addition, the symbolic meaning of the physical setting may contribute to the meanings intended. The social context sets the interlocutors in various social relationships. How people relate to one another will determine both the form and content of communication. Physical and social context together define the actual practice of communication: what to be communicated, where, when, with whom and how it is realized.

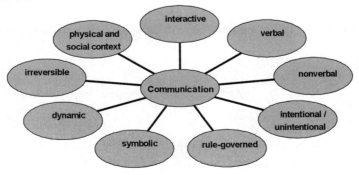

跨文化交际（第2版）
Intercultural Communication (Second Edition)

After You Read

Knowledge Focus

1. **Pair Work: Discuss the following questions with your partner.**
   1) What are the factors that comprise the communication process?
   2) What could be your own map of communication? Describe why.
   3) Are there any more examples to illustrate the factors of communication?
   4) At what stage the Turkish student and the American roommate misunderstand each other in the case at the beginning of this unit?
   5) Can you work out other features of communication?

2. **Solo Work: Match the following terms with their definitions.**

   _____ 1) source   _____ 7) encoding
   _____ 2) message   _____ 8) response
   _____ 3) channel   _____ 9) sender
   _____ 4) feedback   _____ 10) noise
   _____ 5) code   _____ 11) receiver
   _____ 6) decoding   _____ 12) intracultural communication

   a. the person that receives the message in the communication
   b. communication between people from the same cultural background
   c. the interlocutor who initiates the message
   d. any systematic arrangement or comprehensive collection of symbols
   e. the interpretative process of assigning meaning to a message
   f. the content of interaction
   g. information generated by the receiver and made available to a source that allows the source to make qualitative judgments about the communication while it is taking place
   h. the act of putting an idea or thought into a code
   i. the mode by which a message moves from the source of the message to the receiver of the message
   j. the reaction of the receiver to the decoded message
   k. any factor that hinders or distorts the reception of messages
   l. any person that produces the message

Language Focus

1. **Fill in the blanks in the following passage with an appropriate word from those given below in its proper form.**

nonverbal	movement	limit	contact
language	multiply	distinction	further
tone	revealing	remark	gesture

   How do we communicate? The first answer that is likely to come to most people's minds is through (1)_____: we speak, we listen, we read, we write. When we think (2)_____, we become increasingly aware that we also communicate in (3)_____ ways, through gestures and body (4)_____. The signals given by our "body language" are often more (5)_____ than the words we use. Most of us will have had the experience of someone saying something to us — making a flattering (6)_____, for instance—that we felt was insincere. Why did we feel that? Maybe it was the (7)_____ in which it was said, or something in the person's movement or eye (8)_____ with us.

When we turn to communication process across cultures, the complexities and complications (9)_____. Language is again the most obvious example. If you speak only English and the person you try to talk to speaks only Japanese, communication will be (10)_____ — though you will, if you both really try, be able to understand each other to some extent by means of (11)_____. Even with speakers of the same language, problems may be the result of intracultural differences, that is, (12)_____ between subgroups within a culture.

2. **Find the appropriate prepositions or adverbs that collocate with the words in bold letters.**
   1) One can **derive** a lot of pleasure _____ watching and hearing the interplay of speech and movement in a dramatic performance.
   2) A group of plants and animals living and **interacting** _____ one another in a specific region under relatively similar environmental conditions.
   3) Intercultural communication **refers** _____ the exchange of information between individuals who are unalike culturally.
   4) It is really hard to **put** my present feelings _____ words.
   5) He tries not to let his business **interfere** _____ his home life.
   6) The negotiations will **call** _____ considerable dexterity.
   7) All electronic computers **consist** _____ five units although they are of different kinds.
   8) The worse part is he is **unconscious** _____ his mistake during the conversation.
   9) The success of this project **is** _____ a set of specific factors.
   10) Honesty and hard work **contribute** _____ success and happiness.

3. **Error Correction: Each of the following sentences has at least one grammatical error. Identify the errors and make corrections.**
   1) It comes from the Latin "communicare," that means, "to make common" or "to share."
   2) Communication is a form of human behaviors derived from a need to connect and interact with other human beings.
   3) Communication can be taken place on different levels and can be classified into several types.
   4) It is the process of understanding and sharing of meaning in pairs or in small groups. What constitute such interaction?
   5) Speaker A is the source — the point which information or interaction originates.
   6) Feedback in fact makes possible for the source or sender to adjust himself so as to proceed with the interaction.
   7) The context could be as small as a classroom or dinner table, and at the same time it could be as big as the entire cultural environment.
   8) Intercultural communication and intracultural communication consists of the same components.
   9) The following diagram shows components and the process of a communication event.
   10) The following is some of the most distinctive features of communication.
   11) Communication is always done in two ways: the source sends messages to the receiver

and the receiver responds to the message receiving and sends his message or response to the source.
12) We have not to say everything we intend to communicate in words.
13) A sigh or frown accompanied speech, if noticed by the receiver, may also carry unintended messages to the receiver.
14) If the patterns are shared and understood, any communication becomes easy and effective.
15) The physical surroundings serve as the background of our interaction and, to a large extent, defines what we communicate and how we do it.
16) What people relate to one another will determine both the form and content of communication.

Comprehensive Work
1. **Pair Work**
1) **Discuss with your partner the factors that can be barriers to human communication and what people can do to facilitate communication.**

English is widely used the world over. Sometimes its use as a second or foreign language may cause problems in communication. Read the following commercial signs written in English in many different countries and guess the meaning that was originally intended to convey.

a. In a Bucharest hotel lobby...

The lift is being fixed for the next day. During that time we regret that you will be unbearable.

b. In a Bangkok temple...

It is forbidden to enter a woman even a foreigner if dressed as a man.

c. A sign outside a doctor's office in Rome...

Specialist in Women and Other Diseases.

Unit 2 Understanding Communication

d. A sign posted in a German park...

It is strictly forbidden on our black forest camping site that people of different sex, for instance, men and women, live together in one tent unless they are married with each other for that purpose.

You may find these commercial signs are not only quite misleading but amusing as well. What improvement will you make on the above mistranslations? Have you ever found some similar cases of mistranslation in your life?

_____
_____

2) **In communication, the sentence meaning and the speaker's meaning may not be exactly the same. What is important to successful communication is not just knowing the sentence meaning, but also knowing what the speaker actually means by the sentence said. Work with your partner and decide what the second speaker probably means in each of the following short conversations.**

Conversation 1
A: Tea?
B: It would keep me awake all night.

Conversation 2
A: Can you tell me the time?
B: Well, the milkman has come.

Conversation 3
A: Is John a good cook?
B: He's English.

Conversation 4
Reporter: Senator, what is the present state of your marriage?
Senator: Well, we, I think have been able to make some very good progress and it's ...I would say that it's ... it's ... it's delightful that we're able to ...

to share the time and the relationship
that we... that we do share.

2. Group Work

In our life, there are many situations where people tend to use indirect ways to express themselves. For instance, they do not often say "no" directly to others but may express it in some other ways. Form groups of four or five. Interview some people you know and try to find out how they would respond or behave in the following situation. Report your findings in class.

Situation 1

When someone asks if he can copy your homework and you do not want to comply, you will ...

Situation 2

When you are asked by your boss to work overtime at the weekend and you do not really want to, you will ...

Situation 3

When you are asked by your parents about your problems in your studies and you do not want to tell them, you will ...

Situation 4

When you are asked whether you agree with a professor's idea about an issue that you do not really agree with, you will ...

3. Writing — Prompt Writing

1) Spend ten to fifteen minutes on free writing about this picture.
2) Choose an aspect of your free writing exercise as a starting point for a short story. The story does not have to explain the picture, so long as the picture has in some way inspired the resulting work.
3) Share the stories with your classmates, explaining how the picture resulted in the work.

Read More

Text C How Long Does It Take to Say I'm Getting Married (I)

I (Waverly) had taken my mother out to lunch at my favorite Chinese restaurant in the hope of putting her in a good mood, but it was a disaster.

When we met at the Four Directions Restaurant, she eyed me with immediate disapproval. "Ai-ya! What's the matter with your hair?" she said in Chinese.

"What do you mean, 'What's the matter,'" I said. "I had it cut." Mr. Rory had styled my hair differently this time, an asymmetrical bluntline fringe that was shorter on the left side. It was fashionable, yet not radically so.

"Looks chopped off," she said. "You must ask for your money back."

I sighed. "Let's just have a nice lunch together, okay?"

She wore her tight-lipped, pinched-nose look as she scanned the menu, muttering, "Not too many good things, this menu." Then she tapped the waiter's arm, wiped the length of her chopsticks with her finger and sniffed: "This greasy thing, do you expect me to eat with it?" She made a show of washing out her rice bowl with hot tea, and then warned other restaurant patrons seated near us to do the same. She told the waiter to make sure the soup was very hot, and, of course, it was by her tongue's expert estimate "not even lukewarm."

"You shouldn't get so upset," I said to my mother after she disputed a charge of two extra dollars because she had specified chrysanthemum tea instead of the regular green tea. "Besides, unnecessary stress isn't good for your heart."

"Nothing is wrong with my heart," she huffed as she kept a disparaging eye on the waiter.

And she was right. Despite all the tension she places on herself — and others — the doctors have proclaimed that my mother, at age sixty-nine, has the blood pressure of a sixteen-year-old and the strength of a horse.

After our miserable lunch, I gave up the idea that there would ever be a good time to tell her the news: that Rich Schields and I were getting married.

My mother had never met Rich. In fact, every time I brought up his name — when I said, for instance, that Rich and I had gone to the symphony, that Rich had taken my four-year-old daughter, Shoshana, to the zoo — my mother found a way to change the subject.

"Did I tell you," I said as we waited for the lunch bill, "what a great time Shoshana had with Rich? He —"

"Oh," interrupted my mother, "I didn't tell you. Your father, doctors say maybe need surgery. But no, now they say everything normal." I gave up. And then we did the usual routine.

I paid for the bill, with a ten and three ones. My mother pulled back the dollar bills and counted out exact change, thirteen cents, and put that on the tray instead, explaining firmly: "No tip!" She tossed her head back with a triumphant smile. And while my mother used the restroom, I slipped the waiter a five-dollar bill. He nodded to me with deep understanding. While she was gone, I devised another plan. When she returned, I said, "But before I drop you off, let's stop at my place real quick. There's something I want to show you."

My mother had not been to my apartment in months. When I was first married, she used to drop by unannounced, until one day I suggested she should call ahead of time. Ever since then, she had refused to come unless I issue an official invitation.

And so I watched her, seeing her reaction to the changes in my apartment — from the pristine habitat I maintained after the divorce, when all of a sudden I had too much time to keep my life in order to this present chaos, a home full of life and love. The hallway floor was littered with Shoshana's toys, all bright plastic things with scattered parts. There was a set of Rich's barbells in the living room, two dirty snifters on the coffee table, the disemboweled remains of a phone that Shoshana and Rich had taken apart the other day to see where the voices came from.

"It's back here," I said. We kept walking, all the way to the back bedroom. The bed was unmade, dresser drawers were hanging out with socks and ties spilling over. My mother stepped over running shoes, more of Shoshana's toys, Rich's black loafers, my scarves, a stack of white shirts just back from the cleaner's.

Her look was one of painful denial, reminding me of a time long ago when she took my brothers and me down to a clinic to get our polio booster shots. As the needle went into my brother's arm and he screamed, my mother looked at me with agony written all over her face and assured me, "Next one doesn't hurt."

But now, how could my mother not notice that we were living together, that this was serious and would not go away even if she didn't talk about it? She had to say something.

I went to the closet and then came back with a mink jacket that Rich had given me for Christmas. It was the most extravagant gift I had ever received.

I put the jacket on. "It's sort of a silly present," I said nervously. "It's hardly ever cold enough in San Francisco to wear mink. But it seems to be a fad, what people are buying their wives and girlfriends these days."

My mother was quiet. She was looking toward my open closet, bulging with racks of shoes, ties, my dresses, and Rich's suits. She ran her fingers over the mink.

"This is not so good," she said at last. "It is just leftover strips. And the fur is too short, no long hairs."

"How can you criticize a gift!" I protested. I was deeply wounded. "He gave me this from his heart."

"This is why I worry," she said.

And looking at the coat in the mirror, I couldn't fend off the strength of her will anymore, her ability to make me see black where there was once white, white where there was once black. The coat looked shabby, an imitation of romance.

"Aren't you going to say anything else?" I asked softly.

"What should I say?"

"About the apartment? About this?" I gestured to all the signs of Rich lying about.

She looked around the room, toward the hall, and finally she said, "You have career. You are busy. You want to live like mess, what can I say?"

1. **Fill in the blanks.**
   1) Waverly's lunch with her mother turned out _____.
   2) Waverly wanted to put her mother in a good mood because _____.
   3) Waverly's mother _____ the Chinese restaurant they went to.
   4) When Waverly said "There's something I want to show you," she intended to show her mother _____.
   5) Waverly's mother _____ Waverly's apartment and her mink jacket.

2. **The following conversations are from the above story. Please identify the ingredients of communication based on the knowledge in Text A.**

   Conversation 1

   Mother: Ai-ya! What's the matter with your hair?

   Waverly: What do you mean, "What's the matter," I had it cut.

   Mother: Looks chopped off. You must ask for your money back.

   Source: _____

Encoding: _____
Message: _____
Channel: _____
Receiver: _____
Decoding: _____

Conversation 2

Waverly: Aren't you going to say anything else?
Mother: What should I say?
Waverly: About the apartment? About this? (gesturing to all the signs of Rich lying about)
Mother: You have career. You are busy. You want to live like mess, what can I say?

Source: _____
Encoding: _____
Message: _____
Channel: _____
Receiver: _____
Decoding: _____

Books to Read

1. Tan, Amy. *The Joy Luck Club*. New York: G. P. Putnam's Sons, 1989.
- This book is a best-selling novel. It focuses on four Chinese American immigrant families who start a club known as "the Joy Luck Club." There are sixteen chapters divided into four sections, and each woman, both mothers and daughters (with the exception of one mother, Suyuan Woo, who dies before the novel opens), share stories about their lives in the form of vignettes. Each section comes after a parable. This novel explores the clash between Chinese culture and American culture.
2. Mckay, Matthew, Martha Davis and Patrick Fanning. *Messages: The Communication Skills Book*. Oakland: New Harbinger Publications, 1995.
- This is an amazing self-help book that cuts through all big words and psychological concepts. It gets immediately into helping you change. The concise explanations of poor communication patterns will help you change your attitude and methods of communicating with others.

Movie to Watch

Driving Miss Daisy is based on the Pulitzer Prize-winning play by Alfred Uhry. It affectionately covers the twenty-five year relationship between a wealthy, strong-willed Southern matron (Jessica Tandy) and her equally indomitable black chauffeur Hoke (Morgan Freeman). Neither of them could understand each other at the beginning of the movie. However, the two fully realize that they have been friends.

Unit 3
Verbal Communication (I)

> The notion that thought can be perfectly or even adequately expressed in verbal symbols is idiotic.
> —— Alfred North Whitehead
>
> Words have frightening power.
> —— Colin Cherry

Unit Goals

- To understand how language and culture are closely linked
- To understand cultural influences on meanings of words and analyze denotational and connotational differences between English and Chinese words and idioms
- To learn useful words and expressions about verbal communication and improve language skills

Before You Read

It has been realized that basic color terms could arouse intercultural misunderstanding. Discuss the cultural associations of color in different cultures with your partner.

Culture	Red	Yellow	Green	Blue
European and North American				
Chinese				
Japanese				
Arab				

Start to Read

Text A Cultural Differences on Lexical Level

Words are the basic units of meaning. Understanding the meanings of words is, therefore, critical to the sharing of meanings conveyed in verbal communication. Lexical meaning can largely be grouped into two types: denotation and connotation. Denotation is the conceptual meaning of the word that designates or describes things, events or processes, etc. It is the primary, explicit meaning given in the definition of a word in a dictionary. The connotation refers to the emotional or stylistic associations that a word or phrase suggests in one's mind. It is the implicit, supplementary value which is added to the purely denotative meaning of a word or phrase.

Cultural Differences in Denotative Meanings

Each culture creates certain vocabulary to describe its unique physical and social environments as well as the activities its people engage in those contexts. So the absence of certain objects, events, concepts or states in one culture will naturally result in the absence of the necessary vocabulary to refer to them. Words like "炕""节气""关系""太极拳""功夫""德育""三纲五常""五行" etc. can only make sense to the Chinese, and words like "privacy," "Thanksgiving Day," "parliament," "motel," "hostel," etc. are foreign to most Chinese. The unique vocabulary can cause great trouble in translation. For the sake of clarity and accuracy, adequate explanation can be added in such cases.

In addition to the total equivalence of words and absence of equivalents in denoting certain referents, cultures also overlap in the denotation of certain vocabulary. For example, the languages of the Chinese, British and Eskimos all have words that refer to the natural phenomenon "snow," but the Chinese and English languages only have a general term for this while the Eskimos have many words for different kinds of snow. So the meaning of the word "snow" in the English or Chinese language does not coincide with the meanings expressed by the Eskimos' words, which are more specific and minute. So the overlapping of denotative meaning should not lead us to the misbelief that seemingly equivalent words refer to the same thing in both languages of the speaker and listener in an intercultural setting. The English connotation of some words like kinship terms as "uncle," "aunt," "niece," "sister" or "brother" can hardly cover the complex relations reflected in Chinese kinship terms. Without  mentioning the exact reference of the terms used, these words cannot be translated into proper Chinese at all, because it is always necessary in Chinese to make a clear distinction about the relationships of the relative to the persons concerned. Whether the relative is from one's mother side or one's father's side, whether he is younger or older than one's parents or oneself, all influence the exact term a Chinese uses in addressing him.

The implication for foreign language learners and intercultural communicators is that they must learn or use the words in another language with the right denotation. Otherwise, their communication will be based on wrong references and misunderstandings will follow up.

Cultural Differences in Connotative Meanings

A typical example of this kind of distinction is the color language. The Chinese and English both have words denoting the basic colors, but the meanings associated with these color words are quite different. Take "yellow" for example. Yellow in English is usually associated with the state of being cowardly, as in "yellow-bellied" and "yellow streak." In Chinese, however, the word "黄色" carries the meaning of being pornographic and obscene, as in "黄色书刊," "黄色电影." Not knowing such differences, some students translated such Chinese terms directly into English as "yellow books" and "yellow movies," which seem bizarre or ridiculous to English speakers.

Animal words may also have different connotations in different languages. The owl is associated with wisdom in English, as in the saying "as wise as an owl." But in Chinese, the owl is a symbol of bad luck. The proverb "夜猫子进宅,好事不来" means if the owl comes at night, misfortune will follow. The dragon is the totem of the Chinese people. The word "dragon" is in every sense a positive term in Chinese. Its common associations are "good luck and fortune," "wisdom," "royal and noble," etc. There are many phrases to show Chinese love for this legendary animal: "龙凤呈祥," "藏龙卧虎," "龙头企业," "龙子龙孙," etc. In English, the word "Dragon" refers to a dreadful creature like a crocodile or snake (*Oxford Advanced Learner's Dictionary of Current English*), and it is associated with fierceness and derogatory sense when used to describe a person. In another dictionary (COBUND), there is a sentence "if you call a woman a dragon, you mean that she is fierce and unpleasant."

Numbers, due to their sounds or stories about them, may also have special meanings in certain cultures. 13 is most unwelcome in Western countries because of its connection with the "Last Supper" of Jesus Christ. 4 is to be avoided in China, Japan and South Korea for its similar sound with the word "death" or "to die" in all the three languages spoken there. 8 is loved by many Chinese as it sounds like "发" in Cantonese, meaning "to be prosperous" or "to make a fortune." Knowing a few of the nuances behind numbers gives you a better understanding of why many Chinese businesses flocked to the San Gabriel Valley of Southern California. The area code in that vicinity was 818 or "Prosperity guaranteed prosperity!"

After You Read

Knowledge Focus

1. **Pair Work: Discuss the following questions with your partner.**
    1) What are the two layers of meanings?
    2) What is denotation? Give examples to illustrate it.
    3) What is connotation? Give examples to illustrate it.

4) Can you give some examples of the overlapping of denotative meaning in the languages of Chinese and English?
5) Find some expressions with the same denotation but different connotations in the languages of Chinese and English.
6) Find some words with connotations in one language but without the connotation in another.

2. Solo Work: Multiple Choices
 1) Many words from Chinese and English are different in both the denotative meanings and connotative meanings. Which of the following is an example for this?
   A. 鸽子/dove   B. 猫头鹰/owl
   C. 龙/dragon   D. 红/red
 2) Denotation refers to _____.
   A. the figurative meaning of a word
   B. the associated meaning of a word
   C. the set of associations implied by a word
   D. the most specific and direct meaning of a word
 3) "Dumpling" is often used as the translation of the typical Chinese food "jiaozi," but in fact it is quite misleading because of _____.
   A. the cultural difference in denotative meaning
   B. the cultural difference in connotative meaning
   C. the different intercultural settings
   D. the different cultural emphases
 4) Colors have both similar and different meanings in different languages. For example, yellow is the color of _____ in English.
   A. mourning   B. fear   C. danger   D. violence
 5) In Chinese, there are two sets of names zumu/nainai, waizumu/waipo for the English word "grandmother." This reflects that _____.
   A. these so-called equivalents are only partly equivalent
   B. Chinese emphasize more on kinships
   C. terms in one language find no counterparts in the other language
   D. we have to find appropriate words to express ourselves in a foreign language

Language Focus
1. Fill in the blanks with the following words or expressions you have learned in Text A.

convey	designate	explicit	implicit	minute
associate	bizarre	totem	nuance	coincide with

 1) The North American Indians used to make _____ poles.
 2) The town has been _____ a development area.
 3) She _____ happiness with having money.
 4) That rich artistic performance is full of _____.
 5) The demonstration had been carefully stage-managed to _____ the Prime Minister's visit.

6) If you listened carefully, you would find out that her attitude was _____ in the answer she gave us.
7) I had remembered in _____ detail everything that had happened.
8) Mary is a person who calls a spade a spade. She was quite _____ about why she left.
9) The audience cannot help laughing at the grotesque appearance of that _____ actor.
10) He always tends to use more words than necessary to _____ his ideas.

2. **Fill in the blanks with the proper form of the words in the brackets.**
   1) A _____ (supplement) grant may be awarded at the discretion of the committee.
   2) His social pretensions make him appear _____ (ridicule).
   3) He was sentenced to be guilty of intrusion upon my _____ (private).
   4) What if you want to compare the actual contents of an object for _____ (equivalent)?
   5) _____ (Clear) of diction is vital for a public speaker.
   6) She plays with _____ (seem) effortless skill.
   7) There is no further _____ (refer) to him in her diary.
   8) He smiled, with the _____ (imply) that he did not believe me.

3. **Find the appropriate prepositions or adverbs that collocate with the words in bold letters.**
   1) He is going to live by the coast _____ **the sake of** his health.
   2) **In addition** _____ giving a general introduction to computer, the course also provides practical experience.
   3) My religious beliefs do not **coincide** _____ yours.
   4) Judgment should **be based** _____ facts, not on hearsay.
   5) I do not want to **associate** myself _____ them any more.
   6) Can you **translate** the sentence _____ English?
   7) They **attribute** their success _____ their teacher's encouragement.
   8) The television station apologized for the interference, which was **due** _____ bad weather conditions.

4. **Error Correction: Each of the following sentences has at least one grammatical error. Identify the errors and make corrections.**
   1) Understanding the meanings of words are critical to the sharing of meanings conveyed in verbal communication.
   2) Denotation is the conceptual meaning of the word that designates or describes things, events or process, etc.
   3) Denotation is the primary, explicit meaning giving in the definition of a word in a dictionary.
   4) Each culture creates a certain vocabulary to describe its unique physical and social environments as well as the activities its people engage in those contexts.
   5) The absence of certain objects, events, concepts or states in one culture will naturally result in the absence of the necessary vocabulary referred to them.
   6) The unique vocabulary can cause a great trouble in translation.
   7) For sake of clarity and accuracy, adequate explanation can be added in such cases.
   8) The meaning of the word "snow" in the English or Chinese language do not coincide with the meanings expressed by the Eskimos' words.
   9) So the overlapping of denotative meaning should not lead us to the misbelief that seeming equivalent words refer to one and the same thing in both languages of the

speaker and listener in intercultural setting.

10) Whether the relative is from one's mother side and one's father's side, all influence the exact term a Chinese uses in addressing him.

11) Otherwise, their communication will base on wrong references and misunderstandings will follow up.

12) Chinese and English have both words denoting the basic colors.

13) There are many phrases show Chinese love for this legendary animal.

14) Dragon is associated with fierceness and derogatory sense when using to describe a person.

15) In the worst case, translators might find themselves in a dilemma there is almost no way out.

16) Besides physical drives, men devote themselves to wide range of pursuits, such as pleasure, profits, and religions.

Comprehensive Work

1. **Pair Work**

   1) Observe the following paragraph and discuss the meanings of the color words in it.

      Mr. Brown is a very white (　　) man. He was looking rather green (　　) the other day. He has been feeling blue (　　) lately. When I saw him, he was in a brown study (　　). I hope he will soon be in the pink (　　) again.

   2) What are the similarities and differences in the meanings of the following animal words in both Chinese and English?

Chinese word	English word	Associated meaning in Chinese	Associated meaning in English
凤凰	phoenix		
狗	dog		
蝙蝠	bat		

2. **Group Work**

   Discuss the translation of the brand names with your group members.

3. **Writing**

In many cases, the typical Chinese way of writing seems to be the inverse of the approach preferences by westerners. Western writers are generally expected to state their point right at the beginning and even begin each paragraph with a topic sentence. But in Chinese writing, it is more acceptable to build up the point rather than announce it right from the start; statements of main points are delayed till later or even near the end. This difference has often been one of the causes of misunderstanding between Chinese and Westerners in communication.

Read the following article written by an American writer, Donna Pilato. Then rewrite the article in the Chinese way. When you finish, compare the two articles with each other to see what advantages and disadvantages they may have respectively.

A Housewarming Party

Moving into a new home ranks among the more exciting events in life. It is definitely time to break out the bubbly and celebrate. It can also be stressful if you are moving away from friends and family. In either case, holding a housewarming party is a good way to welcome new and old friends to your home.

If you are hosting your own party, you do not need to wait until your home is in perfect shape or until everything is unpacked. People understand that it takes a long time to get settled, and they are more curious to see what the house looks like than critical of the naked windows that do not have custom curtains hung yet.

The good news is that despite all the confusion of your move, a housewarming can be a relatively informal and simple event. Your home is the main attraction so you do not need to plan lots of activities to keep your guests amused. They will be far more interested in touring your house than in playing party games at this time. The only game that might be useful is a simple icebreaker to introduce old friends to new neighbors. In fact, housewarmings are sometimes the only way old neighbors get to see each other with the busy schedules we all live.

As is mentioned earlier, tours of your new home are the main event. Therefore, you should have a plan for handling them. If you plan to conduct the tours, you will need someone to act as host, answering the door, welcoming your guests, and making them comfortable until the next tour begins. You can assign a close friend or family member to act as tour guide for you. You can also allow guests to give self-guided tours. In that case, you might want to give your guests a floor plan of your home. Label each room with its name, purpose and any interesting details you would like to show off. If you have made extensive renovations to your home, post a "before" picture outside each room. You could also post pictures taken of the rooms while under construction. People love to see the magical transformation. This is one occasion where you should clean all of your rooms. Ignore this suggestion if your party is taking place while your boxes are still packed. Then anything goes!

Read More

Text B Translation and Cultures

Pre-reading Exercise

Before reading Text B, translate the following terms into Chinese and look them up in an English-English dictionary. Compare your translation in Chinese and the English definition.

individualism _____
idealist _____
materialism _____
landlord _____
capitalist _____
political _____
ambition _____
propaganda _____
peasant _____
criticism _____

    Among different cultures one can find similar traditions and practices, as well as totally different or even contradictory ones. Shared cultural elements make cross-cultural communication possible, which means translation, a form of cross-cultural communication, is feasible to some extent. Different traditions, however, often present varied social and political concepts, thus posing cultural barriers and putting translators in a difficult situation where lots of cultural elements have to be translated. In the worst case, translators might find themselves in a dilemma where there is almost no way out.

    For example, Chinese medical theory is heavily based on Taoist philosophy from which 气 (chi), 阴阳 (yin and yang), and 五行 (five elements, including Metal, Wood, Water, Fire, and Earth) are developed. For Chinese physicians, a healthy body must maintain balance and harmony of the yin-yang, five elements and the Chi through proper nutrition, even nutritional breathing. Sometimes an illness might be caused by "too much fire" in a patient's liver (肝火过旺). How can a translator convey the same concept to western readers? In this situation, cultural references or connotations outrun the language.

    On the contrary, everyone has the same physical drives regardless of race, color, culture, and age. A man drinks water to quench his thirst and eats food when hungry. It follows that "I am hungry" can be readily translated into Chinese. However, besides physical drives, men devote themselves to a wide range of pursuits, such as pleasure, profits, and religions. People from different cultures generally have varied perspectives on these issues. Western society and Westerners' relations with the spiritual world are influenced by Christianity. In contrast, the Chinese establish relations with world and the society mainly on the basis of Confucianism, Buddhism, and Taoism. In China, proper relations, such as husband-and-wife, supervisor-and-subordinate, and teacher-and-student relations, manifest themselves in the hierarchy of society. Attached to these relations are expectations of behavior, rituals, and face-giving. The cultural differences between Eastern and Western societies pose difficulties to English-Chinese/Chinese-English translators.

Moreover, a figure or creature may have opposing connotations in different cultures. There is a saying that goes, "One person's meat is another person's poison." A symbol sacred in one culture may be deemed evil in another. A typical example is the symbol created by the mythical beast: "the dragon"（龙）. The dragon represents power and authority in Chinese culture. However, it is often used in a derogatory manner to describe a fierce person, as in the sentence "The woman in charge of the accounts department is an absolute dragon." When translating this sentence into Chinese, translators have to either use a different metaphor, such as "母夜叉" (an ugly, female devil in Chinese culture) or just paraphrase it.

It sometimes occurs that metaphors used in the source language do not exist in the target language. In this situation, cultural barriers will be erected and translation dilemmas inevitably ensue. For example, there is an old Chinese saying "不到黄河心不死" (Literally, it means refusing to stop until one reaches the Yellow River). This expression actually means "refusing to give up until one reaches one's goals." Translators have to find equivalent expressions or paraphrase it when doing translation, because the Yellow River, which is inextricably linked to Chinese culture, does not exist in the Western world. Verbatim translation will not create the same image in the minds of western readers as it does with Chinese people.

How should translators deal with cultural barriers that they encounter?

Translators cannot do their job well without taking cultural references into consideration. They ought to keep in mind that both the source language and the target language should be given the same emphasis during the process of translation. The concept of "functional equivalence," first proposed by Eugene A. Nida, provides a guiding principle for translators when dealing with translation problems related to cultural differences. It emphasizes that the equivalence of cultural elements overweighs that of words. The "faithfulness" of a translation lies in whether cultural connotations from the source language have been successfully conveyed to the target language.

An understanding that regards translation as a cultural rather than a linguistic conveyance, should be promoted. The act of translation is no longer "transcoding" but rather an act of communication. As we know, metaphors and culturally charged idioms not only add flavor to texts, but also represent the worlds created by different peoples. Although the importance of metaphors varies depending on text types, keeping the original metaphor(s), or at least transferring them as much as possible, should be put at the top of translators' priorities. With this being said, it is acceptable that translators ignore metaphors when dealing with reports or surveys where metaphors play a relatively less important role and clarity is the top priority. In other words, translators have a wide freedom of seeking alternatives to first comprehend the meaning of the expression under consideration and then use everyday common phrases to get the point across.

In short, a good translation is determined by an excellent trade-off between how to maintain culturally charged expressions and how to avoid unreadability.

Unit 3 Verbal Communication (9)

Notes

Eugene A. Nida (born on November 11, 1914) is the developer of the dynamic-equivalence *Bible* translation theory. He has been a pioneer in the fields of translation theory and linguistics.

Text C   How to Improve Verbal Communication

Pre-reading Exercise
Pair Work
1. People from different countries may use different expressions to convey the same meaning. In the following chart, the left column is the expressions commonly used in Singapore. Work with your partner and figure out the American equivalents. You will find the answers in Text C.

In Singapore, these are common:	In the United States, these are common:
Please queue up.	
Could I have the bill, please?	
Take away, please.	

2. What do the following idioms mean? You will also find the answers in Text C.
    break a leg

    _____
    to hold one's tongue

    _____
    to rain cats and dogs

    _____
    more money down the drain

    _____

In discussing verbal communication, the choice of words and expressions, organization of messages, and clarity of pronunciation will be examined.

Choice of words and expressions
When you are communicating with people of a different culture, you need to pay careful attention to your choice of words and expressions. Avoid ambiguous words, unfamiliar words, acronyms, idiomatic expressions and slang.

37

Ambiguous words

The same word may have very different interpretations in different cultures and this could give rise to miscommunication when interacting with people across cultures. Here are some examples:

When one suggests tabling something for discussion, it means putting it on the meeting agenda in England but it means taking it off the agenda in the US.

Unfamiliar words

The use of unfamiliar words can also cause a breakdown in communication.

e.g.

In Singapore, these are common:	In the United States, these are common:
Please queue up.	Please get in line.
Could I have the bill, please?	Could I have the cheque, please?
Take away, please.	To go, please.

Acronyms

Acronyms that are easily understood by members of one culture may be totally incomprehensible to members of another culture.

e.g. FYI, ASAP, EDB, IPO

Idioms

These expressions can create a breakdown in communication when used in an intercultural context, especially one involving non-native speakers of English. For instance,

to break a leg (to do well at some performance)

to hold one's tongue (to refrain from saying something unpleasant or nasty)

to rain cats and dogs (to rain very heavily)

more money down the drain (more money to spend)

Slang

Cultures may develop their own slang that may be foreign to other cultures using the same language. For instance,

An advertisement by Electrolux worked very well in Europe but was unusable in the United States. The advertisement carries the slogan, "Nothing *sucks* like the Electrolux." The slogan will not go down well with an American audience because the slang expression "it sucks" has negative connotations in the US. In Europe, the word "sucks" has a literal meaning, so the slogan is perfectly all right.

Organization of messages

It is also important to organize your messages in a way that is suitable for your target audience whose culture is different from yours. Many English-speaking countries prefer a direct approach to most messages with the main idea presented first and the details given later. However, for many other cultures like Latin American, Japanese and Arabic cultures, this direct approach is not usually favored and may even sometimes be seen as tactless and rude. This preference can be traced back to the nature of the culture with respect to face-saving.

Clarity of pronunciation

The clear articulation of speech is important in any speaking situation but even more so when speaking in an intercultural communication context. Some words are so close in pronunciation that articulating them wrongly or "lazily" could create confusion in communication as in the following cases.

differ/defer	pot/port	access/assess	tree/three
leaf/lift	pan/pen	paint/pain	cuff/carve

For Fun

Book to Read

Lewis, Richard D. *When Cultures Collide: Leading across Cultures*. London: Nicholas Brealey Publishing, 2005.

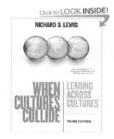

- The successful managers for the next century will be the culturally sensitive ones. You can gain competitive advantage from having strategies to deal with the cultural differences you will encounter in any international business setting. Richard Lewis, a speaker of 12 languages, provides a guide to working and communicating across cultures, and explains how your culture and language affect the ways in which you think and respond.

Movie to Watch

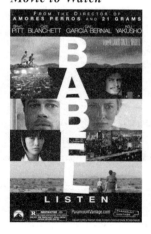

Babel is one of the most intelligent and artfully made films of 2006. The film has two central themes—culture and communication. It brilliantly weaves four deeply interconnected stories engaging five cultures on three continents. The cultures are North American, Mexican, Islamic and Japanese. At the heart of each tragedy is an inability to communicate. The tragedies begin with bad decisions that spin each plot somewhat out of control once cultural interference and miscommunication kick in.

Unit 4
Verbal Communication (II)

> Even if you do learn to speak correct English, whom are you going to speak it to?
> —— Clarence Darrow
>
> Words are, of course, the most powerful drug used by mankind.
> —— Rudyard Kipling

Unit Goals

- To understand how language and culture are closely linked
- To learn to make intercultural comparisons of different pragmatic rules used in various speech acts
- To discuss how superficial behaviors are related to the cultural assumptions of the speakers
- To learn useful words and expressions about verbal communication and improve language skills

Before You Read

Compliments are an expression of praise, respect, or approval. How will Chinese and American respond to the following compliments respectively? Then role-play these situations with your partner in the class.

Compliments	Chinese response	English response
1. This is really a nice sweater.		
2. You did a good job.		
3. I like your scarf. It's very pretty.		
4. Your English is good!		

You may find there is a huge difference between Chinese and English compliments. What do you think may be the cultural root of this difference?

___

Start to Read

Text A Compliments in Chinese and American English (I)

Compliments are commonly and widely used both in Chinese society and American society to greet, encourage, thank, and to open a conversation. As a polite speech act that explicitly or implicitly attributes credit to someone for something that is valued positively by the speaker and hearer, a native speaker of a particular language is taken for granted to know when and how to offer and respond compliment appropriately. For example:

1) 甲：你的字写得真好，学的是什么体啊？
   Your handwriting is beautiful, what style are you following?
   乙：哪里，哪里，我还差得远着呢，什么体也不是。
   No, it's nothing. I am just scratching.
2) A: Your French is good. Where did you learn your excellent French?
   B: Thank you. I learned it at my university.

It is clear that a Chinese and an American respond to a compliment differently. For a simple compliment like the above, a Chinese tend not to accept the compliment though the particular compliment itself to his talent in handwriting is well appreciated. As for an American, he or she normally accepts the compliment with pleasure.

Topics for Chinese and American Compliments

Both in Chinese and American societies, compliments are employed to start a conversation. Appearances, talents, ability, and achievements are common topics in Chinese and American language.

Complimenting appearance

The appearance of a speaker or hearer such as color of skin, clothing, style, etc. is a major topic of compliment, but the difference is that sex is an important factor for consideration when a Chinese is to compliment the appearance of a hearer. For example:

3) 今天你真精神！
   You look handsome today.
4) 多漂亮的毛衣啊！
   What a beautiful sweater!

In the Chinese society, if the hearer is a male, complimenting his appearance as shown in Example 3) is appropriate. But the speaker has to be very careful if he or she is to compliment a female hearer because it is against rules governing the speech act of compliment in Chinese unless the speaker is very intimate to the hearer. But it is all right for a Chinese speaker to compliment a hearer of same sex with regard to the appearance. Besides, age or social status is also a factor that affects the speech act of compliment if this speech act happens between two interlocutors of the same sex. A senior speaker can compliment a junior hearer's appearance but not vise versa. For example:

5) (年长者或上级)小李,你这身打扮真精神。

(A senior speaker to a junior hearer) You look terrific today.

Complimenting the appearance of a hearer is more flexible in the American society, and a female hearer tends to welcome or appreciate compliments of her appearance be it from a male or female speaker.

6) You're wearing a lovely skirt. You look sexy.

7) Your new sweater looks great on you. I really like the style.

Compliments in Examples 6) and 7) are quite appropriate to a female hearer in American English regardless of the sex of the speaker. But it would be inappropriate or even rude in the Chinese context.

Complimenting talent or ability

The talent or ability is another major topic of compliments in both Chinese and American societies. But again there are two differences between the two languages. First, compliments by an American speaker would focus more on the achievements by a hearer as a result of hard work and less on the talent or ability of the hearer. For example:

8) You've done a great job.

9) You made a great presentation. I like it.

But a Chinese speaker tends to compliment a hearer's quality or talent. For example:

10) 你真能干,把家操持得这么好。

What a capable housewife! You take so good care of your family.

11) 你脾气真好,对孩子这么有耐心。

You have got such a good temper and are so patient to kids.

The second difference is that in American society compliments on one's ability are usually made by the speaker of higher social status because they are serious judgments that have to be made by capable people. Obviously it would be inappropriate for a speaker with lower social status to make such compliments to a hearer with higher social status. For example:

12) I am satisfied with what you have done.

13) (A native speaker to a non-native speaker) I must applaud your excellent English. I wish my Chinese were as good as your English.

In the Chinese context, however, it is not uncommon to have compliments from a junior official to his or her superior. For example:

14) 刘教授,您知道得真多,我现在明白了。

You're so knowledgeable, Professor Liu. Now I fully understood this point.

Cleary, Example 14) would be very inappropriate in American context. In fact it could be regarded as a flattery rather than a compliment.

Text B Compliments in Chinese and American English (II)

Formulas of Compliments in Chinese and American English

One may have noticed that examples of compliments above, either Chinese or American English, have been highly formulaic in nature. Manes & Wolfson believe that only three basic syntactic patterns would suffice the expression of compliments. They are:

NP is/looks (really) ADJ (e.g., "Your blouse is beautiful.")

I (really) like/love NP (e.g., "I like your car.")

Pro is (really) (a) ADJ NP (e.g., "That's a nice painting.")

As for Chinese, there has been so far no comprehensive study on the formulas of Chinese compliments. But it is clear that compliments in Chinese context are viewed as a means or intention to show respect, therefore, should be very polite. On many occasions, a Chinese speaker tends to play down himself or herself to show his or her respect to the hearer when making compliments. Instead of "你" (you), its honorific form "您" (you) is often used. Moreover, the honorific form of *you* is often employed at the very beginning of a sentence. For example:

15) 您的设计多有创意啊。

What an original design!

16) 您这件毛衣很漂亮,您看上去年轻多了。

Your sweater is very beautiful. You look much younger.

"Lack of originality" is another feature of compliments in both Chinese and American English. Highly restricted set of adjectives and verbs are used in both Chinese and American contexts when making compliments. The most frequently used adjectives are those words like "nice," "good," "beautiful" and "pretty." For verbs, words such as "like" and "love" are two commonly used ones. And in Chinese one may find a similar feature.

If there is any difference, one feature stands out. An American speaker likes to express his or her view in a direct way, therefore the first person is more often used. For example:

17) I like the way you talk.

18) I am so proud of you.

While a Chinese speaker is more likely to use second person when he or she wants to compliment:

19) 你的房子真漂亮。

Your house is very beautiful.

20) 你儿子真乖。

Your son is so cute.

Responses to Compliments in Chinese and American English

Responses to compliments in Chinese and American English are so different that one can easily find the influence of the two cultures on the usage of compliments. Examples 1) and 2) on page 41 clearly show the two different responses to compliments. An American tends to appreciate a compliment by saying "thank you" while a Chinese would prefer to deny though it does not necessarily mean he or she does not welcome the compliment.

In Chinese context, even for the hearer who wants to accept the compliment, he or she would choose to deny or not to show full acceptance. For example:

21) 甲:好久不见,你越活越年轻了。

Long time no see. You look much younger.

乙：哪能啊，你别拿我开玩笑了。

Oh, no. Don't tease me.

In American English, however, even if the hearer does not fully agree with the speaker's compliment, he or she would prefer to appreciate first then deny, using a strategy of "acceptance or acknowledgement and transfer." For example:

22) A: You did very well in your presentation. You're a great public speaker.

B: Thank you. I made a lot of preparation.

23) A: That's a lovely blouse you're wearing!

B: Well, I went shopping on Saturday and happened to see it in one of the stores.

An interesting point has to be made here is that language teaching and learning would affect the way of responding to compliments. A learner tends to employ the responses of the language he or she is learning. For example, if an English learner comes across with compliment of "Your English is excellent," he or she is more likely to respond with "Thank you," and for a Chinese learner of American, if his or her Chinese is complimented, he or she would react with "哪里，哪里" (No, no). But when the Chinese learner receives Chinese compliments, he is more likely to react in the typical Chinese way. So is the American learner of Chinese.

Many attempts have been made to explain the factors contributing to the differences of compliment strategy between Chinese and American English. It is clear that the compliment, like any other speech act, reflects a variety of cultural norms and values and it serves to express and maintain these values. Compliments in Chinese and American English should not be the exception.

Firstly, in Chinese culture, modesty is always regarded as one of the most important virtues. Denigrating others while elevating self is widely perceived as being "arrogant" or "boasting"; therefore, it should be avoided. In American English, individualism and the value of mutual respect and acknowledgement are highly valued. Therefore, for a particular compliment, an acceptance is preferred over a denial as people tend to believe, respect and acknowledge others and choose to be treated in the same manner in social interactions. Understanding this cultural difference is extremely important in the sense that a modest Chinese who is denigrating or humbling himself or herself should not be misunderstood as incompetent or ineffective. And an acknowledging American should not be viewed as arrogant or boasting.

Secondly, different topics appropriate for complimenting in Chinese and American English are attributed to different values in Chinese and American cultures. While the appearance of females in Chinese can be complimented, it is not as widely as that in American context. Rather it is sex sensitive and restrained. As shown in the examples above, in Chinese context, a male speaker has to be very careful in complimenting a female so as to avoid inappropriateness or even rudeness.

Thirdly, the relationship of the speaker and the hearer is another important point that should be taken into account when a compliment is used. In American society, equality is highly valued and achievements are greatly appreciated. In Chinese society, however, complimenting is sometimes taken as flattery. One has to be very careful so as to make a compliment more appropriate.

After You Read

Knowledge Focus

1. **Pair Work: Discuss the following questions with your partner.**
   1) What are the common topics of Chinese and American compliments? In what way are they different from each other?
   2) Who tend to compliment the appearance of a hearer more flexibly, American or Chinese? Why?
   3) Will Chinese and American interpret "You're so knowledgeable, Professor Liu" the same way?
   4) How does language teaching and learning affect the way of responding to compliments?
   5) What do you think causes the differences in compliments across cultures?

2. **Solo Work: Tell whether the following statements are true or false according to the knowledge you learned and explain why.**
   1) Responses to compliments vary greatly from culture to culture. (　)
   2) Typical Chinese response to "This is really a nice dress" is "Thank you. I am glad you like it." (　)
   3) Cultural differences in response to compliments may result in misunderstandings in social interaction across cultures. (　)
   4) Westerners are prone to efface themselves and look up to others. (　)
   5) In Western countries, compliments of a female's appearance from a male speaker would be more appreciated. (　)
   6) Cultural differences in compliments lie in the fact that the Chinese have traditionally been modest and have tended to underestimate their abilities, qualifications and achievements. (　)
   7) "You have a beautiful wife" would be regarded as almost indecent by many Chinese. (　)
   8) In Chinese society, complimenting is the same as flattery. (　)

Language Focus

1. **Fill in the blanks with proper prepositions and adverbs that collocate with the neighboring words.**
   1) The patient did not respond _____ treatment.
   2) I have nothing to say with regard _____ your complaints.
   3) He was too shortsighted to focus _____ the object.
   4) As _____ the hotel, it was very uncomfortable and miles from the sea.
   5) She tried to play _____ his part in the affair and play up her own.
   6) His height makes him stand _____ in the crowd.
   7) Saying and doing should agree _____ each other.

8) The fall in the number of deaths from heart disease is generally attributed _____ improvements in diet.

2. **Fill in the blanks with the proper form of the words in the brackets.**
    1) We need a foreign policy that is more _____ (flexibility).
    2) I respect him because he is _____ (knowledge).
    3) Children love jokes and riddles that are heavily _____ (formula).
    4) Cut out the soft soap; _____ (flatter) will get you nowhere!
    5) She has a striking _____ (origin) in her use of metaphor.
    6) It would be _____ (appropriate) for me to comment until we know more of the facts.
    7) The reduction in their grant is an _____ (acknowledge) that they have been paid too much.
    8) She was hurt by a bullying and _____ (competency) teacher.

3. **Error Correction: Each of the following sentences has at least one grammatical error. Identify the errors and make corrections.**
    1) Compliments are commonly and widely used all in Chinese society and American society to greet, encourage, thank, and open a conversation.
    2) Chinese tend to not accept the compliment though the particular compliment itself to his talent in handwriting is well appreciated.
    3) As for an American, he and she normally accepts the compliment with pleasure.
    4) The appearance of a speaker or hearer such as color of skin, clothing, style, etc. are a major topic of compliment.
    5) The speaker has to be very careful if he or she is to compliment a female hearer because it is against rules govern the speech act of compliment in Chinese unless the speaker is very intimate to the hearer.
    6) Besides, age or social status are also a factor that affects the speech act of compliment if this speech act happens between two interlocutors of same sex.
    7) A female hearer tends to welcome or appreciate compliments of her appearance it is from a male or female speaker.
    8) You take such good care of your family.
    9) Obviously it would be inappropriate for a speaker with lower social status to make such compliment to a hearer with higher social status.
    10) As for Chinese, there is so far no comprehensive study on the formulas of Chinese compliments.
    11) The most frequently using adjectives are those words like "nice," "good," "beautiful" and "pretty."
    12) In American English, even if the hearer does not fully agree with the speaker's compliment, he or she could prefer to appreciate first then deny.
    13) But when the Chinese learner receives Chinese compliments, he is more likely to react in the typical Chinese way. So the American learner of Chinese is.
    14) For a particular compliment, an acceptance is preferred over a denial as people tending to believe, respect and acknowledge others and choose to be treated in the same manner in social interactions.
    15) In Chinese context, a male speaker has to be very careful in complimenting a female so as to avoiding inappropriateness or even rudeness.

16) One has to be very carefully so as to make a compliment more appropriate.

Comprehensive Work
1. Pair Work

Case Study

Jonathan is a professor in an adult school class in America. After class, he is speaking to Guen, an international student from Vietnam.
Jonathan: Guen, your English is improving. I am so proud of your progress.
Guen: Oh, no. My English is not very good.
Jonathan: Why do you say that, Guen? You're doing very well in class.
Guen: I am not a good student.
Jonathan: You're making progress in this class. You should be proud of your English.
Guen: You're a very good teacher, but I am not a good student.
Jonathan: (Very surprised and does not know what to say. He wonders if he should stop giving compliments to Guen.)
1) Why do you think Guen says that her English is not good?
2) Jonathan is surprised and does not know what to say at the end of the conversation. Do you think he should stop giving compliments to Guen? Why or why not?

2. Role Play
Follow the instruction on the cue cards and interact with your partner. Take turns and practice complimenting and responding to the compliments in the role play activity. Prepare to demonstrate your role play activities in front of the class.

Cue Card X

You are an international student from China:
Imagine your American friend invites you to visit his/her new house.
1. Greet your American friend and compliment his/her house.
2. What would you say to your American friend when he/she dresses up?

Cue Card Y

You are an American:
Imagine you invite your friend from China to visit your new house.
1. Greet your friend and respond to your friend's praises.
2. How would you respond to your friend when he/she compliments your clothes?

3. Writing
Make a list of the compliments you have heard over the past week and the way people respond to the compliments. Note down the time, place, sex, and age of the speakers and their relationships to each other. Find out if there are any patterns in compliments and people's responses to them. Write a short essay to report your findings.

Read More

Text C How to Address People?

Pre-reading Exercise

Before reading Text C, please have a look at the following dialogues.

Dialogue 1
A: Teacher Zhang, could you come over to our farewell party this Saturday?
B: I'd love to. What time?

Dialogue 2
A: Manager Smith, could I schedule your presentation on our new design for Friday morning?
B: I am afraid not. I have something important to do on that morning.

Dialogue 3
A: Uncle policeman, could you tell me the way to the railway station?
B: Walk down this road and turn left at the second crossing.

The above utterances are not at all uncommon for Chinese English learners. These learners use English to address people in the Chinese way. For Chinese listeners, they are understandable and acceptable, but to foreigners, they sound quite awkward and uncomfortable. Therefore, it is necessary to note some differences between Chinese and English when it comes to addressing people.

First of all, we should know that although both Chinese and English people have surnames (last name) and given names (first name or middle names), the order of these names and their use in the two languages is somewhat different. In Chinese, the surname comes first and is followed by the given names, but in English this order is reversed, and that is why a surname is also called last name and a given name first name.

It should be pointed out that Westerners themselves vary in their preference for being called by their surnames or by their given names. The British tend to be more conservative than Americans in this respect, and also older people than younger ones. So it is often safer to use the surname unless an English speaker asks to be called by his or her name or he/she only gives his or her given name.

Secondly, it is necessary to know that many English-speaking people tend to address others by using the first name rather than calling a person Mr. Johnson, Mrs. Powell or Miss Julie, etc. This is especially common among Americans, even when meeting people for the first time. This applies not only to people of roughly the same age, but also to people of different ages, as it is not a sign of disrespect in American culture. Very often it is by no means rude for a child to call a much older person Joe, Dennis or Helen, etc.

There exists a sharp difference between the Chinese and English customs of addressing family members, relatives and neighbors. In Chinese, 二姐, 三哥, 四叔 and 刘大伯 are respectful forms of address, which fit in well with the Confucian ideas that the young should respect the old. People are arranged in order of importance based on their age. In English, however, the name alone, whether it is for a man or woman, will ordinarily be enough, with exceptions to addressing one's parents, grandparents, and sometimes an older relative, e.g., Aunt Jenny or Uncle Jim. Note that the first name rather than the last name is used here. More often than not, Americans tend to use just the given name, leaving out the term of relationship. Therefore, an American girl simply calls her sister-in-law's mother Susan instead of Auntie Susan, even though she is over fifty.

Thirdly, Chinese prefer to address others by using their titles or occupations, such as 宋局长, 高经理, 刘老师 in which the surname comes last in order to show respect for the person concerned. However, this custom is not applicable in English in that only a few occupations or titles are used before a person's last name: "Dr." is used to address medical doctors and university professors who have earned a doctorate degree (PhD); "Mrs." to address a married woman (teacher, director, etc.); "Miss" an unmarried woman (teacher, businesswoman, etc.); "Ms." for an unmarried or married woman (teacher, housewife, professional, etc.); "Mr." for a man (teacher, businessman, etc.); "Judge" for those authorized to try cases in a law court; and "Governor" and "Mayor" for those who hold such offices, although often used without the surname. Teacher Zhang and Manager Smith mentioned at the beginning are not idiomatic usage of English and sound odd to English native speakers.

The final difference in addressing people lies in the ways of getting attention of a stranger, or a person whose name we may not know. The Chinese like to do so by using a general term to address such as 同志(comrade), 师傅(master) or referring to the stranger as a family member or using a kinship term, such as 大哥(big brother), 叔叔(uncle), partially because speakers wish to use such terms to show their respect for the listeners, gain their favor and establish a harmonious relationship with them. In contrast, such expressions as "Excuse me" "Pardon me" are adopted to attract people's attention in English. Often, people resort to nonverbal behavior, such as simply clearing their throat loudly, making some noise or producing meaningful gestures.

Text D Conversation and Culture

Pre-reading questions
If you are asked to compare conversation to a sport, what will it be?

What about American conversation? Why?

What about Japanese conversation? Why?

Conversation is like Double Dutch (jump rope with 2 ropes). Timing when to jump in can be difficult if you do not know the local rhythms and rules.

Conversation is fundamentally interactive. It requires response. This in turn requires a mutual understanding of conversational patterns/conventions.

Conversational patterns are highly structured and very difficult to shift. Even when you speak another language well, you probably still use your native language conversation strategies.

American conversation resembles a tennis or volleyball match. You can either serve a new idea, or aim for the ball another player just hit. You have to move quickly; someone else may get there first.

In contrast, Japanese conversation is like bowling. Everybody watches respectfully and quietly and takes turns. You are not expected to respond to the previous statement, but to aim at the conversation goals.

Ending a conversation

Here is one example of the subtle cultural knowledge one needs to play the conversation game skillfully.

Every culture has rituals for entering or closing a conversation. You cannot just launch into your subject without preamble or suddenly hang up. Here are some of the cues we use to get out of a conversation in mainstream US culture:

- Give less frequent feedback and eye contact
- Sigh, cough, shift gaze away, glance at your watch...
- Shift intonation
- Indicate urgency (invoke the polite fiction "we're both busy people")
- Say "gotta go" or "bye-bye" but add reassurance that you intend to continue a pleasant connection, such as "see you soon," "call me sometime."

An exceedingly polite conversation ending can draw out for many minutes.

Elements structuring a conversation

Negotiating a conversation is quite a challenge, when you consider all the elements involved:

- setting — where you talk
- enter/exit
- purpose
- topics
- formality
- who talks to whom
- turn-taking vs. overlap
- cues
- appreciation
- use of humor
- how/if get to the point
- direct/indirect
- sequencing, order
- pace
- eye contact
- attitude, tone of voice
- silence
- length of each utterance, of conversation as a whole

Differences between speakers in any of these elements can lead to irritation, moral judgments, or misreading of intent. When there are tensions between the participants already, these conversational differences can cause serious ruptures.

We have all listened to and participated in conversation nearly every day of our lives. Changing our communication styles and expectations is like asking the leopard to give up its spots. If you are involved in a cross-cultural or high conflict situation, try to be aware of how your conversational habits may be affecting your negotiations. It may help to raise your observations about communication patterns with the other party (and this is the hard part) without a good/bad evaluation attached.

For Fun

Book to Read

Brick, Jean. *China: A Handbook in Intercultural Communication*. Australia: NCELTR Publications, 1991.
- This book reflects the rapidly changing political, social and cultural situation in China. A detailed description of Chinese attitudes to the individual's place in society, social behavior, values, and attitudes to education and doing business makes this an invaluable resource for those who teach, study, work or trade with China.

Movie to Watch

Tortilla Soup (2001) is a movie remake of Ang Lee's *Eat Drink Man Woman* and directed by the Spanish director, Maria Ripoll. It is set in Southern California involving an atypical but loving Hispanic family. If you are in the mood for a funny, romantic and uplifting film, this is the one you are looking forward to.

Unit 5
Nonverbal Communication (I)

> There's language in her eye, her cheek, her lip.
> —— William Shakespeare
>
> The unspoken dialogue between two people can never be put right by anything they say.
> —— Dag Hammarskjild

Unit Goals

- To understand what nonverbal communication is and what function it serves
- To learn cultural rules governing posture, gesture, eye contact, facial expressions, body touch and smell
- To gain an awareness that successful intercultural communication depends not only on what we say, but also on the behavior we display
- To learn useful words and expressions about nonverbal communication and improve language skills

Before You Read

Body language is the unspoken communication that goes on in every face-to-face encounter with another human being. It tells you their true feelings towards you and how well your words are being received.

Your ability to read and understand another person's body language can result in making a great impression or a very bad one! It could help you in a job interview, a meeting, or a special date.

Please go over the following facial expressions and take a good guess at their meanings.

Unit 5 Nonverbal Communication (I)

1. _____ 2. _____ 3. _____

4. _____ 5. _____ 6. _____

Start to Read

Text A Nonverbal Communication

If anyone asked you what were the main means of communication between people, what would you say? That is not a catch question. The answer is simple and obvious. It would almost certainly refer to means of communication that involve the use of words. Speakers and listeners—oral communication, and writers and readers—written communication. And you would be quite right. There is, however, another form of communication which we all use most of the time, usually without knowing it. This is sometimes called body language. Its more technical name is nonverbal communication. Nonverbal, because it does not involve the use of words, NVC for short.

When someone is saying something with which he agrees, the average European will smile and nod approval. On the other hand, if you disagree with what they are saying, you may frown and shake your head. In this way you signal your reactions, and communicate them to the speaker without saying a word. I referred a moment ago to "the average European," because body language is very much tied to culture, and in order not to misunderstand, or not to be misunderstood, you must realize this. A smiling Chinese, for instance, may not be approving but somewhat embarrassed.

Quite a lot of work is now being done on the subject of NVC, which is obviously important, for instance, to managers, who have to deal every day with their staff, and have to understand what other people are feeling if they are to create good working conditions. Body language, or NVC signals, are sometimes categorized into five kinds:

1. Body and facial gestures;
2. Eye contact;
3. Body contact or "proximity";
4. Clothing and physical appearance;
5. The quality of speech.

I expect you understood all those, except perhaps "proximity." This simply means "closeness." In some cultures — and I am sure this is a cultural feature and not an individual one — it is quite normal for people to stand close together, or to more or less thrust their face into yours when they are talking to you. In other cultures, this is disliked; Americans, for instance, talk about invasion of their space.

Some signals are probably common to all of us. If a public speaker (like a professor, for example) is all the time fiddling with a pencil, or with his glasses, while he is talking to you, he is telling you quite clearly that he is nervous. A person who holds a hand over his mouth when he is talking is signaling that he is lacking in confidence. If you start wriggling in your chairs, looking secretly at your watches or yawning behind your hands, I shall soon get the message that I am boring you. And so on. I am sure you could make a whole list of such signals — and it might be fun if you did.

All the signals I have mentioned so far can be controlled. If you are aware that you are doing these things, you can stop. You can even learn to give false signals. Most public speakers are in fact nervous, but a good speaker learns to hide this by giving off signals of confidence. Other kinds of NVC are not so easy to control, eye contact, for instance. Unless you are confessing intense love, you hardly ever look into someone else's eyes for very long. If you try it, you will find they will soon look away, probably in embarrassment.

I have already mentioned proximity, so here are a few words now about our last two categories, which concern the way people dress and the way they speak. These are both pretty obvious signals. People may dress casually and speak casually, which signals that they are relaxed. Or they can dress formally and speak formally, showing their tenseness. In fact, nonverbal communication can, as the saying goes, speak volumes.

Text B Making a Gesture

One important area in the study of nonverbal communication is that occupied by the language of gesture. This is mainly a matter of how we use our hands to convey a message. As with spoken language, the language of the hands differs from country to country and a gesture which means one thing in one country may well mean something quite different to those living in another, even one quite close by. The ring gesture, where you form an "O" by holding the tip of your thumb, means in Britain that you think something is good. Take a trip through the Channel Tunnel to France, however, and you may find that you fail to impress your French host when you use it to tell him your opinion of his new car. In France it means zero or worthless. Travel further south and you are in even greater trouble, for in Tunisia it means "I'll kill you!" Similar problems occur on the other side of the Atlantic, for in the U.S. the ring gesture has the same meaning as in Britain, but in Latin America it is used as an insult. Unfortunately, former U.S. President Richard Nixon was unaware of this. Landing on a visit to one South American country he came out of the aircraft with both hands held high showing the ring gesture. Having just been told to go to hell by their visitor, his hosts gave the puzzled President a somewhat frosty reception. Had he used the same gesture in Japan, his host would have been equally puzzled, for there it means money.

Try to avoid these misunderstandings by using another gesture to indicate that you think something is good and you may still find yourself in trouble. In Britain, the thumbs-up sign is used when you think something is good, but elsewhere, as in Sardinia in Italy, it is an insult. In Britain the gesture is also used for hitch-hiking. But attempt to use it to request a lift  from a passing motorist in Greece and you had better stand well back from the edge of the road for he is quite likely to try to knock you down. For in Greece, it is an insult.

 Beckoning can also be a source of misunderstanding. Using the index finger to beckon someone to come to you may be acceptable in America, but would be impolite in Malaysia where it is only used for calling animals. In Indonesia and Australia, it is also used for beckoning "ladies of the night."

Pulling down the lower lid of your eye with one finger is usually used to indicate alertness. In France and Greece, it means much the same as when we say "My eye!" in England, meaning: "Do not you think I can see it? You can't fool me." In Spain and Italy, it is also related to being alert, but here it is used as a warning: "Keep your eyes open." In South America, it means you think that a woman is an "eyeful," very attractive.

 The ear-tug means as many as four different things in different Mediterranean countries. In Spain, it accuses someone of being a sponger, in Greece it is a warning, in Malta it says someone is a sneak, and in Italy it insults someone for being a homosexual.

Holding your palm away from you with the index and middle fingers raised in a V-sign is intended to show victory or peace in England. However, keeping the same shape with your fingers but turning the palm towards yourself transforms the gesture into an insult. These two gestures have an interesting history. It is likely  that the use of the V-sign dates back 500 years to when the French used to cut off the forefinger and middle finger of the English archers they captured in battle so that they would no longer be able to draw their bows. After the battle of Agincourt, where the French were heavily defeated by English archers, the French prisoners were taunted by the victorious English. To add insult to injury, the English bowmen waved at them mockingly with palms held up proudly displaying the vital forefinger and the middle finger.

In Greece, the use of the V-sign is avoided because it looks like the greatest Greek insult which is to hold up the palm of your hand towards someone's face. This gesture, known as the moutza, dates back to ancient times when faecal matter and dirt was pushed into the faces of defeated enemies. In Britain and the U.S., however, the gesture simply means "top."

If after all this you think you can avoid making mistakes by simply shoving your hands in your pockets, think again. In a number of countries, ranging from Belgium to Indonesia, keeping your hands in your pockets is regarded as impolite.

After You Read

Knowledge Focus

1. **Pair Work**: Discuss the following questions with your partner.
   1) What is nonverbal communication?
   2) What are the five categories of nonverbal communication?
   3) Which two categories of nonverbal communication are the most important?
   4) Can you illustrate proximity by using specific cultural examples?
   5) How does posture communicate different messages? Use examples to illustrate your answer.

2. **Solo Work**: Tell whether the following statements are true or false according to the knowledge you learned and explain why.
   1) The central idea of Text B is that just as spoken language varies from place to place so does the language of the hands. ( )
   2) The central idea of Text B is that each culture has many gestures to enable people to communicate nonverbally. ( )
   3) Former U.S. President Richard Nixon used the ring gesture when he landed on a visit to a South American country and his gesture puzzled his hosts a lot. ( )
   4) His South American hosts gave former U.S. President Richard Nixon a frosty reception when he arrived because they thought he wanted their money. ( )
   5) If you use the thumbs-up gesture to hitch a ride in Greece, you had better not stand by the edge of the road, as you may be knocked down by drivers who are eager to pick you up. ( )
   6) An American visiting Australia has to be careful in using the index finger to beckon someone. ( )
   7) The French used to cut off the forefinger and the middle finger of the English archers they captured in battle so that they wouldn't show the V-sign for victory. ( )
   8) Since gestures can cause so many cultural misunderstanding, the safest way is to make as few gestures as possible when you travel abroad. ( )

Language Focus

1. The following are some sentences from Text A and Text B. Go through the sentences and explain each of the italicized words or phrases in your own words.
   1) That is not a *catch question*. The answer is simple and obvious.

   2) If a public speaker (like a professor, for example) is all the time *fiddling with* a pencil, or with his glasses, while he is talking to you, he is telling you quite clearly that he is nervous.

3) In fact, nonverbal communication can, as the saying goes, *speak volumes*.

4) Having just been told to go to hell by their visitor, his hosts gave the puzzled President *a somewhat frosty reception*.

5) In Indonesia and Australia, it is also used for beckoning "*ladies of the night*."

6) In South America, it means you think that a woman is an "*eyeful*."

7) In Spain, it accuses someone of being a *sponger*.

8) *To add insult to injury*, the English bowmen waved at them mockingly with palms held up proudly displaying the vital forefinger and the middle finger.

2. **Fill in the blanks — Body idioms and expressions.**

In English, there are all kinds of idioms using fingers, hands, bones and toes. Please complete the following body expressions according to their meanings.

Meanings	Expressions
to welcome very warmly	welcome somebody with open _____
to touch somebody, esp. with the intention of harming them	lay a _____ on somebody
to be ready to spend or give money	put one's _____ in one's pocket
to applaud somebody loudly	give somebody/get a big _____
to comfort or help somebody in a sad or difficult situation	hold somebody's _____
to know all the latest news, development, etc.	keep one's _____ on the pulse
to do an activity occasionally in order to remain skilled at it	keep one's _____ in
something which you can reach easily	within _____'s reach
to propose marriage	ask for a woman's _____
to identify an error, or cause of a problem, exactly	put one's _____ on something
to avoid becoming too friendly or involved with somebody	keep somebody at _____'s length

3. **Find the appropriate prepositions or adverbs that collocate with the words in bold letters.**
   1) These two reports of the accident **disagree** _____ each other.
   2) They refused to compromise their principles by doing a **deal** _____ the terrorists.
   3) He is really into **fiddling** _____ all the knobs and dials.
   4) When wine is fermented it **gives** _____ bubbles of gas.
   5) Man **differs** _____ beasts in that the former is able to laugh, while the latter are not.
   6) Gambling is not **the same** _____ investing in the stock market. It is a horse of a different color.
   7) You will be _____ **trouble** if you do not watch your step.
   8) He was **accused** _____ incompetence.

4. **Error Correction: Each of the following sentences has at least one grammatical error. Identify the errors and make corrections.**
   1) When someone is saying something with that he agrees, the average European will smile and nod approval.
   2) Managers who have to deal every day with their staff and have to understand what other people are feeling if they create good working conditions.
   3) It is quite normal for people to stand close together, or more or less thrust their face into yours when they are talking to you.
   4) I am sure you could make a whole list of such signals—and it must be fun if you did.
   5) One important area in the study of nonverbal communication is occupied by the language of gesture.
   6) This is mainly a matter of what we use our hands to convey a message.
   7) As with the spoken language, the language of the hands differs from country to country and a gesture which means one thing in one country may well mean something quite different to those living in another, even one quite close by.
   8) The ring gesture, where you form an "O" by holding the tip of your thumb, meaning in Britain that you think something is good.
   9) Take a trip through the Channel Tunnel in France, and you may find that you fail to impress your French host when you use it to tell him your opinion of his new car.
   10) Landed on a visit to one South American country he came out of the aircraft with both hands held high showing the ring gesture.
   11) Being told to go to hell by their visitor, his hosts gave the puzzled President a somewhat frosty reception.
   12) Had he used the same gesture in Japan, his host will be equally puzzled, for there it means money.
   13) But the attempt to use it to request a lift from a passing motorist in Greece and you had better stand well back from the edge of the road for he is quite likely to try to knock you down.
   14) Using index finger to beckon someone to come to you may be acceptable in America.
   15) It would be impolite in Malaysia which it is only used for calling animals.
   16) To add insult to injury, the English bowmen waved at them mockingly with palms holding up proudly displaying the vital forefinger and the middle finger.

Comprehensive Work

1. **Pair Work: Matching**

   Different gestures may serve the same function, and the same gestures can have a number of unanticipated consequences when communicating with people from different cultures. Work with your partner and try to match the cultures with the gestures or the meanings they convey.

   1) Hands on hips may signal _____.
      - A. in Mexico
      - B. in Malaysia
      - C. in Argentina
      - a. challenge
      - b. anger
      - c. hostility
   2) To show approval is _____.
      - A. in France
      - B. in Greece
      - C. in Tonga
      - a. to raise one's eyebrows
      - b. to tilt one's head
      - c. to have one's thumb up
   3) To point something or somebody out is _____.
      - A. in India
      - B. in the US
      - C. in Guinea-Bissau
      - a. to point with the chin
      - b. to point with the tongue
      - c. to extend the index finger
   4) Pulling one's eyelid may indicate _____.
      - A. in France
      - B. in Italy
      - C. in South America
      - a. you should be alert
      - b. I find a woman very attractive
      - c. respect or humility
   5) Tapping one's temple with the forefinger may suggest _____.
      - A. in North America
      - B. in most of Africa
      - C. in China
      - a. I am thinking about it
      - b. try to use your brain
      - c. somebody is crazy
   6) The ring gesture may mean _____.
      - A. in Brazil
      - B. in Japan
      - C. in France
      - a. zero or something worthless
      - b. something vulgar
      - c. money
   7) Crossing arms may signify _____.
      - A. in the US
      - B. in Russia
      - C. in Finland
      - a. feeling bored
      - b. arrogance
      - c. being rude
   8) Avoiding direct eye contact may suggest _____.
      - A. in the US
      - B. in Japan
      - C. in France
      - a. unfriendliness
      - b. untruthfulness
      - c. respect or humility

2. **Group Work**

   Case Study

   On the right is the poster of Jackie Chan's 2002 movie — *The Tuxedo*. However, it encountered many problems in Thailand. The locals were much offended by Jackie Chan's posture in this poster.

Discuss with your group members and find out why.

3. Writing

Below is part of a letter written by Mike Fast, an American student studying in Beijing, to his net friend, Sun Liang. In this letter, Mike tells Sun Liang an unpleasant experience.

> Hello Liang,
>
> ...
>
> The other day, I had a rather unpleasant experience. It happened when I went to a supermarket. When I parked my bike in the parking area in front of the entrance, the bicycle accidentally fell over. Unfortunately it also knocked the bike on its right down and then several other bikes also fell over. I naturally felt rather embarrassed and quickly bent over to pick the bikes up. While I was doing so, I happened to notice that one or two passers-by were looking at me and laughing. When I stood up, I found not only one or two, but quite a number of people standing around looking and laughing. You can imagine how humiliated and angry I felt!
>
> ...
>
> Yours,
> Mike Fast

Suppose you are Sun Liang. Write a letter back to Mike, explaining to him your understandings on the passers-by's reaction.

Read More

Text C   Every Body's Talking

In the following text, former FBI agent Joe Navarro describes how our torsos, hands, feet and legs frequently communicate emotions that are not put into words. Before reading the article, discuss with your partner and work out what these gestures mean to you.

Pictures	Descriptions	Interpretations
	☞ leaning away from someone (the man on the right) ☞ leaning toward someone (the man on the left)	

(continued)

Pictures	Descriptions	Interpretations
	☞ fingertips spread apart on a surface	
	☞ crossed arms	
	☞ arms akimbo	

Picture this: I was sailing the Caribbean for three days with a group of friends and their spouses, and everything seemed perfect. The weather was beautiful, the ocean diaphanous blue, the food exquisite; our evenings together were full of laughter and good conversation.

Things were going so well that one friend said to the group, "Let's do this again next year." I happened to be across from him and his wife as he spoke those words. In the cacophony of resounding replies of "Yes!" and "Absolutely!" I noticed that my friend's wife made a fist under her chin as she grasped her necklace. This behavior stood out to me as powerfully as if someone had shouted, "Danger!"

I watched the words and gestures of the other couples at the table, and everyone seemed ecstatic—everyone but one. She continued to smile, but her smile was tense.

Her husband has treated me as a brother for more than 15 years, and I consider him the dearest of friends. At that moment I knew that things between him and his wife were turning for the worse. I did not pat myself on the back for making these observations. I was saddened.

For 25 years, I worked as a paid observer. I was a special agent for the FBI specializing in counterintelligence—specifically, catching spies. For me, observing human behavior is like having software running in the background, doing its job — no conscious effort needed. And so on that wonderful cruise, I made a "thin-slice assessment" (that's what we call it) based on just a few significant behaviors. Unfortunately, it turned out to be right: Within six months of our return, my friend's wife filed for divorce, and her husband discovered painfully that she had been seeing someone else for quite a while.

When I am asked what is the most reliable means of determining the health of a relationship, I always say that words do not matter. It is all in the language of the body. The nonverbal behaviors we all transmit tell others, in real time, what we think, what we feel, what we yearn for or what we intend.

Now I am embarking on another cruise, wondering what insights I will have about my travel companions and their relationships. No matter what, this promises to be a fascinating trip, a journey for the mind and the soul. I am with a handful of dear friends and 3,800 strangers, all headed for Alaska; for an observer it does not get any better than this.

While lining up to board on our first day, I notice just ahead of me a couple who appear to be in their early 30s. They are obviously Americans (voice, weight and demeanor).

Not so obvious is their dysfunctional relationship. He is standing stoically, shoulders wide, looking straight ahead. She keeps whispering loudly to him, but she is not facing forward. She violates his space as she leans into him. Her face is tense and her lips are narrow slivers each time she engages him with what clearly appears to be a diatribe. He occasionally nods his head but avoids contact with her. He will not let his hips near her as they start to walk side by side. He reminds me of Bill and Hillary Clinton walking toward the Marine One helicopter immediately after the Monica Lewinsky affair: looking straight ahead, as much distance between them as possible.

I think everyone can decipher this one from afar because we have all seen situations like this. What most people will miss is something I have seen this young man do twice now, which portends poorly for both of them. Every time she looks away, he "disses" her. He smirks and rolls his eyes, even as she stands beside him. He performs his duties, pulling their luggage alone; I suspect he likes to have her luggage nearby as a barrier between them. I will not witness the dissolution of their marriage, but I know it will happen, for the research behind this is fairly robust. When two people in a relationship have contempt for each other, the marriage will not last.

When it comes to relationships and courtship behaviors, the list of useful cues is long. Most of these behaviors we learned early when interacting with our mothers. When we look at loving eyes, our own eyes get larger, our pupils dilate, our facial muscles relax, our lips become full and warm, our skin becomes more pliable, our heads tilt. These behaviors stay with us all of our lives.

I watched two lovers this morning in the dining room. Two young people, perhaps in their late 20s, mirror each other, staring intently into each other's eyes, chin on hand, head slightly tilted, nose flaring with each breath. They are trying to absorb each other visually and tactilely as they hold hands across the table.

Over time, those who remain truly in love will show even more indicators of mirroring. They may dress the same or even begin to look alike as they adopt each other's nonverbal expressions as a sign of synchrony and empathy. They will touch each other with kind hands that touch fully, not with the fingertips of the less caring.

They will mirror each other in ways that are almost imperceptible; they will have similar blink rates and breathing rates, and they will sit almost identically. They will look at the same scenery and not speak, merely look at each other and take a deep breath to reset their breathing synchrony. They do not have to talk. They are in harmony physically, mentally and emotionally, just as a baby is in exquisite synchrony with its mother who is tracing his every expression and smile.

As I walk through the ship on the first night, I can see the nonverbals of courtship. There is a beautiful woman, tall, slender, smoking a cigarette outside. Two men are talking to her. Both are muscular and handsome. She has crossed her legs as she talks to them, an expression of her comfort. As she holds her cigarette, the inside of her wrist turns toward her newfound friends. Her interest and comfort with them resounds, but she is favoring one of them. As he speaks to her, she preens herself by playing with her hair. I am not sure he is getting the message that she prefers him; in the end, I am sure it will all get sorted out.

At the upscale lounge, a man is sitting at the bar talking animatedly to the woman next to him and looking at everyone who walks by. The woman has begun the process of ignoring him, but he does not get it. After he speaks to her a few times, she gathers her purse and places it on her lap. She has turned slightly away from him and now avoids eye contact. He has no clue; he thinks he is cool by commenting on the women who pass by. She is verbally and nonverbally indifferent.

The next night it is more of the same. This time, I see two people who just met talking gingerly. Gradually they lean more and more into each other. She is now dangling her sandal from her toes. I am not sure he knows it. Perhaps he sees it all in her face, because she is smiling, laughing and relaxed. Communication is fluid, and neither wants the conversation to end. She is extremely interested.

All of these individuals are carrying on a dialogue in nonverbals. The socially adept will learn to read and interpret the signs accurately. Others will make false steps or pay a high price for not being observant. They may end up like my friend on the Caribbean cruise, who missed the clues of deceit and indifference.

This brings me back to my friend and his new wife, who are on this wonderful voyage. They have been on board for four days, and they are a delight individually and together. He lovingly looks at her; she stares at him with love and admiration. When she holds his hand at dinner, she massages it ever so gently. Theirs is a strong marriage. They do not have to tell me. I can sense it and observe it. I am happy for them and for myself. I can see cues of happiness, and they are unmistakable. You cannot ask for more.

Text D Top 10 Nonverbal Communication Tips

Pre-reading Activity

First, videotape yourself while you speak. Make sure you are able to see at least your upper half. Notice any gestures, facial expressions, or tones that can conflict with the message you are giving with your words.

Then brainstorm some tips that you think can help improve nonverbal skills.

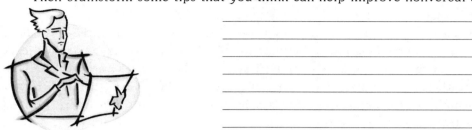

When you finish, use the information from Text D to check if you have the right ones.

Good communication skills can help you in both your personal and professional life. While verbal and written communication skills are important, research has shown that nonverbal behaviors make up a large percentage of our daily interpersonal communication. How can you improve your nonverbal communication skills? The following top ten tips for nonverbal communication can help you learn to read the nonverbal signals of other people and enhance your own ability to communicate effectively.

1. Pay Attention to Nonverbal Signals

People can communicate information in numerous ways; so pay attention to things like eye contact, gestures, posture, body movements, and tone of voice. All of these signals can convey important information that is not put into words. By paying closer attention to other people's nonverbal behaviors, you will improve your own ability to communicate nonverbally.

2. Look for Incongruent Behaviors

If someone's words do not match their nonverbal behaviors, you should pay careful attention. For example, someone might tell you they are happy while frowning and staring at the ground. Research has shown that when words fail to match up with nonverbal signals, people tend to ignore what has been said and focus instead on nonverbal expressions of moods, thoughts, and emotions.

3. Concentrate on Your Tone of Voice When Speaking

Your tone of voice can convey a wealth of information, ranging from enthusiasm to disinterest to anger. Start noticing how your tone of voice affects how others respond to you and try using tone of voice to emphasize ideas that you want to communicate. For example, if you want to show genuine interest in something, express your enthusiasm by using an animated tone of voice.

4. Use Good Eye Contact

When people fail to look at others in the eye, it seems they are evading or trying to hide something. On the other hand, too much eye contact can seem confrontational or intimidating. While eye contact is an important part of communication, it is important to remember that good eye contact does not mean staring fixedly into someone's eyes. How can you tell how much eye contact is correct? Some communication experts recommend intervals of eye contact lasting four to five seconds.

5. Ask Questions about Nonverbal Signals

If you are confused about another person's nonverbal signals, do not be afraid to ask questions. A good idea is to repeat back your interpretation of what has been said and ask for clarification. An example of this might be, "So what you are saying is that..."

6. Use Signals to Make Communication More Effective and Meaningful

Remember that verbal and nonverbal communication work together to convey a message. You can improve your spoken communication by using nonverbal signals and gestures that reinforce and support what you are saying. This can be especially useful when making presentations or when speaking to a large group of people.

7. Look at Signals as a Group

A single gesture can mean any number of things, or maybe even nothing at all. The key to accurately reading nonverbal behavior is to look for groups of signals that reinforce a common point. If you place too much emphasis on just one signal out of many, you might come to an inaccurate conclusion about what a person is trying to communicate.

8. Consider Context

When you are communicating with others, always consider the situation and the context in which the communication occurs. Some situations require more formal behaviors that might be interpreted very differently in any other setting. Consider whether or not nonverbal behaviors are appropriate for the context. If you are trying to improve your own nonverbal communication, concentrate on ways to make your signals match the level of formality necessitated by the situation.

9. Be Aware That Signals Can Be Misread

According to some, a firm handshake indicates a strong personality while a weak handshake is taken as a lack of fortitude. This example illustrates an important point about the possibility of misreading nonverbal signals. A limp handshake might actually indicate something else entirely, such as arthritis. Always remember to look for groups of behavior. A person's overall demeanor is far more telling than a single gesture viewed in isolation.

10. Practice, Practice, Practice

Some people just seem to have a knack for using nonverbal communication effectively and correctly interpreting signals from others. These people are often described as being able to "read people." In reality, you can build this skill by paying careful attention to nonverbal behavior and practicing different types of nonverbal communication with others. By noticing nonverbal behavior and practicing your own skills, you can dramatically improve your communication abilities.

Website to Visit

You will have a chance to learn more about nonverbal communication from http://nonverbal.ucsc.edu/(accessed May 11, 2021).

To learn more about nonverbal communication, you can improve your own ability by reading samples of real nonverbal communication. You will also be taken to different topics in nonverbal communication by reading the description and reviews of the videotapes.

Movie to Watch

Mr. Bean's Holiday is a sweet, warm-hearted and very funny movie with a great soundtrack and good performances. Rowan Atkinson returns to the iconic role that made him an international star. In this misadventure, Mr. Bean—the nearly wordless misfit who seems to be followed by a trail of pratfalls—goes on holiday to the French Riviera and becomes ensnared in a European adventure of cinematic proportions. In this movie, Mr. Bean shows less talking and more of his humor through his over-the-top body language, the facial expressions, and the convincing vibe.

Unit 6
Nonverbal Communication (II)

> The most important thing in communication is to hear what isn't being said.
> —— Peter F. Drucker
>
> What you do speaks so loudly that I cannot hear what you say.
> —— Ralph Waldo Emerson

Unit Goals

- To understand what nonverbal communication is and what function it serves
- To appreciate how attitude toward time and use of space convey nonverbal messages in intercultural encounters
- To learn useful words and expressions about nonverbal communication and improve language skills

Before You Read

Act out the following situations by using your body language.
1) You cannot hear your friend's voice.
2) You want a child to come to your side.
3) Your friend has just walked into the class to take an important examination. Wish him or her good luck.
4) Somebody has asked you a question, and you do not know the answer.
5) You want to tell your friend that the lecture is boring.
6) You signal to your friend that the person on the phone is talking too much.
7) You want to express "Oh, not again!"
8) You want to tell your friend that you have forgotten to bring something.
9) You want to tell your friend to wait a second or slow down.
10) You want to tell your friend that everything is okay.

Intercultural Communication (Second Edition)

Start to Read

Text A How Big Is Your Space Bubble

Do you know that you have a "space bubble" all around you? And do you know that other people have a "space bubble" too?

When people are having conversations with someone else, they generally like to have a little bubble of space all around them. This little bubble of space extends one or two or even three feet all around our bodies. We tend to view this as our personal space, even if we never really think about it.

If we invade too close into someone else's personal space before they are ready to be close to us, they will feel very uncomfortable. And if someone gets too physically close to us during a conversation, we can also feel uncomfortable with them.

Some people misjudge how close they should sit or stand when they are talking to strangers or acquaintances, and they may end up making a poor impression on others either because they get too close, or stay too far away. If someone you do not know very well starts to move too close to you or touches you, you may find yourself taking a step back.

If you do not know the space bubble rules, you might make another person feel uncomfortable by standing too close, or by touching them when they do not want to be touched by you.

We like to keep our space bubble as a personal space for ourselves, and for those who are closest to us. We like it when our loved ones, our family, and our children get physically close to us. However, if a total stranger insists on getting into our personal space and stand just inches away, we may feel alarmed and uncomfortable.

About the only time we willingly allow a stranger into our personal space is when we need medical treatment, or when we cannot prevent it, such as when we are on a crowded bus or an elevator. We also let people get very close to us when we feel a very strong attraction to them.

The size of space bubble we like to have around us and the amount of touching we will permit can be complicated.

There are no cut and dried rules. People from different family backgrounds and different cultures often have different preferences for how big their space bubble will be.

People who come from a British background are likely to be more formal and reserved with strangers and acquaintances than North Americans would be. If you address an English person by his first name without permission, he may feel that you are being too familiar with him. English people will usually feel uncomfortable if you stand close to them while speaking, and will back away to a distance that suits them better.

People from a British background often want to stand quite far away from their conversation partners when making small talk, and are not likely to engage in a lot of public touching with people they do not know.

On the other hand, people from Central and South American countries will often stand extremely close to you while speaking, and may feel offended if you back away. Men from these countries feel comfortable hugging each other in public, whereas most men from a British or North American background will almost never do so.

People from China and Japan are usually much more reserved, and will stand considerably farther away from the other person with whom they are having a conversation.

The size of the space bubble we try to create around us will also change according to circumstances.

When we are on a subway during rush hour, we will tolerate strangers pressing up against us in a way that we would not accept from someone at a business meeting.

When we first meet someone new, we are not likely to stand in each other's zone of private space unless we are both feeling a strong sexual attraction. When people are drunk, they will tolerate a lot of physical closeness with strangers that they might not accept when they are sober.

When you are talking with people, respect the space boundary that your conversation partners want to have around them.

If you find that other people keep moving further back when you stand close to them, it does not necessarily mean they do not like you. It might mean that you are invading territory they consider their personal space. If you notice this happening, they will probably appreciate having a bit more space. Do not move physically closer to them until you know them better and they seem more willing to get close to you.

When people like you a lot, they will often signal this by smiling at you a lot, getting closer to you, and touching you. If they do not feel that this is the right time or place for being close, they will pull back a bit.

You can subtly participate in negotiating the ideal distance by slightly approaching and backing away until you both appear to be comfortable. Thus you will create a better impression on them.

Text B Time Sense: Polychronicity and Monochronicity

Are you a polychron or a monochron?

My guess is you have no idea what I am talking about. And yet, this is one of the most important questions you can ever ask yourself. Knowing if you are a polychron or a monochron will help you understand a lot about yourself, including how you fit into the world and how you get along with others.

The terms monochron and polychron have to do with our time sense: how we perceive and manage time. To a polychron, time is continuous, with no particular structure. Polychrons see time as a never-ending river, flowing from the infinite past, through the present, into the infinite future.

In the workplace, polychrons prefer to keep their time unstructured, changing from one activity to another as the mood takes them. Although polychrons can meet deadlines, they

need to do so in their own way. A polychron does not want detailed plans imposed upon him, nor does he want to make his own detailed plans. Polychrons prefer to work as they see fit without a strict schedule, following their internal mental processes from one minute to the next.

Monochrons see time as being divided into fixed elements that can be organized, quantified and scheduled.

Monochrons relate to time differently. To them, time is discrete, not continuous. Monochrons see time as being divided into fixed elements—seconds, minutes, hours, days, weeks, and so on—temporal blocks that can be organized, quantified and scheduled. Monochrons love to plan in details, making lists, keeping track of their activities, and organizing their time into a daily routine.

Monochrons prefer to do one thing at a time, working on a task until it is finished, then, and only then, moving on to the next task. To a monochron, switching back and forth from one activity to another is not only wasteful and distracting, it is uncomfortable.

Polychrons are different. They love to work on more than one thing at a time. To a polychron, switching from one activity to another is both stimulating and productive and, hence, the most desirable way to work.

Can you see yourself in here somewhere?

I bet you can and, once you do, you can see how easy it would be for a monochron and a polychron who live or work together to butt heads frequently, driving each other crazy without even knowing what is happening.

Here is a common example. Because of the way polychrons see time, they are often late. This only makes sense because, to a polychron, exact times (and even exact dates) are not really meaningful and, hence, are not all that important.

Try telling this to the monochron who is kept waiting for that polychron. While the polychron was finishing a couple of last-minute chores at home, the monochron was at the appointed place five minutes early, anxiously looking at his watch. To a monochron, time is exact and, as he sees it, being late is both rude and disrespectful. To a polychron, any time— even an exact time—is just an approximation. If someone keeps *him* waiting, he does not really care. He just figures that something must have happened to hold up the other person, and it is not that big of a deal.

In order to keep the peace, polychrons do learn to be on time when they really need to be. However, if you can get them to talk truthfully, they will tell you that they do not really understand why so many people feel that punctuality is a virtue.

The important lesson here is that, when it comes to organizing time, we all think that how we do it makes the most sense. The hidden assumption is that there is only one right way to understand time (our way). The truth is there is more than one way to think about time and neither extreme is right or wrong; they are just different.

Of course, this is not to say that, in a particular society, it will not be more advantageous to be either polychronic or monochronic. Indeed, the terms "polychronic" and "monochronic" were first used (by the anthropologist Edward Hall in his book *The Silent Language*, 1959) to describe whole cultures and not individuals.

According to Hall, some cultures are traditionally monochronic. In such a culture, time is thought of as being linear. People are expected to do one thing at a time, and they will not tolerate lateness or interruptions.

In polychronic cultures, time is thought of as being cyclical. In such cultures, it is not important to be punctual, and it is acceptable to interrupt someone who is busy.

If you live in the United States, Canada, or Northern Europe, you live in a monochronic culture. If you live in Latin America, the Arab part of the Middle East, or sub-Sahara Africa, you live in a polychronic culture.

If you are a monochron living in a monochronic culture, you fit in without knowing it. But what if you are a polychron (as I am) living in, say, the United States? You will find yourself at odds with the work habits of most of the people around you, perhaps even disagreeing regularly with family members or spouses.

I have already mentioned that, to a polychron, it is acceptable (and even desirable) to be late, but there is a lot more. Polychrons consider a schedule to be less important than interpersonal relations. So they will, for example, be glad to stop what they are doing to talk to someone, or take a phone call, or to send email. Although polychrons like to handle more than one task at a time, they will not care if someone interrupts them during their work time or even during their break time. To a polychron, all time is the same, and they tend not to separate their work time from their personal time.

Although I live in a monochronic country, I know many polychrons. To my eye, they seem to enjoy their lives a lot more than the majority of monochrons, who live in a highly demanding world that rarely seems to let them relax and just be who they really are.

Perhaps being a polychron in a monochronic country is not all that bad. You get to watch all the busy bees around you, planning, scheduling, and working hard, making sure that things that need to be done are done on time, which means that you get all the advantages of living in a monochronic society.

Moreover, as long as you can finesse your way around the demands of punctuality and mandatory deadlines, you can work when you want to on whatever it is that interests you at that moment. Since you do not need to make an artificial distinction between your work and the rest of your life, you have no need to separate what you think from what you feel. Thus, you can live your life with a great deal of passion, much of which will find its way

into your work.
No wonder I feel as if I am always on vacation!

After You Read

Knowledge Focus
1. **Pair Work**: Discuss the following questions with your partner.
   1) What is "space bubble"?
   2) Use examples to explain how a culture perceives and uses space to communicate messages to others.
   3) How does the size of the space bubble change according to circumstances?
   4) What is Hall's notion of M-time?
   5) What is Hall's notion of P-time?
   6) In what way are polychronic cultures different from monochronic cultures?

2. **Solo Work**: Match the following descriptions with monochronic people and polychronic people respectively.

Monochronic People	Polychronic People

   1) do one thing at a time
   2) do many things at once
   3) consider time commitments an objective to be achieved, if possible
   4) concentrate on the job
   5) are high-context and already have information
   6) take time commitments (deadlines, schedules) seriously
   7) are committed to people and human relationships
   8) are low-context and need information
   9) are committed to the job
   10) change plans often and easily
   11) adhere religiously to plans
   12) are concerned about not disturbing others; follow rules of privacy and consideration
   13) borrow and lend things often and easily
   14) show great respect for private property; seldom borrow or lend
   15) emphasize promptness
   16) are accustomed to short-term relationships
   17) are highly distractible and subject to interruptions
   18) are more concerned with those who are closely related (family, friends, close business associates) than with privacy
   19) base promptness on the relationship
   20) have strong tendency to build lifetime relationships

Language Focus

1. Find the appropriate prepositions or adverbs that collocate with the words in bold letters.
   1) I am afraid we have to call the whole deal off if you still **insist** _____ your original quotation.
   2) You could **end** _____ running this company if you play your cards right.
   3) Politicians should not **engage** _____ business affairs that might affect their political judgment.
   4) A hot cloth **press** _____ your jaw will usually soothe a toothache.
   5) He refused to **back** _____ from his position.
   6) Taper the plug off a bit with the chisel so that it will **fit** _____ the hole.
   7) Jane's performance will **be impressed** _____ my memory for a long time.
   8) He is always _____ **odds** with his father over politics.

2. Fill in the blanks with the proper form of the words in the brackets.
   1) I _____ (judge) how wide the stream was and fell in.
   2) It will be _____ (advantage) if steps are taken to resume our business relationship on the basis of mutual benefit.
   3) The energy shortage of the world results partly from _____ (waste) use of energy by the industrialized countries.
   4) It is _____ (respect) to mourners at the funeral to have unruly children running around.
   5) The project was predicated on the _____ (assume) that the economy was expanding.
   6) It is _____ (desire) that atomic energy should be used for peaceful purpose.
   7) I spent a very _____ (produce) hour in the library.
   8) It is illegal to read people's private letters without _____ (permit).

3. Error Correction: Each of the following sentences has at least one grammatical error. Identify the errors and make corrections.
   1) Some people misjudge how close they might sit or stand when they are talking to strangers or acquaintances.
   2) If someone you do not know very well starts to move too close to you or touches you, you could find yourself taking a step back.
   3) If you do not know the space bubble rules, you could make another person feel uncomfortable by standing too close.
   4) We like to keep our space bubble as a personal space for ourselves and for those which are closest to us.
   5) We like it where our loved ones, our family and our children get physically close to us.
   6) English people will feel uncomfortable if you stand close to them when speaking.
   7) Men from Central and South American countries feel comfortable being hugged each other in public.
   8) People from China and Japan will stand considerably far away from the other person with whom they are having a conversation than South Americans.
   9) When we are on a subway during rush hour we will tolerate strangers pressing against us in a way what we would not accept from someone at a business meeting.
   10) This is one of the most important question you can ever ask yourself.

11) In the work place, polychrons prefer to keep their time changing from one activity to another as the mood taking them.
12) A polychron does not want detailed plans imposed upon them, or does he want to make his own detailed plans.
13) If someone keeps a polychron waiting, he just figures that something must happen to hold that person and it is not a big deal.
14) Polycrons do not understand why so many people feel that punctuality is virtue.
15) When it comes to organize time, we all think that how we do it makes the most sense.
16) In polychronic cultures, time is thought as being cyclical.

Comprehensive Work
1. **Solo Work**
   1) **Fill in the following blanks according to your understanding of the variation of body distance.**

   > At an international conference, two professors (one Ecuadorian, the other American) were talking during a coffee break. Throughout the conversation, _____ kept advancing while _____ kept retreating until _____ was pressed to the corner of the conference hall. The reason is that _____ did not feel comfortable unless he was very close to _____ and _____ in turn did not feel easy unless the distance was greater.

   2) **The Polychronic Attitudes Index Exercise**

   What is your attitude toward time? You can find it out by completing the polychronic attitude index below. Circle your chcice on the scale provided: strongly disagree, disagree, neutral, agree, or strongly agree.

description	scale				
	Strongly Disagree	Disagree	Neutral	Agree	Strongly Agree
☞ I do not like to juggle several activities at the same time.	☐	☐	☐	☐	☐
☞ People should not try to do many things at once.	☐	☐	☐	☐	☐
☞ When I sit down at my desk, I work on one project at a time.	☐	☐	☐	☐	☐

(continued)

description	scale				
	Strongly Disagree	Disagree	Neutral	Agree	Strongly Agree
☞ I am comfortable doing several things at the same time.	☐	☐	☐	☐	☐
☞ Add up your points and divide the total by 4. Then plot your score on the scale on the right.	1.0 1.5	2.0 2.5	3.0 3.5	4.0 4.5	5.0
	Polychronic				Monochronic

What is your score? The lower your score (below 3.0) is, the more polychronic you are, and the higher your score (above 3.0) is, the more monochronic you are.

2. Pair Work: Analyze the following cases with your partner.

Case Study 1

An African-American male went into a convenience store recently taken over by new Korean immigrants. He gave a $20 bill for his purchase to Mrs. Cho who was the cashier and waited for his change. He was upset when his change was put down on the counter in front of him.

1) Why was the African American upset?
2) Why did Mrs. Cho put down the change on the counter?

Case Study 2

An American invited a group of Japanese students over to his house. He and his wife had spent a great deal of time preparing food and getting the house ready. They were looking forward to the party and hoped that the Japanese would enjoy themselves. They came at about 8:00 at night and right away seemed to be enjoying themselves. There was a lot of dancing and singing and good conversation. Then, almost suddenly, one of the students said "Thank you" to the hosts and said that it was time to go. After that, all of the Japanese began to get ready to leave. The American and his wife could not understand why this happened. They felt insulted because everyone left so early and at the same time.

Can you explain what happened?

3. Writing

Based on the result of "The Polychronic Attitudes Index Exercise," write a composition on the following topic in a *humorous* tone.

The Advantages (or Disadvantages) of
Being a Monochronic (or Polychronic) Person

Read More

Text C   Eye Contact

Pre-reading Exercise

Eye contact is an important aspect of body language. One could draw up quite a lot of rules about eye contact: to look or not to look, when to look and how long to look, who and who not to look at, etc. These rules may vary from culture to culture.

What would you do in the following situations according to Chinese customs?

1. You and a stranger sit across from each other in a railway dining car waiting for your dishes.
   A. You look at the stranger for a while and imply that you want to get to know each other.
   B. You try hard to avoid each other's glance.
   C. You look out of the window as if nobody sat nearby.
   D. You two exchange a short glance to show that you have noticed someone else is sitting nearby, and then you can either start to talk or simply keep silent throughout the meal.
2. You are listening to an instruction given by someone who is senior to you.
   A. You gaze intently at him/her all the time to show your respect.
   B. You try to avoid eye contact to show your respect.
   C. You look at him/her only when you are asked to do so.
   D. You look at him/her as naturally as he/she looks at you.

Having looked at some Chinese situations, please check out the following text which deals with rules for eye contact in other cultures.

Eye contact is one way of measuring the degree of closeness of relationship between two speakers, although there are cultural variations in the meaning of eye contact. In the Middle East, for example, it is considered extremely provocative for a woman to let a man catch her eye, let alone return his gaze. Social psychologist Michael Argyle observes that there is more eye contact between people who like each

other than those who are indifferent or hostile towards each other. And the longer the length of the gaze, the more likely it is that the listener is more interested in the person who is speaking, than the actual topic of conversation. Frequently looking down can indicate submissiveness or embarrassment. Looking away repeatedly may express boredom or dislike. Women tend to engage in more eye contact than men, especially when talking to other women.

But too steady eye contact can make one feel uneasy at times. Most people become uncomfortable under the intense gaze of a stare. One scientist suggests that perhaps one reason that man becomes tense under the force of a stare is in his biological ancestors: in apes, a stare signifies aggressiveness and hostility. The person who insistently fixes his eyes on our face is often more successful in arousing our dislike than impressing us with his directness and sincerity.

Similarly, the smile cannot always be interpreted as a sign of friendliness. The person who smiles almost constantly and with little apparent reason makes us uneasy. Even though he may believe that he is expressing friendliness, he may really seem nervous and tense. In other animals, bared teeth are a warning gesture, a danger sign.

Genuine warmth or interest can be revealed in the eyes, suggests Dr. Eckhard Hess of the University of Chicago, who believes that the pupils of the eyes can indicate emotion or interest. The opened pupil tends to be associated with pleasant, satisfying experiences. That special sparkle in the lover's eyes need not be fantasy, for love may make the pupil grow larger. Sometimes when we feel that a person is "warm" or "friendly," it is possible we are reacting to a form of nonverbal communication — his opened pupils.

The next time you are at a party, take note of some of the silent messages being sent around you. Notice which persons seem to draw naturally together to speak, which others try to stay further apart or even avoid meeting each other's eyes. You may find that this silent language is much more fascinating than the actual conversation going on around you.

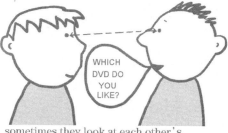

sometimes they look at each other's eyes to check whether the other is interested

Book to Read

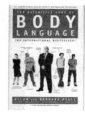

Pease, Allan and Barbara Pease. *The Definitive Book of Body Language*. New York: Bantam Books, 2004.
- This is a great resource for anyone who wants to gain a better understanding of body language. It can help you learn more about how to interpret the nonverbal behavior of other people as well as how to use body language to send the right signals.

Movie to Watch

Date with an Angel is an American movie which was released in 1987. The romantic fantasy/comedy was an updated reworking of 1942 movie *I Married an Angel*. This movie was marketed with the tagline "Jim is about to marry a princess... but he's in love with an angel." It provides wonderful examples of eye gaze, facial expression, spontaneous communication, kinesics and physical appearance. Some important concepts or aspects of nonverbal communication are fully embodied in this movie.

Unit 7

Cross-gender Communication

> When women are depressed, they either eat or go shopping; men invade another country.
> —— Elayne Boosler
>
> When men and women agree, it is only in their conclusions; their reasons are always different.
> —— George Santayana

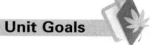

- To understand the differences between male and female in communication
- To learn effective cross-gender communication principles
- To learn useful words and expressions about cross-gender communication and improve language skills

Gender Differences in Communication

1. At public gatherings or in many informal conversations, who talks most?
   A. Men.　　　　　　　　B. Women.
2. Who initiate more interaction in conversations?
   A. Men.　　　　　　　　B. Women.
3. Who interrupt the speech of other people more often?
   A. Men.　　　　　　　　B. Women.
4. Who ask more uncomplicated questions in formal group meetings?
   A. Men.　　　　　　　　B. Women.

5. Who are less likely to have confidence in their ability to make persuasive arguments?
   A. Men.　　　　　　B. Women.
6. Who take up more physical space when sitting or standing, with arms and legs stretched out away from their body?
   A. Men.　　　　　　B. Women.
7. Who tend to lean forward when listening?
   A. Men.　　　　　　B. Women.
8. Who tend to look at the other person directly when listening?
   A. Men.　　　　　　B. Women.
9. Who tend to establish more business relationships through discussing their personal life?
   A. Men.　　　　　　B. Women.
10. Who talk more about what they did, where they went and less about relationships with others in business negotiation?
    A. Men.　　　　　　B. Women.

Start to Read

Text A　Gender Differences in Communication

All of us have different styles of communicating with other people. Our style depends on a lot of things: where we are from, how and where we were brought up, what education we received and how old we are. It can also depend on our gender. Generally speaking, men and women talk differently although there are varying degrees of masculine and feminine speech characteristics in each of us. But men and women speak in particular ways mostly because those ways are associated with their gender.

The styles that men and women use to communicate have been described as "debate vs. relate," "report vs. rapport" or "competitive vs. cooperative." Men often seek straightforward solutions to problems and useful advice whereas women tend to try and establish intimacy by discussing problems and showing concern and empathy in order to reinforce relationships.

Jennifer Coates, in her book *Women, Men and Language* (Longman Inc., 1986) studied men-only and women-only discussion groups and found that when women talk to each other they reveal a lot about their private lives. They also stick to one topic for a long time, let all speakers finish their sentences and try to have everyone participate. Men, on the other hand, rarely talk about their personal relationships and feelings but compete to prove themselves better informed about current affairs, travel, sport, etc. The topics change often and the men try to over time, establish a reasonably stable hierarchy, with some men dominating conversation and others talking very little.

Dr. Lillian Glass' book *He Says, She Says: Closing the Communication Gap Between the Sexes* (The Putnam Berkeley Group, 1993) details her findings on the many differences in the way men and women communicate, both verbally and nonverbally. You can have a look at the differences.

BODY LANGUAGE

Men	Women
They take up more physical space when sitting or standing, with arms and legs stretched out away from their bodies.	They take up less physical space, sitting with arms and legs toward their bodies.
They gesture away from the bodies.	They gesture toward the bodies.
They assume more reclined positions when sitting and lean backward when listening.	They assume more forward positions when sitting and lean forward when listening.
They are not as sensitive to the communication cues of others.	They have greater sensitivity and acuity toward other people's nonverbal communication cues.
They tend to approach women more closely in terms of their personal space.	They do not approach men as closely in terms of their personal space.

FACIAL EXPRESSION

Men	Women
They tend to cock their heads to the side and look at the other person from an angle when listening.	They tend to look at the other person directly facing them with their heads and eyes facing forward when listening.
They provide fewer facial expressions in feedback and fewer reactions.	They provide more facial expressions and more reactions.
They tend to display frowning and squinting when listening.	They display smiling and head-nodding when listening.
They stare more in negative interaction.	They lower their eyes more to avert gaze in negative interaction.

SPEECH PATTERNS

Men	Women
They speak in a louder voice.	They speak in a softer voice.
They use loudness to emphasize points.	They use pitch and inflection to emphasize points.
They sound more monotonous in speech. They use approximately 3 tones when talking.	They sound more emotional in speech. They use approximately 5 tones when talking.
They interrupt others more and allow fewer interruptions.	They interrupt others less and allow more interruptions.
They disclose less personal information about themselves.	They disclose more personal information about themselves.
They make direct accusations (i.e. "You don't call").	They make more indirect accusations. They use "why," which sounds like nagging (i.e. "Why don't you ever call?").
They make more direct statements and "beat around the bush" less often.	They make more indirect statements.
They make more declarative statements (i.e. "It's a nice day").	They make more tentative statements and use "tag endings" or upward inflections which make statements sound like questions (i.e. "It's a nice day, isn't it?").
They use more interjections when changing topics (i.e. "Hey!""Oh!" "Listen!").	They use more conjunctions when changing topics (i.e. "and," "but," "however").
They ask fewer questions to stimulate conversation.	They ask more questions to stimulate conversations.
They rarely discuss their personal life in business.	They tend to establish more business relationships by discussing their personal life.

BEHAVIOUR

Men	Women
They try to solve problems and troubles.	They try to match troubles by relating similar negative experiences.
They have a more analytical approach to problems.	They have a more emotional approach to problems.
They are less likely to ask for help. They try to figure things out on their own.	They are more likely to ask for help and accept it.
They are more task-oriented (i.e. "What is everyone going to do?").	They are more maintenance-oriented (i.e. "Is everyone all right?").
They appear less intuitive and less aware of details.	They appear more intuitive and more aware of details.
They have more difficulty in expressing intimate feelings.	They have less difficulty in expressing intimate feelings.
They are more apt to yell, shout and swear to release anger.	They are more apt to cry to release anger.
They talk more about what they did, where they went and less about relationships with others.	They talk more about how they feel and more about relationships with others.
They tend to take verbal rejection less personally.	They tend to take verbal rejection more personally.

Text B Six Principles for Effective Cross-gender Communication

We are inclined to think what differs from our own standards as wrong. For example, a woman might assume a man is closed because he does not disclose as much as she does, while a man might regard a woman intrusive if she cares too much about his feeling. Instead of debating which is better, either feminine or masculine style of communication, we should learn to see difference as mere difference. The following six principles are constructive in achieving effective cross-gender communication.

Suspend Judgment

This is first and foremost, because as long as we are judging differences, we are not respecting them. When you find yourself confused in cross-gender conversations, resist the tendency to judge. Instead, explore constructively what is happening and how you and your partner might better understand each other.

Recognize the Validity of Different Communication Styles

In cross-gender communication, we need to remind ourselves that there is a logic and validity to both feminine and masculine communication styles. It is inappropriate to apply a single criterion — either masculine or feminine — to both genders' communication. Instead, we need to realize that different goals, priorities, and standards pertain to each.

Provide Translation Cues

Now that you realize men and women tend to learn and apply different rules for interaction, it makes sense to think about helping the other gender understand your communication.

Seek Translation Cues

We can also improve our interactions by seeking translation cues from others.

Enlarge Your Own Communication Style

Studying other culture's communication teaches us not only about other cultures, but also about ourselves. If we are open to learning and growing, we can improve our own communication skills. Men could learn a great deal from feminine communication style about how to support others. Similarly, women could expand the ways they experience intimacy by appreciating "closeness in doing." There is little to risk and much to gain by incorporating additional skills into our personal repertoire.

Suspend Judgment

If you are thinking we have already covered this principle, you are right. It is important enough, however, to merit repetition. Judgment is so thoroughly woven into Western culture as well as Eastern culture that it is difficult not to evaluate others and difficult to resist our own positions. Yet as long as we judge others and defend ourselves, we are probably making no advancement in communicating more effectively. Therefore, suspending judgment is the first and last principle of effective cross-gender communication.

After You Read

Knowledge Focus

1. **Pair Work: Discuss the following questions with your partner.**
   1) In what way do men and women communicate differently?
   2) How do men differ from women in body language, facial expression, speech pattern and behavior?
   3) What is the first and foremost principle for effective cross-gender communication?
   4) Can we apply a single criterion to cross-gender communication? Why or why not?
   5) How can one enlarge his/her communication style?

2. **Solo Work: Complete the following sentences according to the knowledge you have learned in Text A and Text B.**
   1) Men enjoy giving information as a way to _____. Women like sharing information to _____.
      A. show expertise
      B. build relationships

2) Women listen to _____. Men listen to _____.
   A. solve problems   B. gain understanding
3) Men tend to make unilateral decisions and are more comfortable giving and taking _____. Women tend to seek input and consensus and are more comfortable with giving and taking _____.
   A. suggestions   B. orders
4) Men tend to argue more and find it interesting to _____. Women more often seek _____ and see _____ as more threatening to relationships.
   A. disagree   B. disagreement   C. agreement

Language Focus

1. **Fill in the blanks with the following words or expressions you have learned in Text A and Text B.**

squint	avert	repertoire	reclined	tentative
associate	apt	straightforward	intimacy	rapport

   1) I do not want to _____ myself with them any more.
   2) The actor developed a close _____ with his audience.
   3) His _____, modest manner took into camp everybody he knew.
   4) The _____ of the room was enhanced by its warm colors.
   5) She _____ her head against my shoulder.
   6) He _____ in the bright sunlight.
   7) She _____ her eyes from the terrible sight.
   8) The group included some techno in their _____.
   9) The government is taking _____ steps towards tackling the country's economic problems.
   10) Some of the staff are _____ to arrive late on Mondays.

2. **Fill in the blanks with the proper form of the words in the brackets.**
   1) The management took all _____ (reason) safety precautions.
   2) Although he is clever, he is _____ (back) in giving his views.
   3) He banged his fist on the table to _____ (emphasis) his argument.
   4) This _____ (accuse) of bribery is a vile smear on an honorable citizen.
   5) A _____ (maintain) manual gives diagrams and instructions for repairing your car.
   6) Her _____ (reject) of him seems to have made him go back into his shell.
   7) It would be _____ (appropriate) for me to comment until we know more of the facts.
   8) Your trouble is you've got your _____ (prior) back to front!

3. **Find the appropriate prepositions or adverbs that collocate with the words in bold letters.**
   1) The country **depends** heavily _____ its tourist trade.
   2) The new machine is supposed to be the **solution** _____ all our production problems, but the proof of the pudding is in the eating.
   3) Reporter should **stick** _____ investigating the facts.
   4) He is not being any help at all. He is just **taking** _____ space.
   5) Talking _____ **a low voice** were a man and a woman.

6) She is extremely professional in her **approach** _____ her job.
7) In whatever he does, he is **apt** _____ go heels over head.
8) Many of your suggestions have been **incorporated** _____ the new plan.

4. Error Correction: Each of the following sentences has at least one grammatical error. Identify the errors and make corrections.
   1) Both of us have different styles of communicating with other people.
   2) Men and women speak in particular ways mostly. Because those ways are associated with their gender.
   3) Men often seek straightforward solutions of problems and useful advice.
   4) Women stick to one topic for a long time, letting all speakers finish their sentences and try to have everyone participate.
   5) Men take up more physical space when sitting or standing, with arms and legs stretching out away from their body.
   6) Women tend to speak in softer voice.
   7) Men interrupt others more and allow few interruptions.
   8) We are inclined to think that differs from our own standards as wrong.
   9) A woman might assume a man is closed because he does not disclose as many as she does.
   10) You should explore how you and your partner might better understood each other.
   11) We need to remind ourselves that there is a logic and validity to both feminine or masculine communication styles.
   12) We do need realize that different goals, priorities, and standards pertain to each other.
   13) Studying other culture's communication teach us not only about other cultures, but also about our own culture.
   14) If we are open to learn and grow, we can improve our own communication skills.
   15) If you are thinking we already covered this principle, you are right.
   16) Judgment is so thoroughly woven into Western culture as well as Eastern culture that it is difficult to not evaluate others and difficult to resist our own positions.

Comprehensive Work

1. Pair Work: The following are some examples of common problems in communication between men and women. Analyze these cases with your partner.

Case Study 1

Mary is very upset when she meets John for dinner. She explains that she is worried about a friend who has begun drinking heavily. When John suggests she should get her friend counseling, Mary repeats how worried she feels. John tells Mary to make sure her friend does not drive after drinking. At this point Mary explodes, saying that she does not need his advice. Irritated at her lack of appreciation for his help, John asks, "Then why did you ask for it?" Exasperated, Mary responds, "Oh, never mind. I'll talk to Ann. At least she cares how I feel."

Case Study 2

Rita and Mike are colleagues in a marketing firm. One morning Mike drops into Rita's office to discuss a project with her. As Mike presents his ideas, Rita nods and says "Um," "Uh huh" and "Yes." When he finishes and asks what she thinks, Rita says, "I really don't think that plan will work out." Feeling misled, Mike demands, "Then why do you agree the whole time I presented my idea?" Completely confused, Rita responds, "What makes you think I was agreeing with you?"

Case Study 3

Catherine and George have been dating for two years and are very serious. To celebrate their anniversary, Catherine wants to spend a quiet evening in her apartment where they can talk about the relationship and be alone with each other. When George arrives, he has planned to dine out and go to a concert. Catherine feels hurt because he does not want to talk and spend the evening alone with her.

2. Group Work

Form groups of 4. First try to decide whether your communication style is masculine, feminine, or a combination of both. Then make a list of the ways that could help enrich communication style.

_____
_____
_____

3. Writing

First read the following dialogue between a husband and a wife.

He: What would you like for your birthday?
She: I don't care. Anything is OK.
He: No, really, what do you want? I'd like to get you something nice.
She: You don't have to get me anything. Besides we cannot afford much right now.
He: Well, how about our going out for dinner together then?
She: Sure, that's fine. I don't really want anything. You always give me whatever I want anyway.

What do you think of this conversation? Is it based on fact or not? Does it tell you much about gender differences? How should we view such differences if it is really the case in our life?

Please write a composition to comment on it.

Text C Gender Issues

Pre-reading Exercise

The following cases are about the misunderstandings between men and women. Before reading Text C, try to find out the "between the lines meanings."

Misunderstanding 1

> He: I'm really tired. I have so much work to do — I don't know how I'm going to get it done!
> She: Me, too. There just aren't enough hours in the day!
> He: There you go again! You never think my contributions to this marriage are good enough!

Misunderstanding 2

> She: I'm really tired. I have so much work to do — I don't know how I'm going to get it done!
> He: Why don't you take a day off and rest, if you're so tired?
> She: (Sarcastically) Thanks a lot! You think my contribution to this household is so trivial that I can do nothing and the difference will not even be noticed?

Misunderstanding 3

> She: I'm really tired. I have so much work to do — I don't know how I'm going to get it done!
> He: That's ridiculous! Nothing bad is going to happen, so just trust that I'll get there safely! If something bad does happen, I'm sure you'll hear about it!

A lot of media attention has been devoted to the idea that women and men communicate very differently — in fact, it is sometimes stated that women and men communicate so differently from one another that they must come from different planets! Although at times differences in women's and men's communication styles seem to be constant and overwhelming, they are really quite minor. For example, both women and men can be nurturing, aggressive, task-focused, or sentimental. What is important to think about, however, is that women and men sometimes perceive the same messages to have different meanings. In fact, it may be a result of the differences in message interpretation that the "battle of the sexes" occurs.

Studies indicate that women, to a greater extent, are sensitive to the interpersonal meanings that lie "between the lines" in the messages they exchange with their mates. That is, societal expectations often make women responsible for regulating intimacy, or how close they allow others to come. For that reason, it is argued that women pay more attention than men to the underlying meanings about intimacy that messages imply. Men, on the other hand, to a greater extent than women, are more sensitive to "between the lines meanings" about status. For men, societal expectations are that they must negotiate hierarchy, or who is the captain and who is the crew.

These differences in emphasis on interpersonal vs. status implications of messages typically lead women to expect relationships to be based on interdependence (mutual dependence) and cooperation. Women more frequently emphasize the similarities between themselves and others, and try to make decisions that make everyone happy. In contrast, it is more typical for men to expect relationships to be based on independence and competition. Men more frequently emphasize the differences between themselves and others, and often make decisions based on their personal needs or desires.

How are these differences seen in marriage? In the ways women and men communicate! Women tend to be the relationship specialists and men tend to be task specialists. Women are typically the experts in "rapport talk" which refers to the types of communication that build, maintain, and strengthen relationships. Rapport talk reflects skills of talking, nurturing, emotional expression, empathy, and support. Men are typically the experts in task accomplishment and addressing questions about facts. They are experts in "report talk," which refers to the types of communication that analyzes issues and solves problems. Report talk reflects skills of being competitive, lacking sentimentality, analyzing, and focusing aggressively on task accomplishment.

These differences can create misunderstandings. Here are three examples:

Misunderstanding 1

> He: I'm really tired. I have so much work to do — I don't know how I'm going to get it done!
> She: Me, too. There just aren't enough hours in the day!
> He: There you go again! You never think my contributions to this marriage are good enough!

In this conversation, she is trying to communicate something like "We're partners and share similar experiences." Her intended "between the lines" message is: "I understand what you're going through; you're not alone." The "between the lines" message he hears emphasizes competition for status: "What are you complaining about? You aren't any better than I am!" or "Your contributions to our marriage aren't any more significant than mine!"

Misunderstanding 2

> She: I'm really tired. I have so much work to do — I don't know how I'm going to get it done!
> He: Why don't you take a day off and rest, if you're so tired?
> She: (Sarcastically) Thanks a lot! You think my contribution to this household is so trivial that I can do nothing and the difference will not even be noticed?

Here, he is trying to communicate something like "Oh, you need advice and analysis? I'll focus on the details and facts, and offer a solution." His intended "between the lines" message is: "I will help you solve your problem because I think I know something that might help." The "between the lines" message she hears him saying is: "I don't want to understand your feelings; I'm different from you and I know what you should do."

The problems here result from some subtle differences in the ways that women and men approach problems. Women *sometimes* deal with problems (especially emotional concerns) by talking about them, sharing their feelings, and matching experiences with others. This can be frustrating to men, who *more typically* deal with problems by focusing on the facts and seeking an immediate solution. Occasionally, men perceive women to be ungrateful for the advice and solutions they offer and ponder in frustration why women do not want to resolve their problems! Similarly, when men offer a solution, rather than talking about a problem, women may feel hurt, dissatisfied, and put-down by the lack of empathy men show.

Misunderstanding 3

> She: I'm really tired. I have so much work to do — I don't know how I'm going to get it done!
> He: That's ridiculous! Nothing bad is going to happen, so just trust that I'll get there safely! If something bad does happen, I'm sure you'll hear about it!

In this final example, she is trying to communicate something like, "We're connected and I care about you and your safety." Her intended "between the lines" message is: "You are loved and important to me." The "between the lines" message he hears her saying is: "You had better check in with me! I want to know where you are, who you are with, and what you are doing at all times."

The misunderstandings in these examples probably result from differences in the ways that women and men show affection. It is more common for women to show affection through talking, but it is more common for men to show affection by doing things — either doing things together or doing separate things within the same physical space. Sometimes not talking — not having to talk — is a sign of trust and intimacy for men.

What does all this mean to us?

Understanding differences is the key to working them out. When we misunderstand one another, we often think that the other's motives are not reasonable, are mean-spirited, or worse! But by knowing that women and men sometimes see — and hear! — things through different filters, we can begin to share with one other the distortions we experience, and thereby find our way to clarity.

So, the next time you feel surprised, disappointed, or angry with someone's response to something you have said, ask yourself if he or she may have "misheard" you. Is the other responding to your problems with a solution, when you wanted to receive sympathy? Is the other responding to your message of affection with a message of status? If so, you will be able to help the other to understand the source of your miscommunication, and avoid the hurt feelings and conflicts that sometimes follow.

Text D Rapport-Talk and Report-Talk

Text D is an excerpt from Deborah Tannen's *You Just Don't Understand: Women and Men in Conversation*. After you finish your reading, please fill in the following chart based on your understanding of the text.

Items	Female	Male
Conversational Style		
Communication Purpose		
Ways of Communication		

Who talks more, women or men? The seemingly contradictory evidence is reconciled by the difference between what I call "public" and "private speaking." More men feel comfortable doing "public speaking," while more women feel comfortable doing "private" speaking. Another way of capturing these differences is by using the terms "rapport-talk" and "report-talk."

For most women, the language of conversation is primarily a language of rapport: a way of establishing connections and negotiating relationships. Emphasis is placed on displaying similarities and matching experiences. From childhood, girls criticize peers who try to stand out or appear better than others. People feel their closest connections at home, or in settings where they feel at home—with one or a few people they feel close to and comfortable with—in other words, during private speaking. But even the most public situations can be approached like private speaking.

For most men, talk is primarily a means to preserve independence and maintain a status in a hierarchical social order. This is done by exhibiting knowledge and skill, and by holding center stage through verbal performance such as storytelling, joking, or imparting information. From childhood, men learn to use talking as a way to get and keep attention. So they are more comfortable speaking in larger groups made up of people they know less well—in the broadest sense, "public speaking." But even the most private situations can be approached like public speaking, more like giving a report than establishing rapport.

What is the source of the stereotype that women talk a lot? Dale Spender suggests that most people feel instinctively (if not consciously) that women, like children, should be seen and not heard, so any amount of talk from them seems like too much. Studies have shown that if women and men talk equally in a group, people think the women talked more. So there is truth to Spender's view. But another explanation is that men think women talk a lot because they hear women talking in situations where men would not: on the telephone; or in social situations with friends, when they are not discussing topics that men find inherently interesting; or at home alone—in other words, in private speaking.

Home is the setting for an American icon that features the silent man and the talkative woman. And this icon, which grows out of the different goals and habits I have been describing, explains why the complaint most often voiced by women about the men with whom they are intimate is "He doesn't talk to me"—and the second most frequent is "He doesn't listen to me."

A woman who wrote to Ann Landers is typical:

> My husband never speaks to me when he comes home from work. When I ask, "How did everything go today?" he says, "Rough..." or "It's a jungle out there." (We live in Jersey and he works in New York City.)
>
> It's a different story when we have guests or go visiting. Paul is the gabbiest guy in the crowd — a real spellbinder. He comes up with the most interesting stories. People hang on every word. I think to myself, "Why doesn't he ever tell me these things?"
>
> —The Invisible Woman

Ann Landers suggests that the husband may not want to talk because he is tired when he comes home from work. Yet women who work come home tired too, and they are nonetheless eager to tell their partners or friends everything that happened to them during the day and what these fleeting, daily dramas made them think and feel.

Sources as lofty as studies conducted by psychologists, as down to earth as letters written to advice columnists, and as sophisticated as movies and plays come up with the same insight: Men's silence at home is a disappointment to women. Again and again, women complain, "He seems to have everything to say to everyone else, and nothing to say to me."

When something goes wrong, people look around for a source to blame: either the person they are trying to communicate with ("You're demanding, stubborn, self-ccentered") or the group that the other person belongs to ("All women are demanding"; "All men are self-centered"). Some generous-minded people blame the relationship ("We just can't communicate"). But underneath, or overlaid on these types of blame cast outward, most people believe that something is wrong with them.

If individual people or particular relationships were to blame, there wouldn't be so many different people having the same problems. The real problem is conversational style. Women and men have different ways of talking. Even with the best intentions, trying to settle the problem through talk can only make things worse if it is ways of talking that are causing trouble in the first place.

Once again, the seeds of women's and men's styles are sown in the ways they learn to use language while growing up. In our culture, most people, but especially women, look to their closest relationships as havens in a hostile world. The center of a little girl's social life is her best friend. Girls' friendships are made and maintained by telling secrets. For grown women too, the essence of friendship is talk, telling each other what they're thinking and feeling, and what happened that day: who was at the bus stop, who called, what they said, how that made them feel. When asked who their best friends are, most women name other women they talk to regularly. When asked the same question, most men will say it's their wives. After that, many men name other men with whom they do things such as play tennis or baseball (but never just sit and talk) or a chum from high school whom they haven't spoken to in a year.

Men and women often have very different ideas of what's important—and at what point "important" topics should be raised. A woman told me, with lingering incredulity, of a conversation with her boyfriend. Knowing he had seen his friend Oliver, she asked, "What's new with Oliver?" He replied, "Nothing." But later in the conversation it came out that Oliver and his girlfriend had decided to get married. "That's nothing?" the woman gasped in frustration and disbelief.

Many men honestly do not know what women want, and women honestly do not know why men find what they want so hard to comprehend and deliver.

Book to Read

Gray, John. *Men are from Mars, Women are from Venus*. New York: Harper Paperbacks, 1992.

- This book offers many suggestions for improving husband-wife relationships by understanding the communication style and emotional needs of the opposite gender. As suggested by the title, this book asserts the notion that men and women are as different as beings from other planets. In contrast to some psychologists who emphasize similarities between the sexes, Gray writes almost exclusively about differences.

Movie to Watch

A Streetcar Named Desire (1951) was adapted from Tennessee Williams' 1947 Pulitzer Prize-winning play of the same name. This movie discusses the struggle between men and women within downtown American society. Tennessee Williams foregrounds the gender struggle, using different techniques to represent the truth of social attitudes towards masculinity and femininity. He explores both male and female stereotypes as well as society's reaction to those who challenge these preconceptions.

Unit 8
Understanding Culture

> No culture can live, if it attempts to be exclusive.
> —— Mahatma Gandi
>
> As the soil, however rich it may be, cannot be productive without cultivation, so the mind without culture can never produce good fruit.
> —— Lucius Annaeus Seneca

Unit Goals

- To understand the definitions of culture
- To learn to identify the ingredients and functions of culture
- To learn to describe the characteristics of culture
- To be aware of cultural differences
- To learn some useful words and expressions about culture and improve language skills

Before You Read

We can learn culture from a large variety of sources. Proverb is one of them. Let us touch on some of the invisible "instructors" and their "instructions." Read the following proverbs aloud and try to find out the culture behind them.

ITEMS	PROVERBS	CULTURE
American proverbs	☞ Strike while the iron is hot. ☞ Actions speak louder than words. ☞ God helps those who help themselves. ☞ A man's home is his castle.	
Chinese proverb	☞ A journey of a thousand miles begins with a single step.	

Unit 8 Understanding Culture

(continued)

ITEMS	PROVERBS	CULTURE
German proverb	☞ Order is half of life.	
Korean proverb	☞ Even if the bridge be made of stone, make sure it is safe.	
Swedish proverb	☞ He who stirs another's porridge often burns his own.	
Mexican proverb	☞ We are all like well buckets. One goes up and the other comes down.	
Ethiopian proverb	☞ When spider webs unite, they can tie up a lion.	

Jewish proverb: Wisdom is better than jewels.
The culture behind it:

_____

Arabic proverb: A man's tongue is his sword.
The culture behind it:

_____

African proverb: The ill-mannered child finds a father wherever he goes.
The culture behind it:

_____

Start to Read

Text A   What Is Culture?

　　The word culture has many different meanings. For some, it refers to an appreciation of good literature, music, art, and food. For a biologist, it is likely to be a colony of bacteria or other microorganisms growing in a nutrient medium in a laboratory Petri dish. However, for anthropologists and other behavioral scientists, culture is the full range of learned human behavior patterns. The term was first used in this way by the pioneer English Anthropologist Edward B. Tylor in his book, *Primitive Culture*, published in 1871. Tylor said that culture is "that complex whole which includes knowledge, belief, art, law, morals, custom, and any other capabilities and habits acquired by man as a member of society." Since Tylor's time, the concept of culture has become the central focus of anthropology.

　　Culture is a powerful human tool for survival, but it is a fragile phenomenon. It is constantly changing and easily lost because it exists only in our minds. Our written languages, governments, buildings, and other man-made things are merely the products of culture. They are not culture in themselves. For this reason, archaeologists cannot dig up culture directly in their excavations. The broken pots and other artifacts of ancient people that they uncover are only material remains that reflect cultural patterns — they are things that were made and used through cultural knowledge and skills.

There are three layers or levels of culture that are part of our learned behavior patterns and perceptions. The most obvious level is **the body of cultural traditions** that distinguish our specific society. When people speak of Italian, Samoan, or Japanese culture, they are referring to the shared language, traditions, and beliefs that set each of these peoples apart from others. In most cases, those who share our culture do so because they acquired it as they were raised by parents and other family members who have it.

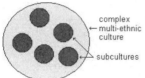

The second layer of culture that may be part of your identity is **subculture.** In complex, diverse societies in which people have come from many different parts of the world, they often retain much of their original cultural traditions. As a result, they are likely to be part of an identifiable subculture in their new society. The shared cultural traits of subcultures set them apart from the rest of their society. Examples of easily identifiable subcultures in the United States include ethnic groups such as Vietnamese Americans, African Americans, and Mexican Americans. Members of each of these subcultures share a common identity, food tradition, dialect or language, and other cultural traits that come from their common ancestral background and experience. As the cultural differences between members of a subculture and the dominant national culture blur and eventually disappear, the subculture ceases to exist except as a group of people who claim a common ancestry. That is generally the case with German Americans and Irish Americans in the United States today. Most of them identify themselves as Americans first. They also see themselves as being part of the cultural mainstream of the nation.

The third layer of culture consists of **cultural universals.** These are learned behavior patterns that are shared by all of humanity collectively. No matter where people live in the world, they share these universal traits.

After You Read

Knowledge Focus

1. **Pair Work: Discuss the following questions with your partner.**
    1) How did English Anthropologist Edward B. Tylor define culture in his book, *Primitive Culture*?
    2) What are the three layers or levels of culture?
    3) What is the body of cultural traditions?
    4) Can you give one or two examples to illustrate subculture?
    5) What are cultural universals? Can you list some that you have found in your life?
2. **Solo Work: Tell whether the following statements are true or false according to the knowledge you learned and explain why.**
    1) Culture means all kinds of things: art, music, literature, related intellectual activities,

beliefs, customs, practices, social behavior of a particular nation or people and so on. (　)
2) Because of their long history, cultures do not change or reinvent themselves. (　)
3) Our written languages, governments, buildings, and other man-made things are culture. (　)
4) When people mention Chinese culture, they mean Chinese language, traditions, and beliefs. (　)
5) People of the same nationality share a common identity, food tradition, dialect or language. (　)
6) A cultural universal refers to an element, pattern, trait or institution that is common to all human cultures worldwide. (　)
7) Culture is static and cannot change with the time. (　)
8) The most obvious level of culture is cultural universals. (　)

Language Focus

1. Fill in the blanks with the following words or expressions you have learned in Text A.

| fragile | dig up | ancestry | anthropology |
| reinforcement | set apart | trait | refer to |

1) Glasses are _____ and must be handled with great care.
2) An athletic supporter has a protective _____ of rigid plastic or metal.
3) For further particulars, please _____ Chapter Two.
4) In mythology and legend, a man, often of divine _____, is endowed with great courage and strength and favored by the gods.
5) He was _____ because he suffered an infectious disease.
6) By _____ a few unsavory details about his past we managed to have him hounded out.
7) One of my friends majored in _____ in a university in Illinois.
8) One of his less attractive _____ is criticizing his wife in public.

2. Fill in the blanks with the proper form of the words in the brackets.

1) There is an _____ (appreciate) of the poet's work in the book.
2) An organism, such as a mosquito or tick, carries disease-causing _____ (organism) from one host to another.
3) Plants absorb minerals and other _____ (nutritious) from the soil.
4) This course is about the cultural, _____ (behave) and sociological aspects of spatial distances between individuals.
5) _____ (excavate) of the site will begin tomorrow.
6) It was two young reporters who _____ (cover) the whole plot.
7) We should study our _____ (ancestry) achievements.
8) The following example uses the _____ (relate) and logical operators.

3. Find the appropriate prepositions or adverbs that collocate with the words in bold letters.

1) I am not free on Sundays, not to **speak** _____ Mondays.
2) This word can also **refer** _____ a conflict or disagreement, often involving violence.

3) For reasons he could not explain he was made to feel different, **set apart** _____ the other boys.
4) I always **see** her _____ my first English teacher.
5) Children need to learn to **relate** _____ other children.
6) The trees outside the windows **deprive** the house _____ light.
7) The treasurer has to **account** _____ the money paid to him.
8) He cannot **adjust** himself _____ the whirl of modern life in this big city.

4. **Error Correction**: Each of the following sentences has at least one grammatical error. Identify the errors and make corrections.
   1) "Culture" is first used in this way by the pioneer English Anthropologist Edward B. Tylor in his book, *Primitive Culture*, published in 1871.
   2) Tylor said that culture was "that complex whole which includes knowledge, belief, art, law, morals, custom, and any other capabilities and habits acquired by man as a member of society."
   3) Since Tylor's time, the concept of culture becomes the central focus of anthropology.
   4) They are things what were made and used through cultural knowledge and skills.
   5) When people speak of Italian, Samoan, or Japanese culture, they are referring to the sharing language, traditions, and beliefs that set each of these peoples apart from others.
   6) In complex, diverse societies which people have come from many different parts of the world, they often retain much of their original cultural traditions.
   7) As the cultural differences among members of a subculture and the dominant national culture blur and eventually disappear, the subculture ceases to exist except as a group of people who claim a common ancestry.
   8) Process of cultural acquisition is called enculturation.
   9) If the environment is different, the culture that each individual learns or acquires will be different, also.
   10) Only when we are deprived of our own culture or put into a completely new culture we can realize the importance of culture to us.
   11) We should make deliberate effort to understand how culture influences our own behavior as well other people.
   12) The learned cultural patterns are not the property of some individuals but shared by the members of the same group or society.
   13) Though individuals may have different preferences over one way of conduct or another, they must share one and the same system which their personal choice is made.
   14) The study of culture and its people could involve not only the learning of the explicit rules but also those implicit beliefs, values and attitudes that relate to them.
   15) We must not assume that any trait of culture should be forever fixed.
   16) Only in this way must we gain a true understanding of a culture and its people.

Comprehensive Work
1. Pair Work
Analyze the following cases with your partner.

> Case Study 1

A female neurologist from Beijing was working on a research project in a Toronto hospital. She shared a small office with a young Canadian physiotherapist who loved peanut butter. He was so fond of peanut butter that he kept a jar in the office. One day he came into the office and exclaimed, "Who took my peanut butter?" The Chinese woman immediately felt accused. After all, there were only two of them in the office.

She was deeply distressed, but she said nothing. Later that day she was working in a room where the physiotherapist was treating a patient who had suffered paralysis of his legs and arms from a motorcycle accident. The physiotherapist moved one of the patient's legs in a way that caused him pain.

"Ouch!" he cried.

"Oh, I didn't do that," said the physiotherapist. "It was that doctor over there," and he pointed to the Chinese woman.

"How could she have done it since she's on the other side of the room?" the patient asked.

"Ah, she has three hands," the physiotherapist replied jokingly, expecting the patient to be amused by his fanciful explanation for his pain.

At these words the Chinese doctor became even more upset. She was very disturbed. She waited until the patient had gone and then said to the physiotherapist, "I'm very upset by what you said." The physiotherapist was taken aback. What had he said? "You said I had three hands." The doctor finally choked. "You think I took the peanut butter."

1) Why do you think the Chinese doctor felt accused when she heard the Canadian say, "Who took my peanut butter?" What did the Canadian mean by saying that?
2) What was wrong when the Canadian told the patient that the Chinese doctor had three hands?

> Case Study 2

A Japanese student, Keiko, who studied at the University of Wisconsin in Madison was on a strict budget. Recently she found a small apartment to share with a friend. Her college friend, knowing of her situation, offered to round up some of the necessary items for apartment living. Keiko politely declined, saying she could manage. Wanting to help out, her friends found some old but still usable household appliances and furniture. Mary had an old desk that was in her garage. Mike had some chairs from his uncle and Joe and Marion had a few extra dishes. They cheerfully brought them over one day. Keiko seemed very embarrassed, but gracefully accepted them, sincerely and profusely thanked them.

The following week they were each presented with a gift from Keiko. Mary got an ornate jewelry box, Mike a volume of woodcuts by a famous Japanese artist, and Joe and Marion a beautiful Japanese vase, all of which were of considerable worth and value, much more than the old things they had donated to her. They all protested that she could not afford to give such elaborate gifts; they really expected nothing as the household items were not really being used and they would rather have her use them. Keiko, however, insisted that they take the gifts. In the end, they accepted the gifts, although they all felt uncomfortable as they knew she was really sacrificing to give them.

1) What do you think of Keiko insisting on giving valuable gifts to her college friends?
2) How would you feel if Keiko presented you with a gift for your help?
3) What would you do if you were Keiko?

2. Group Work

Discuss the following popular metaphors of culture with your group members and comment on them. What is culture to you? Try to work out a metaphor of your own and explain it to the class.

- Culture is the dancing step of the human race.
- Culture is the social adhesive of all human relationships.
- Culture is a computer that programs our everyday conduct.
- Culture is a blueprint for living.

My own metaphor of culture is

_____

3. Writing

First, read the following story.

Rosemary is a woman of about 21. For several months, she has been engaged to a young man named Geoffrey. The problem she faces is that between her and her fiancé there lies a deep, wide river filled with hungry alligators.

Rosemary wonders how she can cross the river. She remembers Sinbad, who has the only boat in the area. She then approaches him, asking him to take her across.

Sinbad replies, "Yes, I'll take you across if you'll spend the night with me."

Shocked at this offer, she turns to another acquaintance, Frederick, and tells him her story.

Frederick responds by saying, "Yes, Rosemary, I understand your problem, but it's your problem, not mine."

Rosemary decided to return to Sinbad, spends the night with him and in the morning he takes her across the river.

Her meeting with Geoffrey is warm. But on the evening before they are to be married, Rosemary feels she must tell Geoffrey how she succeeded in getting across the river.

Geoffrey responds by saying, "I wouldn't marry you even if you were the last woman on earth."

Finally, Rosemary turns to her friend, Dennis.

Dennis listens to her story and says, "Well, I don't love you... but I will marry you."

This story provides us with some clues that help us understand the characteristics of culture. Please write a composition about your interpretation of this story.

Read More

Text B Features of Culture

Examining the features of culture will help us understand the concept of culture and enable us to see how these features influence communication.

Culture is learned behavior.

Patterns of culture are not inherent with any individual. They are not genetically passed down from previous generations; rather, they are acquired through the process of learning or interacting with the individual's environment. The process of cultural acquisition is called enculturation. The learning environment includes the family, neighborhood, schools, social groups, physical surroundings, etc. If the environment is different, the culture that each individual learns or acquires will be different too.

Culture is usually acquired unconsciously.

It should be noted that the learning of culture is usually done unconsciously. Our relationship with culture is like that between birds and the sky, fish and water or people and air. Only when we are deprived of our own culture or put into a completely new culture can we realize the importance of culture to us. Without culture we cannot survive. Since culture is often learned unconsciously, we often fail to account for our behavior. In intercultural studies, we should make deliberate effort to understand how culture influences our own behavior as well as that of other people.

Culture is shared among its members.

The learned cultural patterns are not the property of any individuals but shared by the members of the same group or society. When we say A and B come from the same culture, we assume A and B share the same patterns of living: the same set of symbols used for communication, the same rules of speaking, the same idea about what can be eaten as food and what cannot, the same belief about nature and man, and so on. Though individuals may have different preferences over one way of conduct or another, they must share one and the same system out of which their personal choice is made. Within the same system, individuals can easily understand one another and adjust themselves to their surroundings. If we intend to understand people from other cultures, and communicate effectively with them, we must try to understand their ways of living.

Culture is persistent and enduring.

Culture is not created and developed overnight. It is the deposit of human knowledge and collection of both material and non-material wealth created by man over the long process of human civilization. This nature of culture gives continuity to the development of a culture and provides reinforcement to its members in their lifetime learning of the culture.

Culture manifests itself both implicitly and explicitly.

Some aspects of culture are easily observable and some are not. The ways of dressing, talking, and working are readily noticeable, but the ideas and motivations underlying these superficial behaviors are generally unrecognized. The study of culture and its people should involve not only the learning of the explicit rules but also those implicit beliefs, values and attitudes that relate to them.

Culture is adaptive and changeable.

Though culture is persistent and enduring, it is not static. Any great inventions and progress of mankind will bring about changes in people's ideas, way of life, mode of behavior, etc. These changes often take place on the superficial levels of a culture, while the deep structures, i.e. ideological perceptions, values and value orientations, world views and beliefs, are likely to stay or change slowly. Therefore, the study of culture should take a dynamic perspective. We must not assume that any trait of culture is forever fixed. The belief that culture is adaptive and changeable also makes it possible for us to learn about new cultures and adapt ourselves to them.

Culture is relational.

Any culture is an integrated entity. All the components of culture are interrelated. The change of one aspect of culture will certainly bring about changes in other aspects as well. The study of culture and people should also take a relational approach. In other words, we should study one aspect of culture in relation to other aspects. Only in this way can we gain a true understanding of a culture and its people.

Questions for Discussion or Reflection

1. What do you think are the features of culture?
2. Please use examples to illustrate "culture is usually acquired unconsciously."

Text C How Long Does It Take to Say I'm Getting Married (II)

And the next day, my mother called me (Waverly), to invite me to a belated birthday dinner for my father. My brother Vincent was bringing his girlfriend, Lisa Lum. I could bring a friend, too.

I knew she would do this, because cooking was how my mother expressed her love, her pride, her power, her proof that she knew more than Auntie Su. "Just be sure to tell her later that her cooking was the best you ever tasted, that it was far better than Auntie Su's," I told Rich. "Believe me."

The night of the dinner, I sat in the kitchen watching her cook, waiting for the right moment to tell her about our marriage plans, that we had decided to get married next July, about seven months away. She was chopping eggplant into wedges, chatting at the same time about Auntie Suyuan: "She can only cook by looking at a recipe. My instructions are in my fingers. I know what secret ingredients to put in just by using my nose!" and she was slicing with such a ferocity, seeming inattentive to her sharp cleaver, that I was afraid her fingertips would become one of the ingredients of the red-cooked eggplant and shredded port dish.

I was hoping she would say something about Rich first. I had seen her expression when she opened the door, her forced smile as she scrutinized him from head to toe, checking her appraisal of him against that already given to her by Auntie Suyuan. I tried to anticipate what criticisms she would have.

Rich was not only not Chinese, he was a few years younger than I was. And unfortunately, he looked much younger with his curly red hair, smooth pale skin, and the splash of orange freckles across his nose. He was a bit on the short side, compactly built. In his dark business suits, he looked nice but easily forgettable, like somebody's nephew at a funeral, which was why I didn't notice him the first year we worked together at the firm. But my mother noticed everything.

"So what do you think of Rich?" I finally asked, holding my breath.

She tossed the eggplant in the hot oil and it made a loud, angry hissing sound. "So many spots on his face," she said.

I could feel the pinpricks on my back. "They're freckles. Freckles are good luck, you know," I said a bit too heatedly in trying to raise my voice above the din of the kitchen.

"Oh?" she said innocently.

"Yes, the more spots the better. Everybody knows that."

She considered this a moment and then smiled and spoke in Chinese: "Maybe this is true. When you were young, you got the chicken pox. So many spots, you had to stay home for ten days. So lucky, you thought."

I couldn't save Rich in the kitchen. And I couldn't save him later at the dinner table.

He had brought a bottle of French wine, something he did not know my parents could not appreciate. My parents did not even own wine glasses, and then he also made the mistake of drinking not one but two full glasses, while everybody else had a half-inch "just for taste."

When I offered Rich a fork, he insisted on using the slippery ivory chopsticks. He held them splayed like the knock-kneed legs of an ostrich while picking up a large chunk of sauce-coated eggplant. Halfway between his plate and his open mouth, the chunk fell on his crisp white shirt and then slid into his crotch. It took several minutes to get Shoshana to stop shrieking with laughter.

And then he had helped himself to big portions of the shrimp and snow peas, not realizing he should have taken only a polite spoonful until everybody had had a morsel.

He had declined the sautéed new greens, the tender and expensive leaves of a bean plant plucked before the sprouts turn into beans. And Shoshana refused to eat them also, pointing to Rich: "He didn't eat them! He didn't eat them!"

He thought he was being polite by refusing seconds, when he should have followed my father's example, who made a big show of taking small portions of seconds, thirds, and even fourths, always saying he could not resist another bite of something or other, and then groaning that he was so full he thought he would burst.

But the worst was when Rich criticized my mother's cooking, and he didn't even know what he had done. As is the Chinese cook's custom, my mother always made disparaging remarks about her own cooking. That night she chose to direct it toward her famous steamed pork and preserved vegetable dish, which she always served with special pride.

"Ai! This dish is not salty enough, no flavor," she complained, after tasting a small bite. "It is too bad to eat."

This was our family's cue to eat some and proclaim it the best she had ever made. But before we could do so, Rich said, "You know, all it needs is a little soy sauce." And he proceeded to pour a riverful of the salty black stuff on the platter, right before my mother's horrified eyes.

And even though I was hoping throughout the dinner that my mother would somehow see Rich's kindness, his sense of humor and boyish charm, I knew he had failed miserably in her eyes.

Rich obviously had a different opinion on how the evening had gone. When we got home that night, after we put Shoshana to bed, he said modestly, "Well, I think we hit it off A-o-kay."

"Uh-hmm," I said. I was still shuddering, remembering how Rich had firmly shaken both my parents' hand with that same easy familiarity he used with nervous new clients. "Linda, Tim," he said, "we'll see you again soon, I'm sure." My parents' names are Linda and Tim Jong, and nobody, except few older family friends, ever calls them by their first names.

"So what did she say when you told her?" And I knew he was referring to our getting married, when at every possible moment we were alone, she seemed to remark on how much expensive wine Rich liked to drink, or how pale and ill he looked, or how sad Shoshana seemed to be.

Rich was smiling. "How long does it take to say, Mom, Dad, I'm getting married?"

"You don't understand. You don't understand my mother."

Rich shook his head. "Whew! You can say that again. Her English was so bad. You know, when she was talking about that dead guy showing up on *Dynasty*, I thought she was talking about something that happened in China a long time ago."

1. **Discuss with your partner the following questions.**
1) When Waverly's mother mentioned "spots" on Rich's face, what did she intend to say?

2) Why did Waverly say she could not save Rich at the dinner table?
3) Why did Waverly's mother take Rich unfavorably?
4) How did Rich perceive the dinner with Waverly's family?
5) Did Rich correctly interpret Waverly's words "You don't understand my mother"?

2. **Apparently, Rich did not know much about Chinese culture. What Chinese dinner etiquette did he violate?**

1) _____
2) _____
3) _____
4) _____

For Fun

Books to Read
1. Samovar, Larry A., Richard E. Porter and Lisa A. Stefani. *Communication Between Cultures*(跨文化交际). Beijing: Foreign Language Teaching and Research Press, 2000.
- Going beyond traditional coverage, this book focuses on the deep structure of culture with special emphasis on religion, family and history. You will explore how differences in perception, world views, values and verbal and nonverbal messages all affect communication. And you will have the benefit of the book's many current examples and

concrete strategies for improving your skills.

2. Snow, Don 编著.《跨文化交际技巧——如何跟西方人打交道》(学生用书). 上海：上海外语教育出版社，2004.

- This book aims to help you improve your English language skills and develop intercultural communication habits and skills. It also familiarizes you with basic concepts of intercultural communication and teach you basic aspects of western culture.

Movie to Watch

A Walk in the Clouds is a movie in which a young man returning from war meets a young Mexican woman who got pregnant out of wedlock. She is terrified about confronting the situation with her conservative parents (specially her father). In comes Paul Sutton (Reeves) who agrees to pose as her husband for a couple of days in order to trick her father into believing she is happily married.

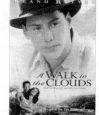

This beautiful movie clearly depicts the cultural differences between Latin and American families. The clean-cut American boy comes in to rescue the misunderstood Mexican lady. You will get a couple of good laughs and a warm feeling once the credits begin to run.

Unit 9
Cultural Diversity

> It were not best that we should all think alike; it is difference of opinion that makes horse race.
> —— Mark Twain
>
> We have become not a melting pot but a beautiful mosaic. Different people, different beliefs, different yearning, different hopes.
> —— Jimmy Carter

Unit Goals

- To understand the difference between different cultures
- To be aware of cultural differences
- To learn useful words and expressions about intercultural communication and improve language skills

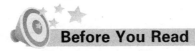

Before You Read

Below are some statements about various cultures throughout the world. Try to decide which one best completes the statement.

An Intercultural Quiz

1. In Japan, loudly slurping a soup is considered as _____.
   a. rude and obnoxious
   b. a sign that you like the soup
   c. normal at home but not in public
   d. something only foreigners do

2. **In Brazil, it is considered normal to show up for a social event _____.**
   a. ten to fifteen minutes early
   b. ten to fifteen minutes late
   c. fifteen minutes to an hour late
   d. one to two hours late

3. **The doors in German offices and homes are generally kept _____.**
   a. wide open to symbolize a welcome of friends and strangers
   b. slightly ajar to suggest that people should knock before entering
   c. half open suggesting that some people are welcome and some are not
   d. tightly shut

4. **You should select a prospective manager, for your Joint Venture with a Shanghai enterprise, on his or her proven ability to _____.**
   a. improve profit by cost cutting
   b. acquire more money from the government
   c. manage people on different levels
   d. learn new technology

5. **For your second visit to your Egyptian partner's office, your associate asks you to come between ten and eleven o'clock in the morning to continue the discussion. You should arrive at _____.**
   a. 9:30 a.m.
   b. 10:00 a.m.
   c. 11:00 a.m.
   d. 10:30 a.m.

6. **An Arab businessman offers you a cup of Arabian coffee at his office. You do not drink coffee. You should say _____**
   a. "No, thank you."
   b. "Thank you but I do not drink coffee."
   c. "Thank you," and accept the cup of coffee.
   d. "No, thank you. Coffee makes me nervous."

7. **You are discussing a subject with a Japanese team. Suddenly everyone becomes quiet. You should _____.**
   a. tell a joke to wake them up
   b. give your discount now
   c. be quiet too
   d. ask them what the problem is

(continued)

8. You have been working and living in Chile for some time, and have gained a lot of valuable business contacts. You would like to do something nice for one of your Chilean business acquaintances. What do you do?
   a. You invite him to your home for a quiet dinner.
   b. You take him to the best nightclubs for a night of drinking.
   c. You invite him for a round of golf at your club.
   d. You buy a bottle of expensive French wine and give it to him.

9. You are in a negotiation team with one of the biggest Russian distributors of your goods. After you offer the price level the Russian senior negotiator, one of the shareholders, shows lack of interest and intention to quit the negotiation. He means _____.
   a. your offer is not common sense
   b. you do not show enough respect to him
   c. he does not have enough authority to respond
   d. he is using "dirty tactics" in order to create pressure

10. An Egyptian executive, after entertaining his Canadian guest, offered joint partnership in a business venture. The Canadian, delighted with the offer, suggested they meet again the next morning with their respective lawyers to finalize the details. The Egyptian never arrived. This happened because _____.
    a. the Egyptian interpreted inviting lawyers as a sign of the mistrust from the Canadian side
    b. the Egyptian executive expected a counteroffer from the Canadian guest
    c. it is difficult to find a good lawyer in Cairo in such a short time
    d. the Canadian should not have set up the next meeting time so soon

Start to Read

Text A The Basic Unit of Society: The Individual or the Collective?

When business in the United States first began exploring the reasons for Japanese success and ways to market products in Japan, they found surprisingly different attitudes in Japanese organizations. In Japan, an individual is a fraction of a unit; the group is the fundamental unit. An often-quoted proverb in Japan is "The nail that sticks up will be pounded down." Any assertion of individualism—valuing the individual over the group—is regarded as a threat to the group and will result in punishment by the group.

Individualism in Japan is tantamount to selfishness. It is the opposite of self-denial for the good of the group, which is highly valued in Japan. That means Japanese managers are closely tied to the department they manage, which is also highly cooperative and close-knit.

Organizations can count on the loyalty and wholehearted commitment of their employees. Organizations have their own songs, their own uniforms, and their own ways to build loyalty and groupness.

Individuals in Western cultures make career choices on the basis of personal needs and goals. If a job offers insufficient advancement, for example, or personality conflict arises with a superior, or the tasks become boring, an ambitious individual likely moves to another job. If lifestyle changes—for instance if a child's schooling or care for an elderly relative becomes a priority—an individual may very well change employers. When the employer wants more overtime from an employee but the employee prefers a job that does not require overtime, the employee may change employers.

In Japan, however, none of these situations is reason for a move. Changing employers is an admission of failure and brings loss of face both to the one who could not cooperate in harmony with the organization and to the organization for spawning such an antisocial misfit. In Japan, if personal goals are not met by work, the employee is persuaded to change or defer the goals. When lifestyle changes create new needs, the superior expects to be told and share the concerns. Child care is typically the responsibility of a wife who stays at home, and health insurance is available from all employers, yet employees discuss changes in their personal lives with their superiors. It is not because they may link these changes to a need for more income or housing; it is because the boss is owed the information and is expected to take an interest in the family life of the employee. When the organization demands overtime, employees eagerly respond. In many organizations in Japan, employees come in for overtime work even when they have little actual work to do, just to show their solidarity with other members of their corporate group.

In cultures where individual is a unit of society, a single person can earn credit or blame for the outcome of an organizational project. In cultures where the collective is important, credit or blame goes to a group. Collectivism values the group above the individual, and individuals have a responsibility to the group that supersedes individual needs or rights. The United States and Japan are among the least similar cultures in the individualism-collectivism cultural dimension that attempt to do business together.

Throughout Asia, in varying degrees, collectivism is celebrated. This is not surprising, considering the high value given to relationships in these cultures. What matters is the close-knit interlocked human network; individual recognition is less important, particularly if it means a penalty or some kind of ostracization. Harmony among the interdependent group members is the key, and it takes priority above nearly all other values. In collectivist cultures where interdependence is valued, individuals do not seek recognition and are uncomfortable if it is given; the reluctance to be singled out, even for praise, can present obstacles to a manager who is trained to motivate subordinates by offering personal rewards.

In the United States, where individualism is valued, competitiveness is encouraged as a means for determining the best. When individuals compete against one another, inevitably there are many more losers than winners, but the competitiveness principle asserts that as long as you can enter into competition again and again, you too may one day win. In other words, consolation for losing lies in having a chance to compete. The United States has passed legislation for equal opportunity that is probably based in part on the value of having a chance to compete.

The individual-collectivist priorities mean cultures interpret obligation differently. Everyone has had an experience in which someone came to rescue and offered help just when it was needed. Maybe it was a friend who agreed to drive you to an important event when your own arrangements for transportation failed. Maybe it was a colleague who agreed to represent you at a meeting so you could attend another important function. In the United States, a slang expression sums up the feeling that accompanied gratitude: "I really owe you one." It means one feels indebted to the favored-grantor. But obligation has rules, determined by different cultural priorities, and that can cause problems in intercultural encounters.

To consider the issue of indebtedness, we will turn to a situation that generates obligation. Person A must meet a visitor at the airport, but finds the means of transportation relied upon to get to the airport is not available. So Person A asks Person B to provide transportation to the airport. In India, friendship means a willingness to be indebted. In fact, in some languages in India, no word exists for "thanks"; if one is in a relationship, one incurs indebtedness and one is expected to repay the debt owed. No words are necessary. Nor does one hesitate to request a favor of a friend; that is what friendship means.

Compare this with obligation in the United States where someone might preface a request with, "I really hate to ask you, but ..." or "I wouldn't dream of asking you, only ..." This opening is usually followed by a detailed explanation of why the asker has no alternative but to become indebted. The request finishes with elaborate thanks: "Thanks a million; I'm so grateful." In a culture that values individual achievement, independence, and control over events by personal action, a request that puts someone in another's debt is almost an admission of failure.

After You Read

Knowledge Focus

1. **Pair Work: Discuss the following questions with your partner.**
    1) How do you understand the Japanese proverb, "The nail that sticks up will be pounded down"?
    2) What does individualism mean in Japan?
    3) How do people in Western countries and Japan differ in making career choices?
    4) Could you tell the differences between individualism and collectivism?
    5) How do individual-collectivist priorities interpret obligation differently?
2. **Solo Work: Match the countries with their respective cultural characteristics.**

The United States	Japan

   a. collectivist society
   b. individual society

Unit 9 Cultural Diversity

c. Competitiveness is encouraged.
d. Individualism is equal to selfishness.
e. Changing employers is encouraged.
f. Superiors are expected to take an interest in the employees' family life.
g. Standing out is seen as shameful.
h. Relying or being dependent on others is seen as shameful.

Language Focus
1. **Fill in the blanks with the following words or expressions you have learned in this text.**

fraction	result in	tantamount	priority	misfit
assertion	count on	arise	spawn	supersede

   1) The car stopped within a _____ of an inch of the wall.
   2) The problem may not _____, but there is no harm in keeping our powder dry.
   3) He always feels a bit of a _____ in the business world.
   4) Motorways have already _____ ordinary roads for long-distance travel.
   5) The king's request was _____ to a command.
   6) Excessive dosage of this drug can _____ injury to the liver.
   7) The computer industry has _____ a lot of new companies.
   8) Such a questionable _____ is sure to provoke criticism.
   9) I am afraid that was the only thing they could _____.
   10) The government gave top _____ to reforming the legal system.

2. **Fill in the blanks with the proper form of the words in the brackets.**
   1) A knowledge of economics is _____ (fundament) to any understanding of this problem.
   2) _____ (individual) lies at every corner of American society.
   3) He was angered by the _____ (self) of the others.
   4) The government has issued a _____ (deny) of election in May.
   5) Do not allow personal _____ (loyal) to color your judgement.
   6) His children were dwarfed by _____ (suffice) food.
   7) His _____ (advance) to the position of manager was greeted with enthusiasm.
   8) He is a coward by his own _____ (admit).
   9) Jane is very friendly, but her husband is rather _____ (society).
   10) We must overcome cultural obstacles between different minorities and promote national _____ (solid).

3. **Find the appropriate prepositions or adverbs that collocate with the words in bold letters.**
   1) Pollution poses a **threat** _____ the continued existence of this species.
   2) Her statement is **tantamount** _____ a confession of guilt.
   3) That was the only thing they could **count** _____.
   4) His tastes are _____ **harmony** with mine.
   5) He is **indebted** _____ his memory for his jest and to his imagination for his fact.
   6) They **blamed** the rise in oil prices _____ the big increase in inflation.
   7) Can you **single** _____ good books from bad?

8) After we accomplished this task, we sat down to **sum** _____ experience.

4. **Error Correction: Each of the following sentences has at least one grammatical error. Identify the errors and make corrections.**
   1) When business in the United States first began exploring the reasons for Japanese success and ways to market products in Japan, they find surprisingly different attitudes in Japanese organizations.
   2) A often-quoted proverb in Japan is "The nail that sticks up will be pounded down."
   3) It is the opposite of self-denial for good of the group, which is highly valued in Japan.
   4) If lifestyle changes—for instance if a child's schooling or care for an elderly relative become a priority—an individual may very well change employers.
   5) In Japan, none of these situations is reason of a move.
   6) In many organizations in Japan, employees come in for overtime work even when they have little actual work to do, just showing their solidarity with other members of their corporate group.
   7) In cultures that individual is a unit of society, a single person can earn credit or blame for the outcome of an organizational project.
   8) The United States and Japan are among the least similar cultures in the individualism-collectivism cultural dimension that attempts to do business together.
   9) This is not surprising, considered the high value given to relationships in these cultures.
   10) In collectivist cultures, individuals do not seek recognition and are uncomfortable if they are given.
   11) The individual-collectivist priorities mean cultures which interpret obligation differently.
   12) But obligation has rules, determined by different cultural priorities, and which can cause problems in intercultural encounters.
   13) Person A must meet a visitor at the airport, but finds the means of transportation relying upon to get to the airport is not available.
   14) This unit probably varies much among cultures than any other variable.
   15) Filipinos are dedicated to help their children and will sacrifice greatly for their children to get an education.
   16) The Vietnamese family consists of people currently living as well as the spirits of the dead and of the as-yet unborn.

Comprehensive Work

1. **Pair Work: Analyze the following cases with your partner.**

   Case Study 1

   Janice is a young American engineer working for a manufacturing joint venture near Nanjing. She and her husband George, who is teaching English at a university, are learning Chinese and enjoying their new life. They have been eager to get to know Chinese people better, so they were pleased when Liu, Janice's young co-worker, invited them to her home for dinner.

When Janice and George arrived, Liu introduced them to her husband Yang and asked them to sit down at a table containing 8 plates of various cold dishes. Half-an-hour later she came back and sat down and the three began to eat. Yang came in from time to time, putting hot dishes on the table. Most of the food was wonderful, though neither George nor Janice could eat the fatty pork in pepper sauce or the sea cucumbers, and there was much more than they could eat. They kept wishing Yang would sit down so they could talk to him. Finally he did sit down to eat a bit, but quickly turned on the TV to show them all its high tech features. Soon it was time to go home.

Janice and George felt slightly depressed by this experience, but returned the invitation two weeks later. They decided to make a nice American meal and felt lucky to find olives, tomato juice, crackers and even some cheese in the hotel shop. They put these out as appetizers. For the main course they prepared spaghetti and a salad with dressing made from oil, vinegar and some spices they found in the market.

When Liu and Yang arrived and began to have dinner, they took small tastes of the appetizers and seemed surprised when both George and Janice sat down with them. They ate only a little spaghetti and did not finish the salad on their plates. George urged them to eat more but they refused and looked around expectantly. After a while, George cleared the table and served coffee and pastries. Yang and Liu each put four spoons of sugar into their coffee but did not drink much of it and ate only a bite or two of pastry.

After they left, George and Janice were upset. "We left their place so full that we couldn't walk and they're going to have to eat again when they get home. What went wrong?"

1) Why did Janice and George feel somewhat depressed by their experience of having dinner at Liu's home?
2) Why did Yang and Liu eat very little when they were invited by Janice and George for dinner?

Case Study 2

Joe is an American professor in an American university. Two years ago, he made friends with Hong, a Chinese visiting scholar in another American university when he was in the final year of his Ph.D. program. He began teaching in a university after graduation. Hong, back to China, recommended Joe to her university. Soon, Joe was invited by Hong's university for a five-day visit to give lectures.

Joe was very excited about the trip, as it was his first time in China. Hong and the Chair of her department met him at the airport, then put him up in a very nice hotel. They had arranged a big dinner for him for meeting and made Joe very welcome. At the end of the evening, Hong gave him the itinerary for the next few days. Apart from the lectures, all his time would be filled with meals, concerts, shopping, and a one-day trip to a nearby resort, all paid for by the university. Joe had thought he would have time to explore the city and the area, but the itinerary would leave him no free time.

Joe was grateful to Hong and the host department who took great care of him during his visit. At the end of the visit, he insisted on treating Hong and the Department Chair to dinner to thank them. But they said a dinner had been arranged. Joe was very frustrated. He was not very happy at the dinner, and did not show any enthusiasm when the Department Chair said that they hoped Joe would come back for another visit.

As soon as Joe left, Hong was very relieved. She felt Joe's visit had been successful but it had required most of her time to make sure that Joe's visit would be a smooth one. She never knew that Joe, complained to the person next to him on the plane, "While in China, I sometimes felt like a prisoner."

1) Why do you think Joe sometimes felt like a prisoner while he was in China?
2) What do you think is the appropriate way we should treat our foreign friends?

2. Writing

The drawing below was done by Suzannah, a 4th grader in the Art Club at New York public school. What did this girl want to illustrate through her drawing? Brainstorm and write a short essay to interpret this drawing.

Text B: Create an Asian Community of Shared Future Through Mutual Learning

The following text is an excerpt from Xi Jinping's keynote speech at the opening ceremony of the Conference on Dialogue of Asian Civilizations. Before reading the text, please share your understanding of "community of shared future" with your partner.

……

Ladies and gentlemen,
Friends,
Diversity spurs interaction among civilizations, which in turn promotes mutual learning and further development. We need to promote exchanges and mutual learning among countries, nations and cultures around the world, and strengthen popular support for a community of shared future for both Asia and humanity as a whole. To that end, I believe it

is imperative that we take the following actions:

First, we need to respect each other and treat each other as equals. All civilizations are rooted in their unique cultural environment. Each embodies the wisdom and vision of a country or nation, and each is valuable for being unique itself. Civilizations vary from each other only as human beings differ in terms of skin color and the language used. No civilization is superior to others. It is foolhardy to think that one's own race and civilization are superior and to insist on remolding or replacing other civilizations. To act these out will only have catastrophic consequences. If world civilizations are reduced to one single color or one single model, the world will become monolithic and a dull place to live. What we need is to respect each other as equals and say no to hubris and prejudice. We need a deeper understanding of the differences between our own civilizations and others, and we must work to promote interaction, dialogue and harmony among civilizations.

In the many places I have visited around the world, what fascinates me most is civilizations in their rich diversity. I cannot but think of the Central Asian city of Samarkand, the Luxor Temple in Egypt, Sentosa in Singapore, Wat Phra Kaew in Bangkok, and the Acropolis in Athens, to mention just a few. China is ready to work with other countries to protect Asian cultural heritage and better preserve and sustain our civilizations.

Second, we need to uphold the beauty of each civilization and the diversity of civilizations around the world. Each civilization is the crystallization of human creation, and each is beautiful in its own way. An aspiration for all that is beautiful is common to all humanity, and nothing can hold it back. Civilizations do not have to clash with each other; what is needed is to see the beauty in all civilizations with eyes. We should keep our own civilizations dynamic and create conditions for other civilizations to flourish. Together we can make the garden of world civilizations more colorful and vibrant.

The beauty of a civilization finds concrete expression in the classic works of philosophy and social sciences and works of literature, music, film and TV drama. Now, a large number of outstanding cultural works from other countries are being brought into China, and a lot of fine Chinese cultural products are being introduced to other countries. China is happy to launch initiatives with other countries to translate Asian classics both from and into Chinese and to promote film and TV exchanges and cooperation in Asia. This will help people in Asia better understand and appreciate each other's cultures and build a platform of exchanges and mutual learning for the best of Asian civilizations to spread and be better known to the world.

Third, we need to stay open and inclusive and draw on each other's strengths. All living organisms must renew themselves through metabolism; otherwise, life would come to an end. The same is true for civilizations. Long-term self-imposed isolation will cause a civilization to decline, while exchanges and mutual learning will sustain it. A civilization can flourish only through exchanges and mutual learning with other civilizations. Such exchanges and mutual learning should be reciprocal, equal-footed, diverse, and multidimensional; they should not be coercive, imposed, one-dimensional, or one-way. We need to be broad-minded and strive to remove all barriers to cultural exchanges. We need to be inclusive and always seek nourishment from other civilizations to promote the common development of Asian civilizations through exchanges and mutual learning.

People are the best bridge for exchanges and mutual learning among civilizations.

Increased people-to-people exchanges and mutual learning, for that matter, are a sure way to eliminate estrangement and misunderstanding and to promote mutual understanding among nations. Over the years, in collaboration with other countries, China has established many platforms and channels for cooperation in education, culture, sports, health, and other fields. China will work with other countries to step up exchanges among youths, NGOS, subnational entities, and media organizations, to create a network of exchanges and cooperation between think tanks, to explore new models of cooperation, and to deliver more solid outcomes in diverse forms. Such efforts will boost exchanges and mutual learning among civilizations.

Fourth, we need to advance with times and explore new ground. To sustain a civilization, it must be kept vibrant and built on its heritage from one generation to the next. More importantly, a civilization needs to adapt itself to the changing times and break new ground. The history of world civilizations tells us that every civilization needs to advance with the times and take in the best of its age in order to progress. We need to come up with new ideas to add impetus and inspiration to our civilizations. Through these efforts we will deliver achievements for our civilizations to transcend time and space and endure.

To spur people's innovation and creativity, the best way is to come into contact with different civilizations, see the strengths of others, and draw upon them. Last year, Chinese tourists made over 160 million overseas trips, and more than 140 million foreign tourists visited China. These visits played an important role in promoting exchanges and mutual learning between China and the rest of the world. In this connection, China will work with other countries to implement a plan to promote tourism in Asia. This will further boost economic development in Asia and deepen friendship among the Asian people.

> Xi, Jinping. (2020) *Xi Jinping: The Governance of China* (Volume Ⅲ).
> Beijing: Foreign Languages Press, pp. 543—546.

Text C Family Structure

Pre-reading Excecise

Family is the basic unit of the society and it is also the cradle of every individual. Before reading Text C, please discuss the following two questions with your group members:

> What is a typical Chinese family?   What is a typical American family?

Family structure is the core of any culture. This unit probably varies more among cultures than any other variable.

A major function of the family is to socialize new members of a culture. As children are raised in a family setting, they learn to become members of the family as well as members of the larger culture. The family provides the model for all other relationships in society. Through the observations and modeling of the behavior of other family members, children learn about the family and society including the values of the culture.

Family structure and their inherent relationships and obligations are a major source of cultural difference.

The family is the center of most traditional Asians' lives. Many people worry about their families' welfare, reputation, and honor. Asian families are often extended, including several generations related by blood or marriage living in the same home. An Asian person's misdeeds are not blamed just on the individual but also on the family—including the dead ancestors.

Traditional Chinese, among many other Asians, respect their elders and feel a deep sense of duty to ward them. Children repay their parents' sacrifices by being successful and supporting them in old age. This is accepted as a natural part of life in China. In contrast, taking care of aged parents is often viewed as a tremendous burden in the United States, where aging and family support are not honored highly.

Filipinos, the most Americanized of the Asians, are still extremely family-oriented. They are dedicated to helping their children and will sacrifice greatly for their children to get an education. In turn, the children are devoted to their parents, who often live nearby. Grown children who go away and leave the country for economic reasons typically send large parts of their salary home to their parents and the rest of the family.

The Vietnamese family consists of people currently alive as well as the spirits of the dead and of the as-yet unborn. Any decisions or actions are done from family considerations, not individual desires. People's behavior is judged on whether it brings shame or pride to the family. Vietnamese children are trained to rely on their families, to honor elderly people, and to fear foreigners. Many Vietnamese think that their actions in this life will influence their status in the next life.

Fathers in traditional Japanese families are typically stern and aloof. Japanese college students in one study said they would tell their fathers just about as much as they would tell a total stranger. The emotional and communication barrier between children and fathers in Japan appears very strong after children have reached a certain age.

Traditional Latin Americans are as family-centered as the traditional Asians. The family is the number one priority, the major frame of reference. Latin Americans believe that family members must help each other. Children in Latin America are taught to respect authority and are given many responsibilities at home. The Latin American family emphasizes authorities with males and older people being the most important. The family in most parts of Latin America includes many relatives, who remain in close contact. Family connections are the main way to get things done; dropping names is often necessary to accomplish even simple things.

Although there has been much talk about "family values" in the United States, the family is not a usual frame of reference for decisions in U.S. mainstream culture. Family connections are not so important to most people. Dropping the names of wealthy or famous people the family knows is done in the United States, but it is not viewed positively. More important is a person's own individual "track record" of personal achievement.

Thus, many cultural differences exist in family structures and values. In some cultures, the family is the center of life and the main frame of reference for decisions. In other cultures, the individuals, not the family, is primary. In some cultures, the family's reputation and honor depend on each person's actions; in other cultures, individuals can act without permanently affecting the family life. Some cultures value old people, while other cultures look down on them.

Questions for Discussion or Reflection

1) What cultural values underlie the different family structures?
2) What is your family like? In what aspects is it the same as or different from the traditional?
3) What problems may arise when people from different family backgrounds communicate with one another?

Text D Friendship of American Style

What are some important qualities of true friendship? Discuss with your partner and make a list of the qualities that you will give priority to when making friends with other people.

Steve and Yaser first met in their chemistry class at an American university. Yaser was an international student from Jordan. He was excited to get to know an American. He wanted to learn more about American culture. Yaser hoped that he and Steve would become good friends.

At first, Steve seemed very friendly. He always greeted Yaser warmly before class. Sometimes he offered to study with Yaser. He even invited Yaser to eat lunch with him. But after the semester was over, Steve seemed more distant. The two former classmates did not see each other very much at school. One day Yaser decided to call Steve. Steve did not seem very interested in talking to him. Yaser was hurt by Steve's change of attitude. "Steve said we were friends," Yaser complained. "And I thought friends were friends forever."

Yaser is a little confused. He is an outsider to American culture. He does not understand the way Americans view friendship. Americans use the word friend in a very general way. They may call both casual acquaintances and close companions "friends." Americans have school friends, work friends, sports friends and neighborhood friends. These friendships are based on common interests. When the shared activity ends, the friendship may fade. Now Steve and Yaser are no longer classmates. Their friendship has changed.

In some cultures, friendship means a strong life-long bond between two people. In these cultures friendships develop slowly, since they are built to last. American society is one of rapid change. Studies show that one out of five American families moves every year. American friendships develop quickly, and they may change just as quickly.

People from the United States may at first seem friendly. Americans often chat easily with strangers. They exchange information about their families, hobbies and work. They may smile warmly and say, "Have a nice day" or "See you later." Schoolmates may say, "Let's get together sometime." But American friendliness is not always an offer of true friendship.

After an experience like Yaser's, outsiders may consider Americans to be fickle. Learning how Americans view friendship can help non-Americans avoid misunderstandings. It can also help them make friends the American way.

Here are a few tips on making friends with Americans:
1. Visit places Americans enjoy: parties, churches, western restaurants, parks, sports clubs.
2. Be willing to take the first step. Do not wait for them to approach you. Americans in China may not know you speak English. They may be embarrassed if they cannot speak your language.
3. Use small talk to open the conversation. Ask them where they are from, why they came to China, etc. Remember: Be careful to avoid personal questions about age, salary, marital status and appearance.
4. Show an interest in their culture, their country or their job. (Americans like to talk about themselves!)
5. Invite them to join you for dinner or just for coffee or tea. Try to set a specific time. Americans sometimes make general invitations like "Let's get together sometime." Often this is just a way to be friendly. It is not always a real invitation.
6. Do not expect too much at first. Maybe they are just being friendly. But maybe they do want to be your good friends. It will take time to tell.

People like Yaser should not give up trying to make American friends. Americans do value strong, life-long friendships, even with non-Americans. When making friends, it helps to have a good dose of cultural understanding.

Questions for Discussion or Reflection

1. What do you think of the above tips? Are they very helpful?
2. What tips would you like to give to the Americans who want to make friends with Chinese?

For Fun

Movie to Watch

Based on a Chinese folk-tale, *Mulan* is a 1998 American animated feature film produced by Walt Disney. Mulan is a young high-spirited girl who tries hard to please her parents but always feels like she is disappointing them. Her father is drafted into the army which amounts to certain death because of his old age. Mulan disguises herself as a man and takes her father's place in battle, guided by a guardian dragon, Mushu. At the height of her success her secret is revealed and she is banished from home. But, undaunted she fights and defeats enemy invaders and saves the Emperor, bringing great honor to her family. This movie evidences Chinese culture, history and belief from an American perspective.

Unit 10
Cultural Influence on Perception

> Everyone thinks that all the bells echo his own thoughts.
> —— German proverb
>
> We know what we perceive; we don't know what we don't perceive. Since there is no way that we can know what we don't perceive, we assume that we perceive "correctly"—even if we don't.
> —— Bryan Singer

Unit Goals

- To discover the ways in which culture influences our selections and perception
- To understand the variety of ways our interpretation are influenced by culture
- To learn useful words and expressions about cultural influence on perception and improve language skills

Before You Read

Perception and culture are closely related. Culture teaches us how to perceive and it strongly influences our values. Finish the following chart with your partner to find out the differences between American and Japanese perceptions. Put a check (√) in the corresponding column.

Items	American Perceptions	Japanese Perceptions
☞ adapt to nature	☐	☐
☞ confront and exploit nature	☐	☐
☞ have independent interpersonal relationships	☐	☐

(continued)

Items	American Perceptions	Japanese Perceptions
☞ have interdependent interpersonal relationships	☐	☐
☞ have analytical thinking patterns	☐	☐
☞ have synthetic thinking patterns	☐	☐
☞ tend to be more realistic	☐	☐
☞ tend to be more idealistic	☐	☐

Start to Read

Text A Shakespeare in the Bush

Just before I left Oxford for West Africa, in a conversation one of my friends said, "You Americans often have difficulty with Shakespeare. He was, after all, a very English poet, and one can easily misinterpret the universal by misunderstanding the particular."

I protested that human nature is pretty much the same the whole world over; at least the general plot and motivation of the greater tragedies would always be clear — everywhere — although some details of custom might have to be explained and difficulties of translation might produce other slight changes.

It was my second field trip to that African tribe. I eventually settled on the hillock of a very knowledgeable old man, the head of a homestead of some hundred and forty people, all of whom were either his close relatives or their wives and children.

When it rained, people would often sit inside their huts, drinking and telling stories. One day, they threatened to tell me no more stories until I told them one of mine. I protested that I was not a storyteller. But I protested in vain. Realizing that here was my chance to prove *Hamlet* universally intelligible, I agreed.

I began in the proper style, "Not yesterday, not yesterday, but long ago, a thing occurred. One night three men were keeping watch outside the homestead of the great chief, when suddenly they saw the former chief approach them."

"Why was he no longer their chief?"

"He was dead," I explained. "That is why they were troubled and afraid when they saw him."

"Impossible," began one of the elders, handing his pipe on to his neighbor, who interrupted, "Of course it wasn't the dead chief. It was an omen sent by a witch. Go on."

Unit 10 Cultural Influence on Perception

Slightly shaken, I continued. "One of these three was a man who knew things" — the closest translation of scholar, but unfortunately it also meant witch. The second elder looked triumphantly at the first. "So he spoke to the dead chief saying, 'Tell us what we must do so you may rest in your grave,' but the dead chief did not answer. He vanished, and they could see him no more. Then the man who knew things — his name was Horatio — said this event was the affair of the dead chief's son, Hamlet."

There was a general shaking of heads round the circle. "Had the dead chief no living brothers? Or was this son the chief?"

"No," I replied. "That is, he had one living brother who became the chief when the elder brother died."

The old men muttered: such omens were matters for chiefs and elders, not for youngsters; no good could come of going behind a chief's back; clearly Horatio was not a man who knew things.

"Yes, he was," I insisted. "In our country the son is next to the father. The dead chief's younger brother had become the great chief. He had also married his elder brother's widow only about a month after the funeral."

"He did well," the old man beamed and announced to the others, "I told you that if we knew more about Europeans, we would find they really were very like us. In our country also," he added to me, "the younger brother marries the elder brother's widow and becomes the father of his children. Now, if your uncle, who married your widowed mother, is your father's full brother, then he will be a real father to you. Did Hamlet's father and uncle have one mother?"

His question barely penetrated my mind. Rather uncertainly I said that I thought they had the same mother, but I wasn't sure — the story didn't say. The old man told me severely that these genealogical details made all the difference and that when I got home I must ask the elders about it.

I took a deep breath and began again. "The son Hamlet was very sad because his mother had married again so quickly. There was no need for her to do so, and it is our custom for a widow not to go to her next husband until she has mourned for two years."

"Two years is too long," objected one of the old man's wife, "Who will hoe your farms for you while you have no husband?"

"Hamlet," I retorted without thinking, "was old enough to hoe his mother's farms himself. There was no need for her to remarry." No one looked convinced. I gave up. "His mother and the great chief told Hamlet not to be sad, for the great chief himself would be a father to Hamlet. Furthermore, Hamlet would be the next chief: therefore he must stay to learn the things of a chief. Hamlet agreed to remain."

While I paused, perplexed at how to render Hamlet's disgusted soliloquy to an audience convinced that Claudius and Gertrude had behaved in the best possible manner, one of the younger men asked me who had married the other wives of the dead chief.

"He had no other wives," I told him.

"But a chief must have many wives! How else can he brew beer and prepare food for all his guests?"

I said firmly that in our country even chiefs had only one wife, that they had servants to do their work, and that they paid them from tax money.

I decided to skip the soliloquy. More hopefully I resumed, "That night Hamlet kept watch with the three who had seen his dead father. The dead chief again appeared, and although the others were afraid, Hamlet followed his dead father off to one side. When they were alone, Hamlet's dead father spoke."

"Omens can't talk!" The old man was emphatic.

"Hamlet's dead father wasn't an omen. Seeing him might have been an omen, but he was not." My audience looked as confused as I sounded. "It was Hamlet's dead father. It was a thing we call a 'ghost'." I had to use the English word.

"Anyhow," I resumed, "Hamlet's dead father said that his own brother, the one who became chief, had poisoned him. He wanted Hamlet to avenge him. Hamlet believed this in his heart, for he did not like his father's brother." I took another swallow of beer. "In the country of the great chief, living in the same homestead, for it was a very large one, was an important elder who was often with the chief to advise and help him. His name was Polonius. Hamlet was courting his daughter but her father and her brother warned her not to let Hamlet visit her when she was alone on her farm, for he would be a great chief and so could not marry her."

"Why not?" asked the wife.

"He could have," I explained, "but Polonius didn't think he would. After all, Hamlet was a man of great importance who ought to marry a chief's daughter, for in his country a man could have only one wife. Polonius was afraid that if Hamlet made love to his daughter, then no one else would give a high price for her."

"That might be true," remarked one of the shrewder elders.

I continued, "One day Hamlet came upon Polonius's daughter Ophelia. He behaved so oddly he frightened her. Indeed" — I was fumbling for words to express the dubious quality of Hamlet's madness. "Many people thought that he had become mad." My audience suddenly became much more attentive.

"Why," inquired a bewildered voice, "should anyone bewitch Hamlet on that account?"

"Bewitch him?"

"Yes, only witchcraft can make anyone mad, unless, of course, one sees the beings that lurk in the forest."

"Now Hamlet's age mates," I continued, "had brought with them a famous storyteller. Hamlet decided to have this man tell the chief and all his homestead a story about a man who had poisoned his brother because he desired his brother's wife and wished to be chief himself. Hamlet was sure the great chief could not hear the story without making a sign if he was indeed guilty, and then he would discover whether his dead father had told him the truth."

The old man interrupted, with deep cunning, "Why should a father lie to his son?" he asked.

I hedged: "Hamlet wasn't sure that it really was his dead father."

"You mean," he said, "it actually was an omen."

"Yes," I said, abandoning ghosts and the devil; a witch sent omen it would have to be. "It was true, for when the storyteller was telling his tale before all the homestead, the great chief rose in fear. Afraid that Hamlet knew his secret he planned to have him killed."

"The great chief told Hamlet's mother to find out from her son what he knew. But because a woman's children are always first in her heart, he had the important elder Polonius hide behind a cloth that hung against the wall of Hamlet's mother's sleeping hut. Hamlet started to scold his mother for what she had done."

There was a shocked murmur from everyone. A man should never scold his mother.

"She called out in fear, and Polonius moved behind the cloth, shouting, 'A rat!' Hamlet took his machete and slashed through the cloth." I paused for dramatic effect. "He had killed Polonius!"

The old men looked at each other in supreme disgust. "That Polonius truly was a fool and a man who knew nothing! What child would not know enough to shout, 'It's me!'" With a pang, I remembered that these people are ardent hunters, always armed with bow, arrow, and machete; at the first rustle in the grass an arrow is aimed and ready, and the hunter shouts "Game!" If no human voice answers immediately, the arrow speeds on its way. Like a good hunter Hamlet had shouted, "A rat!"

I rushed in to save Polonius's reputation. "Polonius did speak. Hamlet heard him. But he thought it was the chief and wished to kill him to avenge his father."

This time I had shocked my audience seriously. "For a man to raise his hand against his father's brother and the one who has become his father — that is a terrible thing. The elders ought to let such a man be bewitched."

I nibbled at my kola nut in some perplexity, then pointed out that after all the man had killed Hamlet's father.

"No," pronounced the old man, speaking less to me than to the young men sitting behind the elders. "If your father's brother has killed your killer, you must appeal to your father's age mates; they may avenge him. No man may use violence against his senior relatives." Another thought struck him. "But if his father's brother had indeed been wicked enough to bewitch Hamlet and make him mad that would be a good story indeed, for it would be his fault that Hamlet, being mad, no longer had any sense and thus was ready to kill his father's brother."

There was a murmur of applause. Hamlet was again a good story to them, but it no longer seemed quite the same story to me.

"That was a very good story," added the old man, "and you told it with very few mistakes. Sometime you must tell us some more stories of your country. We, who are elders, will instruct you in their true meaning, so that when you return to your own land your elders will see that you have not been sitting in the bush, but among those who know things and who have taught you wisdom."

After You Read

Knowledge Focus

1. Pair Work: Discuss the following questions with your partner.

   1) Why did the author believe that great tragedies like *Hamlet* would be universally intelligent the world over?

   2) What did the author mean by "a man who knew things"? How did the local people understand it?

3) Why did the old men say "He did well" when they heard that Claudius married Hamlet's newly widowed mother?
4) Why did the old men ask if Hamlet's father and uncle had one mother?
5) Why did the author finally decide to skip Hamlet's soliloquy in telling the story?
6) Why did the old man ask the author to tell more stories of his country to them?

2. **Solo Work:** Finish the following chart with the knowledge learned from Text A.

Apparently the local people have different interpretations of *Hamlet* because of their distinct cultural experiences. To what extent are they different in the understanding of this great tragedy?

Items	The Local People's Interpretations
Seeing former chief approaching	
Younger brother marrying the elder brother's widow	
Hamlet's mother getting married one month after his father's death	
The dead chief having only one wife	
Hamlet's dead father talking	
Hamlet getting mad	
Hamlet killing his father's brother	

Language Focus

1. Read the following words and explanations. First match each word in the left column with its explanation in the right column. Write the number of the word in the brackets provided. Then choose five of the words to complete the sentences that follow.

   1) hillock   a sign of something about to happen (　)
   2) homestead   become clear or enter one's consciousness or emotions (　)
   3) omen   a dramatic speech intended to give the illusion of unspoken reflections (　)
   4) witch   feel about uncertainly or blindly (　)
   5) fumble   a low continuous indistinct sound (　)
   6) mutter   a female sorcerer or magician (　)
   7) beam   be a mystery or bewildering to (　)
   8) penetrate   a small natural hill (　)
   9) perplex   smile radiantly (　)
   10) soliloquy   the home and adjacent grounds occupied by a family (　)

   i. In some culture, crow is a bird of ill _____.
   ii. She _____ about in her handbag for a pen.

iii. Actors often _____ to themselves when rehearsing their lines.
iv. Nothing we say _____ his thick skull!
v. Faced with that dilemma, he was _____.

2. **Fill in the blanks with the proper form of the words in the brackets.**
    1) Jack is an intelligent student but he lacks _____ (motive).
    2) The regimental band _____ (triumph) piped the soldiers in.
    3) I wobbled _____ (certain) for a couple of paces, then over I went.
    4) We were all _____ (witch) by the pretty dancer.
    5) After a _____ (drama) pause, the lawyer finished her summation.
    6) It is a problem of such _____ (perplex) that it was impossible to solve.
    7) The book is _____ (intelligence) to anyone.
    8) _____ (fortune) the restaurant he recommended fell far short of our expectations.

3. **Find the appropriate prepositions or adverbs that collocate with the words in bold letters.**
    1) His lawyer decided to take an **appeal** _____ a higher court.
    2) Day after day she waited _____ **vain** for him to telephone her.
    3) Please **hand** _____ the magazine to your friends.
    4) She **fumbled** _____ the key in her handbag.
    5) _____ that **account**, you should pay more attention to his behavior.
    6) It appears that what I said was untrue, but I did not knowingly **lie** _____ you.
    7) They went to the teacher _____ **fear** and trembling to tell her that they had broken a window.
    8) The boy received a bad **scolding** _____ cutting up in the swimming pool.

4. **Error Correction: Each of the following sentences has at least one grammatical error. Identify the errors and make corrections.**
    1) I protested that human nature was pretty much the same the whole world over.
    2) I eventually settled on the hillock of a very knowledgeable old man, the head of a homestead of some hundred and forty people, all of them were either his close relatives or their wives and children.
    3) When it rained, people often sit inside their huts, drinking and telling stories.
    4) One night three men were keeping watch outside the homestead of the great chief, then suddenly they saw the former chief approach them.
    5) The old man told me severely that these genealogical details made all the difference and that I got home I must ask the elders about it.
    6) It is our custom for a widow not to go to her next husband until she mourns for two years.
    7) "Two years are too long," objected one of the old man's wife.
    8) I was perplexed at how to render Hamlet's disgusted soliloquy to an audience convincing that Claudius and Gertrude had behaved in the best possible manner.
    9) Hamlet decided to have this man told the chief and all his homestead a story about a man who had poisoned his brother.
    10) Hamlet started to scold his mother for what she did.
    11) There was a shocked murmur from everyone because a man may never scold his mother.
    12) "No," pronounced the old man, speaking less to me than the young men sitting

behind the elders.

13) Sometime you could tell us some more stories of your country so that we will instruct you in their true meaning.

14) In one sense, generalizations are the culture, and without generalizations would there be no culture.

15) Stereotypes are dangerous because they may trick us into believing that knowing a few stereotypes is the same thing as understanding the other culture.

16) At most, this is the only first step toward understanding how British people view formality, and it needs to be followed by many other steps.

Comprehensive Work

1. Pair Work: Analyze the following cases with your partner.

Case Study 1

Some years ago, several international businessmen were on a conference cruise when the ship began to sink.

"Go tell those fellows to put on life jackets and jump overboard," the captain directed his first mate.

A few minutes later the first mate returned. "Those guys won't jump," he reported.

"Take over," the captain ordered, "and I'll see what I can do."

Returning moments later, he announced, "They're gone."

"How'd you do it?" asked the first mate.

"I told different people different things. I told the Englishman it was the sporting thing to do, and he jumped. I told the Frenchman it was chic; the German that it was a command; the Italian that it was forbidden; the Russian that it was revolutionary; so they all jumped overboard."

"And how did you get the American to jump?"

"No problem," said the captain, "I told him he was insured!"

1) What do you think of this story? Does it tell you something that is true of people of those different nations?

2) If there had been a Chinese businessman on board, what should the captain have said in order to make him jump overboard?

Case Study 2

A public opinion survey was once conducted in the United States on American perceptions of Japan. One of the questions asked the respondent to select an animal that seemed to characterize Japan best. The largest percentage of Americans chose a fox. When this was reported in the Japanese press, many Japanese were shocked. Japanese commentators were quoted as saying that Japanese people had better mend their ways, if this

was the image they projected in the world.

1) Why do you think most Americans chose a fox to characterize Japan?
2) Why were many Japanese shocked when they learned that Americans had characterized Japan as a fox?

2. Writing

Almost everything in the world may be viewed very differently by different people. It is interesting for us Chinese to learn how we are viewed by Americans and other foreign people. The following are the results of Gallup Polls taken in 1966 and 1972, indicating the qualities, positive and negative, that Americans attributed to Chinese people. In the table, you will find the numbers of people who chose particular adjectives to describe Chinese they perceived.

Quality	In 1966	In 1972
hardworking	37	74
honest	-	20
brave	7	17
religious	14	18
intelligent	14	32
practical	8	27
ignorant	24	10
artistic	13	26
progressive	7	28
sly	20	19
treacherous	19	12
warlike	23	13
cruel	13	9

Write a report describing the information shown above and explaining the changes concerning some qualities.

Read More

Text B   Generalizations and Stereotypes

Not all people who live in the same country share exactly the same culture. For example, in China there are cultural differences between coastal and inland areas, between urban and rural areas, and between Han people and minority peoples. There are also differences between individual Chinese; for example, some are more independent-minded than others, some believe more firmly in tradition than others, and so forth.

However, it is still valid to generalize about "Chinese culture" because, despite their differences, there are many things that the great majority of people of China share in

common, such as:
- Shared knowledge. For example, almost all Chinese people know the stories of people like Qu Yuan, Yue Fei and Sun Yat-Sen.
- Shared values. For example, almost all Chinese consider being a good host important.
- Shared perspectives. For example, virtually all Chinese consider the Great Wall an important symbol of Chinese culture.
- Shared beliefs. For example, most Chinese traditionally believed that their departed ancestors had the power to help them (although this belief is less common now).
- Shared behavior. For example, most Chinese eat with chopsticks, and usually bathe in the evening instead of in the morning.

It is almost impossible to talk about cultures without making generalizations because a culture is based on things that a group of people share in common. In one sense, generalizations are the culture, and without generalizations there would be no culture.

However, we need to be careful that generalizations about cultures do not become "stereotypes," generalizations that are too broad. A generalization like "British people are formal" becomes a stereotype if we believe that all British people are always formal, or even that most British people are formal most of the time.

It is quite natural to have stereotypes about foreigners and their cultures, and stereotypes can be the first step toward learning more about another people or culture. However, stereotypes can also be dangerous. One problem with stereotypes is that they are not very accurate. Some stereotypes may have a basis in fact, but they are too broad and shallow, and they give us the mistaken idea that a people's culture can be summed up easily in a few short, simple statements. This simply is not true. A culture is not like a simple painting in which everything is black or white. Instead, a culture is a richly detailed painting with many lines and different shades of color. Some of the colors and shapes in the painting are more dominant than others, and these give the painting its distinctive character, but there are also many less dominant colors and shapes in the painting which should not be ignored.

Stereotypes are also dangerous because they may trick us into believing that knowing a few stereotypes is the same thing as understanding another culture. For example, once a Chinese student learns that "British are formal," he may be tempted to think that he really understands British people. Even worse, he may be tempted to think that he does not need to learn more about British culture. The problem is that a stereotype like "British are formal" only represents a shallow level of understanding. At most, this is only the first step toward understanding how British people view formality, and it needs to be followed by many other steps.

In order to really understand another culture, you need to learn much more than a few simple stereotypes. To become an effective intercultural communicator, you need to understand not only some of the basic general features of other cultures, but also what the limits of those generalizations are. Perhaps most important, you should not be stratified with just knowing a few simple generalizations about other cultures, and should always keep trying to learn more.

After You Read

The following is a list of cultural stereotypes, which Spaniards between ages 15 and 21 who have never been to the U. S. or who have never had any American friends might have about Americans. Which of them do you think are stereotypes and which are accurate descriptions of American culture?

Statements	Stereotypes	Accurate Descriptions
Men in the U. S. have muscular builds; they resemble Arnold Schwarzenegger or Sylvester Stallone.		
American women are either unusually fat or unusually thin.		
Americans wear very bright colors and mixed patterns, and they wear summer clothes even in winter. They have no sense of style.		
Americans divorce repeatedly and have very complicated private lives.		
American cities are so dangerous that a person has a good chance of being killed in the street.		
Americans eat almost nothing but hamburgers, hot dogs, popcorn, and Coke.		
Americans speak very quickly and very loudly. They use their hands a lot, often gesturing in an exaggerated way when they talk.		

Text C American Stereotypes of China

Pre-reading Exercise

Before reading the following text, please discuss with your partner and list your views of Americans and your views of Chinese.

My Views of Americans

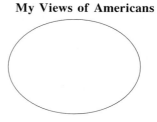

My Views of Chinese

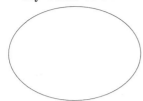

US writer Todd C. Ames concludes his two-part discussion of the ways in which Chinese and Americans think of each other, and the most common misunderstandings that arise.

Americans do not know much about China. What they do know comes from three main sources: movies, the news, and history classes. This can be a sensitive subject, and I do not wish to offend anyone — my goal is only to give you an overview of American stereotypes of China.

Just as I have encountered many stereotypes that the Chinese have of America (some accurate, some absurd, some insulting), one can similarly encounter American stereotypes of China in the US.

- All Chinese know kungfu and dress like Huang Feihong. (Source: Jet Li, Jackie Chan, and Bruce Lee [Li Xiaolong] movies)
- Anything to do with China is "ancient" and "mysterious." (Source: the fact that Chinese language seems to be made up of "mysterious symbols" to Western eyes, movies about Chinese history)
- "Guangdonghua" (Cantonese) is the official language of China. (Source: Hong Kong movies, Chinese-American immigrants who came to the US from Guangdong and Hong Kong during the 19th and 20th centuries)
- Chinese culture is basically the same today as it was 1,000 years ago (e.g., "traditional, conservative, polite," etc.). (Source: studying Chinese history without being familiar with modern China)
- Chinese (and all "Asians") are good at maths. (Source: I do not know)
- China and Japan are basically the same. (Source: ignorance)
- "Asian" women are generally subservient to men, anti-feminist, and more "morally pure" than Western women. (Source: movies about ancient Japan, cultural differences. This stereotype is again the result of ignorance of modern China — and thinking that today's China is really 12th-century ancient Japan.)

Chinese stereotypes of the US

As an American, I can give you a unique perspective on the Chinese stereotypes of the US that I have encountered. Some of them really made me laugh — as I am sure some of the above American stereotypes of China made you laugh.

- Americans do not care about their families very much. The opposite is true. Almost every American will tell you that family is the most important thing in life.
- Mixed ethnic background = intelligence. The more mixed your ethnic background, the smarter you must be. This kind of thinking is truly confusing and shocking to most Americans. Many Americans would even consider this kind of thinking "racist," as some sort of inversion of Hitler's "race purity" theories. In any case, I was really surprised to hear this from virtually every Chinese I know. Almost all Americans have a diverse and

mixed ethnic background — so we must all be geniuses.
- The crime rate is so high in the US that your life is always in danger. This is a vast exaggeration.
- The US has the most socially liberal society in the world, especially when it comes to sex. This idea comes from Hollywood — and it could not be more false. The US in general (especially the Midwest) is very socially conservative.
- All "Western" countries are basically the same. This stereotype is the mirror of the American stereotype that all "Eastern" countries (China, Japan, South Korea, etc.) are basically the same. Both stereotypes are completely false and are purely based on the perception that "all foreigners look alike."
- Most American college students do not study, party all the time, and are ignorant of the outside world. This stereotype is pretty accurate.
- Every American owns a gun. Roughly 25 percent of American adults own a gun, which is extremely high compared to most other countries. But still, the vast majority of Americans do not own guns.

Food

In general, Americans love Chinese food. Chinese food and Italian food are probably the two most popular types of food in the US. However, most of the Chinese food you will find in US restaurants is "Americanized." You probably will not find things like stomach or intestines on the menu. Also, pork is not so popular in the US. Beef and chicken are much more popular in the US than pork. So do not be surprised if many Americans you meet do not like pork.

One "food stereotype" that I have encountered among Chinese (and everyone else outside the US) is that all Americans eat McDonald's. I do not have any friends who like McDonald's. I hate it. Everyone I know hates it. I think McDonald's is probably more popular in other countries than it is here in the US. Of course, it is popular to some degree; but it tends to be more popular among certain segments of society than others.

Book to Read

Gudykunst, William B. *Cross-cultural and Intercultural Communication*. Shanghai: Shanghai Foreign Language Education Press, 2007.
- This book contains state-of-the-art summaries of research and theory in cross-cultural communication and intercultural communication. A large number of theories from a wide variety of theoretical perspectives are included. This book is divided into two parts: cross-cultural communication (Part I) and intercultural communication (Part II). Each part of this book begins with an introduction to the part, then there is a chapter on theory and each part ends with a chapter on research issues. In between the theory and research chapters are chapters containing reviews of major substantive areas of research.

Movie to Watch

 The Forbidden Kingdom (2008) is about an American teenager who is obsessed with Hong Kong cinema and kungfu classics. He makes an extraordinary discovery in a Chinatown pawnshop: the legendary stick weapon of the Chinese sage and warrior, the Monkey King. With the lost relic in hand, the teenager unexpectedly finds himself traveling back to ancient China to join a crew of warriors from martial arts lore on a dangerous quest to free the imprisoned Monkey King. One will find how Chinese culture is interpreted from an American perspective in this movie.

Unit 11
Culture Shock

> Interacting with people from other cultures and/or ethnic groups is a novel situation for most people. Novel situations are characterized by high levels of uncertainty and anxiety.
> —— Gundykunst and Kim
>
> We trust people whose behavior we can predict. When we see people with strange customs, we become anxious and hostile, because we cannot predict what they are going to do.
> —— H. C. Triandis

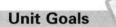

- To understand cultural differences
- To learn to appreciate how differences in cultural values shape behaviors
- To avoid pitfalls in cross-cultural communication and adjust more smoothly to a new cultural environment
- To learn useful words and expressions about culture shock and improve language skills

 Before You Read

A Survey

Quickly survey some of your classmates and be prepared to report your findings in class.

1. How did you feel about the first time you spoke to a foreigner in English?

2. Have you ever lived in an unfamiliar place? If so, do you remember your feelings during your first few days there?

3. What do you think would be the hardest to adapt to for a Chinese living in the West?

4. Try to list several things a Westerner could do that would help him/her deal with culture shock and adjust successfully to the life in China.

Start to Read

Text A Culture Shock

Culture shock is a feeling of frustration, uneasiness, or uncertainty that many people experience in unknown settings. There are many potential things that can cause culture shock. Most often, we feel culture shock because the new culture has different rules from our own; we are no longer in the world taken for granted. We get upset when the new society's unspoken rules, gestures, and assumptions about behavior are not the same as our own. We do not know how to act appropriately in our new environment and others do not act as we expect them. It makes us uncomfortable when expectations are placed upon us for reasons that were not explained in terms that we could understand. We feel unhappy and confused those things are not turning out as we had thought. This is culture shock.

Culture shock is a multifaceted experience resulting from numerous stressors occurring in contact with a different culture. Culture shock occurs for immigrant groups, businessmen on oversees assignments as well as for Euro-Americans in their own culture and society. The multicultural nature of society in the United States makes culture shock an important source of interpersonal stress and conflict for many. Culture shock reactions may provoke psychological crises or social dysfunctions when reactions to cultural differences impede performance. Because our society is becoming increasingly multicultural, we all experience varying degrees of culture shock in unfamiliar cultural or subcultural settings.

The circumstances provoking culture shock and the individual reactions depend on a variety of factors, including previous experience with other cultures and cross-cultural adaption; the degree of difference in one's own and the host culture; the degree of preparation; social support networks; and individual psychological characteristics. The multivariate nature of culture shock requires the development of "programs of preparation, orientation and the acquisitions of culturally appropriate social skills."

Aspects of Culture Shock

Culture shock was initially conceptualized as the consequence of strain and anxiety resulting from contact with a new culture and the feelings of loss, confusion, and impotence resulting from loss of accustomed cultural cues and social rules.

Although the clinical model of culture shock as a psychological and

cognitive reaction has been dominant, the implications of culture shock are more extensive. Culture shock derives from both the challenge of new cultural surroundings and from the loss of a familiar cultural environment. Culture shock stress responses cause both psychological and physiological reactions. Psychological reactions include physiological, emotional, interpersonal, cognitive and social components, as well as the effects resulting from changes in sociocultural relations, cognitive fatigue, role stress, and identity loss.

Causes of Culture Shock

Stress reactions. Exposure to a new environment causes stress, increasing the body's physiological reactions that can cause dysfunction in the rise of pituitary-adrenal activity. Stress induces a wide range of physiological reactions involving mass discharges of the sympathetic nervous system, impairment of the functioning of the immune system, and increased susceptibility to all diseases. Therefore, a normal consequence of living in and adjusting to a new culture is the experience of stress caused by both physiological and psychological factors. In a psychosomatic interaction, psychological states affect the body and its physiological reactions, which in turn increases feelings of stress, anxiety, depression, uneasiness, and so on. Culture shock results in an increased concern with illness, a sense of feeling physically ill, a preoccupation with symptoms, minor pains, and discomforts, and may increase both psychosomatic and physical illness from stress-induced reductions in immune system functioning.

Cognitive fatigue. A major aspect of culture shock and the resultant stress is cognitive fatigue, a consequence of an "information overload." The new culture demands a conscious effort to understand things processed unconsciously in one's own culture. Efforts must be made to interpret new language meanings and new nonverbal, behavioral,  contextual, and social communications. The change from a normally automatic, unconscious, effortless functioning within one's own culture to the conscious effort and attention required to understand all this new information is very fatiguing and results in a mental and emotional fatigue or burnout. This may be manifested in tension headaches and a desire to isolate oneself from social contact.

Role shock. Roles central to one's identity may be lost in the new culture. Changes in social roles and interpersonal relations affect well-being and self-concept, resulting in "role shock." One's identity is maintained in part by social roles that contribute to well-being through structuring social interaction. In the new cultural setting, the prior roles are largely eliminated and replaced with unfamiliar roles and expectations. This leads to role shock resulting from an ambiguity about one's social position, the loss of normal social relations and roles, and new roles inconsistent with previous self-concept.

Personal shock. The notion of personal shock as an aspect of culture shock results from diverse changes in personal life. This includes loss of personal intimacy and loss of interpersonal contact with significant others such as occurs in separation grief and bereavement. One's psychological disposition, self-esteem, identity, feelings of well-being, and satisfaction with life are all created within and maintained by one's cultural system. Losing this support system can lead to a deterioration in one's sense of well-being and lead to pathological manifestations. Scholars suggested that the major and severe symptoms of culture shock may include withdrawal and excessive sleeping, compulsive eating and drinking, excessive irritability and hostility, marital and family tensions and conflicts, loss of work

effectiveness, and unaccountable episodes of crying.

After You Read

Knowledge Focus

1. **Pair Work: Discuss the following questions with your partner.**
   1) What is culture shock?
   2) What are the symptoms of culture shock?
   3) What are some of the causes of culture shock?
   4) What are the aspects of culture shock?
   5) What will the changes in social roles and interpersonal relations bring about?

2. **Solo Work: Explain the following terms in your own words.**
Stress reactions: _____
Cognitive fatigue: _____
Role shock: _____
Personal shock: _____

Language Focus

1. **Fill in the blanks with proper prepositions and adverbs that collocate with the neighboring words.**
   1) Liquid fuels also burn only when the surface of the liquid is _____ contact with air.
   2) Hasty marriage seldom turns _____ well.
   3) Since their son was not interested in their family business, the old couples' expectation was placed _____ their daughter.
   4) The increase in debt result _____ the expansion program.
   5) After retirement, he derived great pleasure _____ gardening.
   6) After staying in the states for a couple of months, she still had problems adjusting herself _____ the new environment.
   7) He was very clear that two yellow cards would result _____ disqualification.
   8) The testimony was consistent _____ the known facts.

2. **Fill in the blanks with the proper form of the words in the brackets.**
   1) He went on talking, lest he should expose his _____ (easy).
   2) The quality of urban living has been damaged by _____ (immerse) noise levels.
   3) The theory is based on a series of wrong _____ (assume).
   4) She became demandingly _____ (dominate) over the years.
   5) Repeated use is the major reason of _____ (physiology) tolerance to a drug.
   6) He seemed to have a rather _____ (clinic) view of the breakup of his marriage.
   7) She is quick to notice the _____ (ambiguous) in the article.
   8) Even when the mother was asleep, she was _____ (conscious) listening for her baby's cry.

3. **Error Correction: Each of the following sentences has at least one grammatical error. Identify the errors and make corrections.**
   1) Culture shock is a feeling of frustration, uneasiness, or uncertainty that many people

experience in unknown setting.
2) There are many potential things can cause culture shock.
3) We are no longer in the world taking for granted.
4) We do not know how to act appropriately in our new environment and others do not act what we expect them.
5) Culture shock is multifaceted experience resulting from numerous stressors occurring in contact with a different culture.
6) Culture shock reactions may provoke psychological crisis or social dysfunctions when reactions to cultural differences impede performance.
7) The circumstances provoked culture shock and the individual reactions depend on a variety of factors.
8) A normal consequence of living and adjusting to a new culture is the experience of stress caused by both physiological and psychological factors.
9) One's psychological disposition, self-esteem, identity, feelings of well-being, and satisfaction with life is created within and maintained by one's cultural system.
10) It might seem like a drag, particularly when you are tired and do not know anyone, but it will be worth in the long run.
11) Sometimes worst culture shock of all comes when you return home.
12) Reverse culture shock is the name people give that feeling of not fitting into your home country.
13) If you are the kind of person who loves to travel a lot, you might have trouble understand this.
14) You might be lucky enough to have a like-minded friend who would be interested in your experiences no matter who they were.
15) You probably will not find any incredible historic attractions that you do not know about, too.
16) But for your friends or colleagues who have not left your homeland, will these kinds of issues not have the priority that they do for you.

Comprehensive Work

1. Pair Work: Analyze the following cases with your partner.

Case Study 1

Kazko, an international student from Japan, was keen to study for an International Business degree in America. Although excited to be in America at first, she now misses home increasingly. Her studies have not been as successful as she would have liked. She is faced with a lot of reading to do for her study, but is not sure how to finish her assignments. At the end of her first semester, she passed two of her four subjects. Everything feels difficult and although she knows her parents want her to complete her studies in America, she is considering quitting and going back to Japan.

1) Can you give some suggestions on the problem Kazko is faced with?
2) If you were Kazko, what preparations would you make before you go to America?

Case Study 2

The following conversation is between a Chinese visiting scholar, Guang and an Australian professor, Alice. Alice is Guang's newly met friend and she promised to show Guang around her campus. This is the second time they have met.

First complete the opening of the conversation with your partner.

Alice: You're very punctual.
Guang: _____.
Alice: Are you hungry?
Guang: _____.

How did you manage the above conversation? The following is what Guang actually did and thought during their conversation.

Alice: You are very punctual.
Guang: The traffic is very smooth today.
Alice: Are you hungry?
Guang: No, not really. (This is true.) And you?
Alice: No, let me show you my office first. Would you like to have something to drink?
Guang: That'll be lovely. Thank you.
(They sat down and had coffee. After about two hours of talking, Guang was starving, but Alice never mentioned lunch again.)
Guang: How much time do you have this afternoon?
Alice: I have a meeting at 3 o'clock.
Guang: It's nearly 2 o'clock. Will you show me around?
Alice: Sure.
(Alice showed Guang around the campus. Just before 3 o'clock, they finished touring. Alice saw Guang off.)
Guang: Thank you very much for your time. It's been a lovely afternoon.
Alice: You're welcome.

1) Why did not Alice invite Guang to lunch since their appointment was to have lunch first?
2) What would you do if you were Guang?

2. Oral Practice

Imagine you are attending your first invitation to dinner at the home of a foreign friend. How would you respond in the following situations? Tick (√) if the expressions are polite English. If they are abrupt and impolite, please correct them.

Situation 1

You are eating, or have been offered some food which you have never tried before. What would you say?
- _____ What's this?

- _____ Is this food sweet or salty?
- _____ Is this food sweet or savory?
- _____ What are the materials?

Situation 2

You are offered some food you do not really like. What would you say?
- _____ No, thanks, I don't like it.
- _____ No, thanks, I don't want any.
- _____ No, thanks, I am doing very well for the moment.

Situation 3

In a Western meal, you are offered a second helping but you have already had enough. What would you say?
- _____ No, thanks. I am full.
- _____ That was really delicious but I've already had plenty, thanks.

3. Writing

People go through different stages in getting used to life in a new country. Suppose you are an exchange student studying in the United States. Write four postcards to your friends and relatives. Each postcard is expected to illustrate one stage of cultural shock.

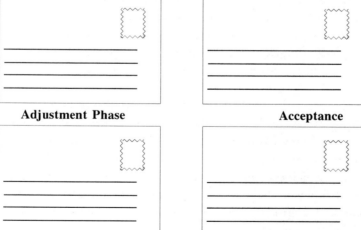

Intercultural Communication (Second Edition)

Text B　How to Survive Culture Shock

Pre-reading Exercise

Are you ready to study abroad? The following text will give you a prescription for culture shock. Before reading Text B, please finish your own list first and then compare it with the list of strategies suggested in Text B.

Things to Do Before My Going Abroad

1. Practice my oral English
2. _____
3. _____
4. _____
5. _____
6. _____
7. _____
8. _____

When you are preparing for your college adventures abroad, it is easy enough to make sure you get all the right forms filled out, have your passport ready, your bags packed, and your textbooks waiting for you at the other end, but how do you prepare for the adjustment to a new place? Especially, how to survive culture shock?

If your language is not the main language spoken, make sure you take some classes in the local language school before you go. Phrase books are all very well, but listening is the best way to learn. Audiotapes are a good alternative.

Any travel agent can tell you what the average rainfall will be and where the best tourist destinations are, but that does not help much. Ask around to find out if anyone you know has been there. Ask the travel agent for any less tourist-oriented information and check libraries and bookstores. Make sure you pack toiletries, medicines, and personal items before you leave. Sure, you can find a lot of things in the new country, but the brands and ingredients might be different and confusing, so go prepared. That will make it easier when you eventually do have to do some shopping.

Take a phone card so you can phone home for the sound of a familiar voice.

When you get on the plane, set your watch to the new time zone and try and place yourself in it. Drink plenty of water because flying dehydrates you. Stretch your legs and get some sleep.

Make sure you know where your consulate office is in case of emergencies. If you do not know, ask airport staff, university staff or use a phone book, but find it before you need it.

Remember, if you take an umbrella, it will not rain. Use the university resources available to you. Be diligent about attending things like orientation. It might seem like a drag, particularly when you are tired and do not know anyone, but it will be worth it in the long run. Prepare a list of questions before you go to orientation or welcome functions so that you do not forget to ask for information you need. How do I get a driver's license? Open a bank account? Get a bus into town? Can I use my electric razor/hair dryer here? Where is the nearest medical center? Ask to be put in touch with other students from your country or who speak your language. Many colleges offer a mentor or buddy system and if you are not staying with a family, making new friends can really help you settle in. Go for short walks to familiarize yourself with your area, and set yourself a task each time, maybe to find a newspaper stand that sells international papers, or to find a restaurant that serves familiar food, locate a currency exchange center, laundromat or cinema.

Later on. Remember, culture shock takes a while to get used to, so give yourself time. Even the most simple things are not always the same in another country. Buses are different, so get maps and timetables. Road rules are different, so use extra care. The currency is different, so familiarize yourself with the money. Habits are hard to break. To get the most out of your study abroad experience, find a happy medium between home and your new environment. It is important to look for the balance. This is a little bit like changing the water in a fish tank. You are supposed to keep one third of the old water and replace two thirds with fresh water. That way, the fish do not completely freak out. Their new environment is diluted with some water from their old environment. That makes sense to the students who study at another country. And once you think you got the water right, you can start to enjoy the swim!

Text C Can You Survive Reverse Culture Shock?

Pre-reading Questions

The following sentences are quoted from K. Merck, a student from Murdoch University who just came back from Perth:

> I definitely was affected more severely upon my return, and missed Perth a lot. It took a while to get used to being back, adjusting to the food, the accent, etc. I absolutely want to go back, as do many of my American friends whom I keep in touch with. Just give yourself time to be open to life there — you will not regret it.

Please discuss the following questions with your classmates before reading Text C.
1. Have you ever heard "reverse culture shock"? Is Merck suffering from reverse culture shock?
2. What do you think are the symptoms of reverse culture shock?
3. How would you walk out of reverse culture shock?

Everybody knows about experiencing culture shock when you visit a country with different customs, cuisine or language. But sometimes the worst culture shock of all comes when you return home. Reverse culture shock is the name people give to that feeling of not fitting into your home country, and you are especially at risk of it if you return home after living abroad for an extended time.

The best way to beat reverse culture shock is to be aware of how it might strike. Here are a few of the experiences you could expect to have once you return home:

Nobody Cares about Your Travels

Really, you will be surprised how few people show even the slightest bit of interest in the life-changing trip or stint abroad you have just returned from. If you are the kind of person who loves to travel a lot, you might have trouble understanding this, because you are probably the exception to the rule. I am the exception who always asks to see everybody's holiday photographs and get the rundown on the kinds of places they stayed in and any interesting people they met.

Basically, just keep your exciting experiences to yourself until someone asks. You might be lucky enough to have a like-minded friend or two, or a mother like mine who would be interested in my experiences no matter what they were — take advantage of these people and share some of the interesting tales you have with them, but be careful not to overload them. You might need them to still be listening when you return from your next big overseas jaunt.

And a corollary to this: do not take it personally when people you know and care for have no idea what you have been doing all this time. I have lost count of the number of people who introduced me to other friends as someone who had just returned from teaching in Slovenia, or Czech... had not they read the dozens of emails I sent from Slovakia? The difference was absolutely clear to me, and I felt almost insulted on behalf of my Slovak friends, but I learned that I was not going to be the one who would change the world. I did correct them, though — gently.

Normality Will Hit Hard

Once you have drunk your favorite coffee again or visited the best CD shop in your neighborhood, the routine normality of home could hit you hard. While you were living or traveling abroad, even mundane everyday tasks might have seemed a bit more exotic or interesting, but at home, going to the supermarket is not a place where you will find a dozen new foods. And if home is a place you lived most of your life, you probably will not find any incredible historic attractions that you do not know about, either.

Every time I have returned from long periods abroad in countries where I did not speak the language well, one thing that really hit me is how tedious it is to hear everyday conversations in a language you understand well. Hearing people discuss how long it takes to get to the next bus stop or complaining about their partner not putting the toilet seat down sounds a whole lot more interesting in a foreign language.

People Just Will Not Understand You

It is a pretty common thread that people who have spent an extended time abroad tend to come home with some new opinions. Usually — hopefully — these come along with a big dose of open-mindedness and a heightened interest in other cultures. But for your friends or colleagues who have not left your homeland, these kinds of issues just will not have the priority that they do for you.

Take this as an example. On a short trip back home in between jobs on different continents, someone I knew asked me: "How do you be friends with somebody who doesn't speak English as a first language?" They already had trouble grasping how I could teach English to Japanese people when I could not speak their language, but when I told them that people like these had become good friends of mine, their understanding completely failed them.

Some Might Be Jealous

Be careful not to drop your travel tales into too many conversations. After traveling pretty widely, I know I am guilty of this at times, and there is a clear reaction from some people if I begin a story with "When I was on the Trans-Siberian ...", which seems like one of jealousy. Not everybody has the same opportunity as you to travel abroad, but they might want to—so be sensitive about who you discuss your experiences with.

Can You Survive Reverse Culture Shock?

My reverse culture shock was so bad on visits home while I lived overseas that I wondered if I could ever return to Australia. Eventually, I met and married a German who convinced me that we should give it a go. And it is turned out fine, but not without some reverse culture shock.

For me, the best way to deal with all of these problems is to ensure the world around me is both multicultural and supportive. I have gone out of my way to make friends with people who speak the languages I have picked up, or who have had similar experiences living abroad. That makes all the rest of the crazy reactions and fears of normality subside enough for me to deal with life happily. So far. But I am still itching to get away again.

Movie to Watch

Lost in Translation is a 2003 comedy-drama film starring Bill Murray and Scarlett Johansson. The film explores themes of loneliness, alienation, existential ennui, and culture shock against the background of the modern Japanese cityscape.

Unit 12
Cultural Differences in Education

> Very often certain values, attitudes, and behavioral patterns of the general culture are directly reflected in and reinforced by the educational setting. Cultural values, the role of the teacher, modes of learning, teacher-student interaction patterns, and norms of interaction must all be considered in cross-cultural analysis.
>
> —— P. R. Furey

Unit Goals

- To understand the differences in education among different cultures
- To learn effective principles in coping with cultural differences in education
- To learn useful words and expressions about cultural differences in education and improve language skills

Before You Read

A Survey of Classroom Interaction

Mark the box that indicates what classroom interaction was like in your high school days.

Items	Always	Usually	Sometimes	Rarely	Never
☞ The teacher asked the class questions.	☐	☐	☐	☐	☐
☞ Students volunteered to answer the teacher's questions.	☐	☐	☐	☐	☐
☞ Students air their opinions freely in class.	☐	☐	☐	☐	☐

(continued)

Items	Always	Usually	Sometimes	Rarely	Never
☞ Students speak only when the teacher calls on them.	☐	☐	☐	☐	☐
☞ Students tell the teacher in class when they do not understand.	☐	☐	☐	☐	☐
☞ Students listen quietly when the teacher or classmates talks.	☐	☐	☐	☐	☐
☞ Students consult with classmates before answering teachers' questions.	☐	☐	☐	☐	☐
☞ Students are afraid of making mistakes.	☐	☐	☐	☐	☐
☞ Teachers encourage students to risk making mistakes.	☐	☐	☐	☐	☐
☞ Students do homework as directed.	☐	☐	☐	☐	☐
☞ Students ask teacher for help.	☐	☐	☐	☐	☐
☞ Students ask for the teacher's opinions in class.	☐	☐	☐	☐	☐
☞ Students want to sit in the front rows of the room.	☐	☐	☐	☐	☐
☞ Teachers ask students to discuss in groups.	☐	☐	☐	☐	☐
☞ Students sleep in class.	☐	☐	☐	☐	☐
☞ Students copy answers from others during tests.	☐	☐	☐	☐	☐
☞ Teachers are easy to talk to after class.	☐	☐	☐	☐	☐

Compare your frequencies checked on the survey with other group members. Discuss the patterns of Chinese high school classroom interaction.

Start to Read

Text A Classroom Expectations

Class participation, as is well known, is one of the cornerstones of the American education system. At the very least, what this means is that, upon entering college, the average student in America is already quite accustomed to doing group work, answering questions posed by the instructor, and even, on occasion, making presentations. But what participation looks like in the classroom can vary depending on factors such as the level of education (e.g., elementary school or high school), the type of class, and the size of the institution. In short, while much of education in the United States is informed by the value of student-centered learning, what that looks like in practical terms may vary quite a lot. While students in an average American high school may participate in a fair number of group projects, at the college level, much depends on the type of course involved. Thus, whereas business courses might require frequent presentations of case studies, instructors of English literature courses may only occasionally assign group presentations. Class participation for science majors, for the most part, centers around conducting laboratory experiments.

An important thing to remember is that the size of the university or college matters. For large public research universities, basic-level lower division courses are usually large (up to several hundred students) and lecture focused, with class participation limited to occasional exchanges of questions and answers. But in addition to the lecture portion of the course, students will also enroll in smaller course sections (often a maximum of twenty students) led by graduate students to discuss specific course-related readings and topics. Advanced-level upper division courses, on the other hand, are usually taught solely by the professor, are smaller in size, and allow the professor greater flexibility in terms of mixing lectures with discussions.

In contrast, private liberal arts colleges promote themselves as having the advantage of providing small classes that allow for much greater levels of interaction with the professor. Moreover, at many of the top liberal arts colleges such as Macalester College and Grinnell College, class participation can often include paid internships to work alongside professors in the laboratory or even accompanying a professor to an archaeological dig in a faraway country. Professors at these institutions are actively encouraged to involve students in their own research projects and are provided funds by the college to support these endeavors.

American university professors are given much autonomy to determine how they will teach their courses, and different professors will use varying degrees of creativity to engage their students in the classroom. But regardless, discussion is one of the most prized values of the American college classroom. Why is discussion so important? Discussion, facilitated by the professor, helps students understand that intellectual knowledge is always the product of a messy process of trial and error, of inquiry, and of the realization

of multiple perspectives. Of course, professors always lead discussions with a learning goal in mind. Though open-mindedness, mutual respect, and even disagreement is allowed and encouraged, in the end, professors usually adhere to high academic standards, and in almost all cases, students are given grades based on their performance and mastery of the course subject.

Students are expected to take responsibility for their own learning. What this means is that while professors are responsible for covering the course subject, mastery of the material is the responsibility of the student. Because students have the ability to choose their courses, there is the basic assumption that each student is personally invested in the learning process. Students who fail courses face the possibility of expulsion from the university if their overall grade point average falls  below satisfactory. There are no make-up exams. However, many universities are recognizing that first-generation college students (whose parents never attended college) face many challenges, economically and academically, and thus, are providing special programs catered to this student population to help them succeed in college.

Professors always have set office hour times for each course and students are encouraged to see the professor if they have questions about the course. At large public universities, professors are often busy with their research, and thus, outside of set office hour times, are often not available to interact with students. However, professors at smaller private liberal arts universities are known to have a lot of interaction with their students, both inside and outside of the classroom. This may include meals together on campus and students inviting professors to attend their extracurricular activities, such as sports competitions.

After You Read

Knowledge Focus

1. **Pair Work: Discuss the following questions with your partner.**
   1) What is classroom participation at American universities?
   2) What are the factors that influence the level of class participation at an American college?
   3) How important do you think discussion is to the overall learning process? Why?
   4) In your opinion, what is the least attractive aspect of student participation in American college education? Why?

2. **Solo Work: Comment on the following teaching methods. Compare the attitudes and practice of American and Chinese teachers and students.**
   1) Students and the instructor have to maintain open minds.
   2) Students and the teacher can respectfully disagree with each other.
   3) Students choose their own courses but are responsible for their own learning outcomes.

Intercultural Communication (Second Edition)

Language Focus

1. Fill in the blanks with the following words or expressions you have learned in Text A.

| cornerstone | accustomed to | enroll | flexibility | endeavor |
| engage in | adhere to | expulsion | cater to | interact |

1) This club faces _____ from the football league.
2) It is pointless to _____ hypothesis before we have the facts.
3) They only publish novels which _____ the mass-market.
4) The mascot of the exhibition will _____ every visitor.
5) The active participation of individuals in greenism is a worthwhile _____.
6) College students should cultivate the ability to ask questions, the _____ of critical thinking.
7) In traditional classes, students were _____ taking in whatever their teachers taught them.
8) The _____ of distance learning would be particularly suited to busy managers.
9) The university plans to _____ four doctoral students starting next year.
10) All the members of the association _____ a strict code of practice.

2. Choose the best modal auxiliaries for the following sentences.

The importance that Americans place on indirect expression of authority is a frequent barrier to communication — both linguistically and culturally. When an American teacher tells an ESL student on a program in the United States "You __1__ move you chair over here close to me so you will not be tempted to talk to Jose," the student rarely understands the message as "Stop talking to Jose."

Teachers __2__ word their orders as orders, not requests. Then, the grammatical structure is more comprehensible, and the students recognize the statement as one requiring a specific response rather than truly offering a choice. This lack of communication became clear to me when I urged a group working on a project to stop gossiping and get down to business. I said, "You __3__ stop visiting and get down to work. You will not get anything done before class is over." The students smiled politely and nodded at me; the gossip continued, and nothing was done that day. I was furious; the students were puzzled by my anger. They had understood the words completely; what had not been communicated was my demand that "they do something" different from "what they were doing." The students honestly felt that I was offering a suggestion, which they were free to act on or to ignore as they saw fit.

I now think that ESL teachers __4__ make their expectations clear at the beginning of the term or assignment, even if they seem obvious to the teachers. While teachers __5__ respect the dignity of their students, they __6__ also be sure that they have clearly communicated their orders and instructions.

3. Find the appropriate prepositions or adverbs that collocate with the words in bold letters.

1) A good marriage is **based** _____ trust.
2) The government **calls** _____ the youth to donate their blood voluntarily.
3) As soon as you create an account for the user, the user can **participate** _____ a secure domain.

4) All things invariably **divide** _____ two.
5) They swore an oath to **carry** _____ their duties faithfully.
6) The chauffeur was **put** _____ **prison** because of much drinking.
7) All the classmates burst into laughter when David **acted** _____ the episode.
8) Who is **responsible** _____ the terrible mess?

4. **Error Correction: Each of the following sentences has at least one grammatical error. Identify the errors and make corrections.**
   1) Upon entering college, the average American students are already quite accustomed to do group work and make presentations.
   2) But that participation looks like in the classroom can vary depending on factors such as the level of education, the type of class, and the size of the institution.
   3) While students in an average American high school may participate in a fair number of group projects, on the college level, much depends on the type of course involved.
   4) Private liberal arts colleges promote themselves as having the advantage of providing small classes that allow much greater levels of interaction with the professor.
   5) Participation in the American classroom not only is accepted but also expected of students in many countries.
   6) The ideal student is considered to be one who is motivated to learn for the sake of learning, not the one is interested only in getting high grades.
   7) At many of the top liberal arts colleges, class participation can often include paying internships to work alongside professors in the laboratory or even accompanying a professor to an archaeological dig in a faraway country.
   8) Because students have the ability to choose their courses, so there is the basic assumption that each student is personally invested in the learning process.
   9) What this means is that professors are responsible for covering the course subject, mastery of the material is the responsibility of the student.
   10) Students who fail courses face the possibility of expulsion by the university if their overall grade point average falls below satisfactory.
   11) At large public universities, professors are often busy with their research, and thus, outside of set office hour times, often not available to interact with students.
   12) This may include meals together on campus and students invite professors to attend their extracurricular activities, such as sports competitions.
   13) Many universities are recognizing that first-generation college students face many challenges, economical and academical and thus, are providing special programs to help them succeed in college.
   14) You have not to agree with every statement the professor makes and all comments by a professor are open to discussion.
   15) Of course, professors always lead discussions with a learned goal in mind.
   16) Different professors will use varying degrees of creativities to engage their students in the classroom.

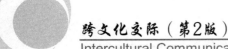

Comprehensive Work

1. Pair Work: Analyze the following cases with your partner.

How Do Students Learn?

Karen Randolph had been teaching high school English in the United States before she accepted a teaching job at a teacher's college in China. She found her new environment and her new teaching assignment exciting. Both her students and her colleagues seemed a bit shy of her, but Karen was sure that in time they would all come to be friends.

In the classroom, however, Karen was very frustrated. When she asked a question, the class was silent. Only if she called on a particular student would she get an answer, often a very good one. She could not understand why they would not volunteer when they obviously knew the answers. They were very quiet when she was speaking in front of the class, and never asked questions, let alone interrupt with an opinion, but as soon as the class ended, they would cluster around her desk to ask their question one-by-one. They would also offer their suggestions about the lesson at this time.

Karen often asked her students to work in small groups during class, especially when they were editing each other's writing. They were slow to move into groups and when they did, they often simply formed a group with the people sitting next to them. Finally she devised her own system of forming groups to get them to interact with students sitting in another section of the classroom.

Most frustrating of all, after she taught her class how to edit essays, she found that the students were likely to write vague remarks on their classmates' papers. They usually accepted her criticism of their writing with good spirits and promises to improve. In fact, they frequently asked for more correction of their English from her than she wanted to give. She felt that one hundred percent grammatical correctness was not as important as learning how to correct what they had written on their own and with the help of others. After all, they would not always have a teacher to tell them what was good and not so good about their English writing.

1) If you were Karen's Chinese colleague, how would you explain to her why students behave in the way she experiences?
2) What do foreign teachers do in class that makes Chinese students uncomfortable?
3) What do you appreciate about the traditional Chinese way of learning? What do you appreciate about the foreign teacher's way of teaching?
4) What suggestions would you give to foreign teachers on how to teach Chinese students well?
5) What suggestions would you give to Chinese students on how to learn well with foreign teachers?

Why Were They Late for the Class?

John Rohrkemper was an American professor. It was his first time to teach in a Brazilian university and he was quite excited about it. His two-hour class was scheduled to begin at

10 a.m. and end at noon. On the first day, to his surprise, there was no one in the classroom when he arrived on time. Many students came after 10 a.m.; several arrived after 10:30 a.m. Two students came after 11 a.m. Although all the students greeted him as they arrived, few apologized for their lateness. Dr. Rohrkemper was very angry about students' rude behaviors and decided to study their behavior.

1) What do you think Dr. Rohrkemper will find in his study about Brazilian students' lateness?
2) What suggestions would you like to give to both Dr. Rohrkemper and his Brazilian students?

2. Group Work

Read the following comments and discuss in groups:
1) What assumptions do you think American and Chinese teachers/students bring to the class in the following situations?
2) What are the Chinese and Western attitudes to learning and teaching?
3) What is the role of the teacher and what is the role of the student in Chinese and Western classrooms respectively?

The trouble with Chinese teachers is that they've never done any real teacher-training courses so they don't know how to teach. All they do is to follow the book. They never give us any opportunities to talk. How in the world do they expect us to learn?

An American student in Beijing in 2002

American teachers are very friendly, but they often cannot teach very well. I never know where they are going — there is no system and I just get lost. Also, they're often badly trained and don't really have a thorough grasp of their subject.

A Chinese exchange student in New York in 2003

3. Writing — Mimetic Writing

The following article, written by an American student, is about how American students prepare for Spring Vacation. Please imitate this article and write a composition on how

Chinese students prepare for their Winter/Summer vacation.

SAMPLE ARTICLE

Students Prepare for Spring Vacation

It is time for the annual spring pilgrimage to Florida. Thousands of college students are packing their bags, leaving the cold north and traveling south.

About one million students will spend part of March or April in Florida, forgetting their books, problems and sometimes their manners. They eat like bears, drink like fish, and search for sun, fun and sex.

Thousands will go to Fort Lauderdale, but most (about 300,000) will go to Daytona Beach. In spite of inflation and recession, more students are expected this year than last year. "Students aren't affected by the economy," said an author of a guide book to Florida.

In order to save money, six or seven students will stay in one hotel room, or stay in a tent at a campground. And many students sleep on the beach during the day and wander the streets at night.

Though most of the students are not rich, local merchants welcome them. If each students spent only $100 during his stay on Daytona Beach, that would add $30 million into the area's economy. "The community is very glad they're here," said one businessman.

But the student invasion makes life difficult for the police. "The majority of them are decent kids just down here to have a good time," said one policeman. "But it takes only one jerk and we've got a problem."

One woman who has worked for thirty-two years as a bartender believes that every spring is basically the same, though the students change. "If you've seen one spring break, you've seen them all," she said. "It's insane all the time."

Read More

Text B 15 Important Cultural Differences in the Classroom

Pre-reading Activity

Work with your group members and develop a plan for how you would approach a classroom with the following student clientele: six Hispanics, eight European Americans, five African Americans, four Japanese and five Chinese.

Then read Text B and you may draw inspiration from it.

Although the personality of two individuals in one country can vary much more than the average personality in two different countries, having some knowledge of how cultures vary from each other can at least give teachers a starting point in knowing how to approach a student or class until teachers get to know the individual preferences of the class. Here is, by no means, an exhaustive list of some cultural differences that can come up in class.

1. Body Language and Gestures

The list of gestures by the teacher or students that could be misinterpreted or even found offensive is huge. In fact, the number of totally universal human gestures is very few. You can fairly easily research the typical body language and gestures of the country your students are from or are interested in, but particular things to look out for in the classroom include pointing at people, gesturing "okay," and holding up various fingers to illustrate numbers, etc. The main point to note with any of these is that people do not stop finding a gesture offensive just because they understand that it means something else in other countries.

2. Dress

This could be a matter of avoiding even brief and accidental showing of parts of the body like shoulders and belly, or could be more a case of certain clothes such as bright colors or overly sturdy shoes being taken as tacky and/or unprofessional. Other things to bear in mind include avoiding holey socks if you might have to take your shoes off. There might also be issues with students wanting to keep on head wear that blocks eye contact and so makes communication difficult. Students might also use dress as a clue to try and work out the financial position of foreign teachers.

3. The Teacher's Role

Different cultures can show different attitudes to the teacher admitting they could not be wrong, letting students make classroom decisions, pair work correction, and pair work more generally. For native speakers, there might also be issues of differing reactions to your knowledge and use of the students' L1 (first language).

4. Asking Questions/Saying "You Do Not Understand"

To give an example, in a Japanese company it is normal for a subordinate to say "Yes, I understand" to any instructions from the boss, and then find out from elsewhere whatever they did not understand. Some people can show the same reaction to grammar explanations and game instructions in the classroom.

5. Making Mistakes and Correction

As with most of these, the embarrassment at making mistakes and being corrected varies more from person to person than culture to culture, but general national characteristics can also be discerned. There might also be issues with how much correction they expect, if that correction can come from other students, and if it can be in front of other people.

6. Status

Students might feel they cannot interrupt or correct people who are older, in a higher status job, male etc., or may be shocked when the teacher or another student does not pay attention to such distinctions.

7. Gender Roles

This is mainly just one subset of "Status" above. If students think that women (especially younger or other "lower status" women) are lower in the ranking, that will exaggerate any negative reactions they have to being interrupted, corrected, told to do things in the classroom that are unfamiliar, etc.

8. Food and Drink

In Islamic countries, you might have to take account of low blood sugar levels and varying break times during Ramadan. In other places, there might be a taboo against the teacher taking in certain drinks or drinking straight from the plastic bottle, or indeed drinking anything if that is seen as rudeness towards students who do not have drinks. There might also be strong reactions in various places against smelling of or admitting to liking certain foods.

9. Taboo Topics

A very much less than exhaustive list of taboo topics in various places included female family members, dogs, politics, social classes, certain periods of history, the Royal Family, the police, the underclass, being mixed race, and homosexuality.

10. Eye Contact

The frequency and length of eye contact changes a lot from country to country, as does the time when eye contact is and is not considered suitable. One frequently misunderstood example is that East Asian students often close their eyes when concentrating.

11. Small Talk

There can be cultural differences in the amount and the timing of small talk that are expected in the classroom. For example, Japanese meetings tend to start and finish with quite a lot of small talk but have a clear transition, whereas British will often try to move cleverly and smoothly between the small talk and the start of the first lesson topic. Other cultures might expect small talk to be shorter or even absent until the end of the lesson.

12. Silence

In some countries, most famously Japan and Finland, silence between conversation turns is quite normal. The danger is that the teacher or another student might jump in to fill the silence and so prevent them from speaking, or that they will make others feel uncomfortable with their silence. The best short term solution is to teach phrases to fill thinking time like "Well, let me see," with the next stage being teaching sentence stems to at least get them started quickly, e.g. "I think that..."

13. Writing Styles

Most of the things that native English speakers are taught in school are good writing style, such as a clear progression of ideas and one topic per paragraph, exist less or in different forms in other cultures. This can make the writing of even higher level students difficult to follow. Guided planning and reading tasks that identify topic sentences to solve these problems (eventually) are fairly common in Academic English and IELTS textbooks.

14. Interrupting

In some cultures, it is normal that several people talk over each other, whereas in others, people will wait until there is complete silence before making their contribution. This can be a problem when you have students from different cultures working together or in EFL tests where the ability to split the speaking 50/50 between partners is assessed. Methods to tackle it include giving the speaker something to hold, making a third student judge each pair on the percentage each person talks, and teaching language forms like tag questions that aid turn taking.

15. Directness

Students who prefer to get straight to the point in L1 often find it easier to communicate in English, but there is a chance of them or other students who do not have the language level to be polite seeming too direct and offending people. They also might miss polite requests to stop doing things etc., for the same cultural, personality and language reasons. This can also be an issue when writing student progress reports, when the same constructive criticism to two different students could offend one but seem like a compliment to the other. Teaching functional language and asking them to judge the politeness of different forms are two good approaches, as is giving realistic reactions when students are rude or overly indirect in class.

Ramadan: This is an Islamic religious observance that takes place during the ninth month of the Islamic calendar; the month in which the Qur'an was revealed to the Prophet Muhammad. It is the Islamic month of fasting, in which participating Muslims do not eat or drink anything from true dawn until sunset. Fasting is meant to teach the person patience, sacrifice and humility.

Text C　Classroom Culture

Pre-reading Activity

1. Discuss the differences in high school education between China and America in groups of three or four. Your discussion is guided by the following chart.

Items	China	America
Teachers' teaching methods		
Classroom activities		
Significance of classroom participation		

2. Work in pairs. Suppose your partner is a teacher from the UK. Describe the higher education system in China to your partner and find out: In what ways does Chinese higher education differ from that in the UK?

_____
_____
_____
_____
_____
_____

Read Text C and you will find out the Chinese classroom culture from a British professor's perspective.

The first day I set foot in the classroom in China, I had to put aside the whispers from Chinese and foreign colleagues alike, that the students in China were quiet. I did not want to judge my new students from another person's opinion. As a person and as a teacher, I do not like rumors, and prefer to make up my own mind from what I see.

The reception I eventually received while walking into the university classroom bowled me over—the students applauded my entrance. I think I bowed my way in muttering thank-yous, reserved, humbled and embarrassed. Through initial introductions and later lessons, I have come to understand that my students are—if only out of politeness—kind, peaceful people, who speak freely and happily of dreams and aspirations, eager to learn of cultural differences and customs. But it seems that there are real fundamental differences between higher-education experiences here and abroad.

In the West, as an undergraduate student, you have minimal contact with lecturers or any university authorities. There is no curfew, and there are no morning exercises, even relatively few mandatory classes. If you want advice from a lecturer, you schedule an appointment, just like you would to see the dentist. It is a formal occasion, 20 minutes of allotted time and that's it. In China, however, I have become accustomed to text messages, emails and phone calls from my students wanting to talk and chat. I am also touched by invitations to restaurants, dormitories and KTV. When I was a student in the UK, it never crossed my mind to take my lecturers out for dinner, perhaps they too would have appreciated it, or perhaps it is only feasible in this situation because I am a foreign teacher, I am not sure.

In conversations about education and teaching, Chinese students have told me that they noticed big differences in instruction and relationships with foreign and Chinese teachers. One student told me that she found her foreign teachers overly strict, while she perceived her Chinese teachers as more friendly, less authoritative and demanding. On what basis she drew her conclusions I do not know, but she was absolute in her view that foreign teachers require too much general interaction. She said that it was their demands in the classroom for students to speak, which put them on the spot and made them feel shy.

I am unable to summate with any degree of expertise the apparently vast differences between Chinese and Western education systems. Yet from experience as a teacher in one and a student in the other, I think there are lessons to learn on both sides from the attitudes of students, teachers and their academic institutions. As I slowly adjust to my position here in China, my objective remains the same as it was in London — to learn and understand without prejudice, and to encourage my students to do the same. Perhaps I have a chip on my shoulder regarding stereotypes, but I am driven to reiterate over and over again — I do not like hamburgers, I can eat with chopsticks, and I do not mind at all if you ask me my age, or if I am married.

Cultures are rich and the people that make them up are an ocean of diversity; just think of all different characters that you meet in any restaurant, any elevator or any corner shop. It is true that we categorize each other but we only do this according to our own agenda, whether it is conscious or sub-conscious. There is no real measure of the degrees of difference between us all and any attempt at one is surely bound to failure. I can only conclude that if we are to reach any degree of sophistication in our learning systems, prejudices should be sidelined in favor of the differences, which insurmountably influence the environments in which we learn, work and live.

For Fun

Book to Read
Gonzales, Frank. *Recognizing Cultural Differences in the Classroom: Training Module Ⅲ*. San Antonio: Intercultural Development Research Association, 1988.
- This training module is designed for trainers to familiarize classroom teachers with cultural elements that some national origin minority populations may bring to the school environment. This book will help participants define culture and the categories of culture. Participants can become familiar with elements of surface culture and deep culture from several ethnic groups. Participants can also generate ideas for validating the culture of their students.

Movie to Watch
L'Auberge Espagnole (The Spanish Apartment, 2002) is a funny and very realistic depiction of the lives of a group of exchange students from all over Europe, who study in Barcelona and live in the same shared apartment. No director could have made this movie without personal experience to draw from. The scenes, the dialogues, and the sets are just too realistic to have been made up. From the messy fridge to arguments over who is next to clean the bathroom, to cultural clashes between the students, director Cédric Klapisch pays close attention to detail in order to bring the movie to life. This movie has won several prizes at international film festivals.

Unit 13
Cultural Differences in Etiquette and Protocol

> There is no accomplishment so easy to acquire as politeness, and none so profitable.
> —— George Bernard Shaw
>
> Good manners will open doors that the best education cannot.
> —— Clarence Thomas

Unit Goals

- To understand the importance of appropriate etiquette and protocol in intercultural communication
- To understand how cultural difference in social entertainment may affect intercultural communication in terms of gift-giving, dining practice, business card exchanging and tipping
- To learn useful words and expressions about cultural differences in etiquette and protocol and improve language skills

Before You Read

Study the following picture and the story in pairs. Try to find out the misunderstanding about gift-giving between Sitti and the Australian lecturer.

Once at a conference, an Indonesian student, Sitti, met an Australian lecturer who she really admired. In her culture, they are always very keen to give something to a special guest and she thought very hard about what she could give the lecturer to express her appreciation. Finally, she decided to give him some special jackfruit crackers. But what happened when she gave her gift to this Australian lecturer? The Australian lecturer gave it straight back to her and said in front of many people: "Thanks, but I cannot take them with me. I can find these easily in Australia."

Sitti was totally shocked by his response and felt very confused. This is because in Indonesian culture, even though they do not like something given by someone, they always say thanks and praise them for their thoughtfulness.

List the factors you would consider when giving gifts.
1. _____
2. _____
3. _____
4. _____
5. _____

Start to Read

Text A International Gift-giving Etiquette

Within the interdependent, global and multi-cultural marketplace of the 21st century, cross-cultural differences in the approaches to and practices of business people across the world are important to learn.

A lack of cross-cultural understanding can lead to misunderstandings which may result in offense. Cross-cultural awareness and an understanding of foreign etiquette are important for today's globe trotting business person.

One area of importance in cross-cultural awareness is in the different gift-giving etiquettes of the world. Understanding gift-giving and the etiquette surrounding it can help international business people cement better relationships with foreign colleagues, clients or customers.

Cross-cultural gift-giving etiquette involves considering the following points:
- Who is receiving the gift? Is it a person or a group? What is the status of the receiver(s)?
- What types of gifts are acceptable or unacceptable?
- What is the protocol associated with gift-giving and receiving?
- Should gifts be reciprocated?

In many countries or regions like North America or the UK, gift-giving is rare in the business world. In fact, it may carry negative connotations as gift-giving could be construed as bribery. However, in many other countries, gift-giving and its etiquette have a central place in business practices.

As a general rule, countries/regions fall into categories based on the importance they place on gift-giving protocol.

High Priority	Medium Priority	Low Priority
Japan	South Korea China Thailand Malaysia Indonesia The Philippines Singapore the Middle East Latin America Russia	United States Canada Australia Europe

In order to highlight some of the different aspects of cross-cultural gift-giving etiquette, a few examples shall be presented.

Gift-Giving Etiquette in China

It is the proper etiquette for gifts to be exchanged for celebrations, as thanks for assistance and even as a sweetener for future favors. It is, however, important not to give gifts in the absence of a good reason or a witness. When the Chinese want to buy gifts it is not uncommon for them to ask what you would like. It would be wise to demonstrate an appreciation of Chinese culture by asking for items such as ink paintings or tea.

Business gifts are always reciprocated. Failing to do so is bad etiquette. When giving gifts, avoid giving cash.

Do not be too frugal with your choice of gift; otherwise, you will be seen as an "iron rooster," i.e. getting a good gift out of you is like getting a feather out of an iron rooster. Depending on the item, avoid giving a single one of something. Chinese philosophy stresses harmony and balance, so give gifts in pairs.

Gift-Giving Etiquette in Japan

Gift-giving is a central part of Japanese business etiquette.

Bring a range of gifts for your trip. So if you are presented with a gift, you will be able to reciprocate. The emphasis in Japanese business culture is on the act of gift-giving, not the gift itself. Expensive gifts are common. The best time to present a gift is at the end of your visit.

A gift for an individual should be given in private. If you are presenting a gift to a group of people, have them all present. The correct etiquette is to present/receive gifts with both hands. Before accepting a gift, it is polite to refuse at least once or twice before accepting. Giving four or nine of anything is considered unlucky. Give gifts in pairs if possible.

Gift-Giving Etiquette in Saudi Arabia

Gifts should only be given to the most intimate friends. Gifts should be of the highest quality. Never buy gold or silk as a present for men. Silver is acceptable. Always give/receive gifts with the right hand. Saudis enjoy wearing scent — "itr." The most popular is "oud" which can cost as much as £1,000 an ounce. It is not bad etiquette to open gifts when received.

Gift-Giving Etiquette in America

Wrapping a business gift is not necessary.

Gifts are opened in front of the giver. The gift is admired, and appreciation is expressed verbally. The oral expression of thanks is followed by a written note of appreciation unless the gift is small and is used as an advertisement (e.g. a paperweight with the company logo). Business gifts to the office or department, such as a basket of fruit or a box of candy, are opened immediately and shared by all. (The manager's taking the gift home to share with his or her family is considered to be in poor taste.)

Gift-Giving in Some Other Cultures

Be aware of taboos related to gifts in different cultures:

- Avoid giving gifts to the French until a personal relationship has been developed. Avoid gifts of perfume or wine; those are their specialties. A bottle of wine in France, could also be viewed by the host as the insult that he does not serve good wine.
- Gifts to Germans should not be wrapped in black, brown, or white.
- A striped tie is not an appropriate gift to a British man; it may represent a British regiment other than his own.
- Avoid gifts of a knife or handkerchief to persons in Latin America. The knife is interpreted as a desire to cut off the relationship; the handkerchief is associated with tears.
- Avoid gifts of liquor or wine for an Arab. Since alcohol is illegal in Islamic cultures, the gift would be confiscated by customs.
- In Germany, roses and chrysanthemums are not considered appropriate. Roses are for lovers, and chrysanthemums are for funerals. Flowers must be in uneven numbers in Germany, and they must be taken out of the paper before being presented, unlike the custom in Britain.

The above are a few of many examples of cross-cultural differences in gift-giving etiquette. It is advisable to try and ascertain some facts about the gift-giving etiquette of any country you plan to visit. By doing so, you maximize the potential of your cross-cultural encounter.

After You Read

Knowledge Focus

1. **Pair Work: Discuss the following questions with your partner.**
    1) How do gift-giving practices vary from culture to culture?
    2) Why is it important to know about the customs associated with gift-giving?
    3) How to classify countries or regions according to the importance they place on gift-giving protocol?
    4) What is the gift-giving etiquette in Japan?
    5) In what way is the gift-giving etiquette in China different from that in America?

2. **Solo Work: According to the knowledge you have learned in Text A, fill in each of the blanks with the appropriate name of a nation or people from those given below, some of**

跨文化交际（第2版）
Intercultural Communication (Second Edition)

which may be used several times.

| Saudi Arabia | America | Germany |
| Japan | Latin America | Chinese |

1) In _____, do not give knives because it means that a relationship is breaking up.
2) In _____, do not give four of anything because four is an unlucky number.
3) In _____, do not give red roses because of their romantic connotation, unless you intend romance.
4) Avoid giving tea to _____ because tea is their specialty.
5) In _____, remember to present your gift with your right hand.
6) In _____, wrapping a business gift is unnecessary.

Language Focus

1. Fill in the blanks with the following words or expressions you have learned in Text A.

| frugal | highlight | reciprocate | taboo |
| insult | cement | trot | offence |

1) Her new job certainly keeps her on the _____.
2) Our object is to further _____ trade relations.
3) Do not be upset by what he said; he meant no _____.
4) When he spoke I was expected to _____ with some remark of my own.
5) Your resume should _____ your skills and achievements.
6) As children we were taught to be _____ and hard-working.
7) There are _____ against appearing naked in public places.
8) Their offer was so low I took it as a(n) _____.

2. Fill in the blanks with the proper form of the words in the brackets.

1) America is a _____ (culture) society.
2) There must have been some _____ (understand). I did not order all these books.
3) Education has become a _____ (center) issue in public debate.
4) We've only been able to rebuild the theatre with the _____ (assist) of the National Lottery.
5) These tax cuts are just a pre-election _____ (sweet).
6) In Japan there is a lot of _____ (emphasize) on politeness.
7) It is not socially _____ (accept) for parents to leave children unattended at that age.
8) The restaurant offers a wide variety of local _____ (special).

3. Find the appropriate prepositions or adverbs that collocate with the words in bold letters.

1) A diet with no exercise is bad for the health, because it will **result** _____ a loss of both fat and muscle tissue.
2) The lecture series **falls** naturally _____ three parts.
3) They will very likely **ask** _____ an increase in the budget.
4) Although (he was) cheerful in company, he was often sad _____ **private**.
5) Cuff-links are only sold _____ **pairs**.
6) We were **cut** _____ in the middle of our conversation.

7) Her best qualities **come** _____ in a crisis.
8) All electronic computers **consist** _____ five units although they are of different kinds.

4. **Error Correction: Each of the following sentences has at least one grammatical error. Identify the errors and make corrections.**
   1) Cross-cultural awareness and an understanding of foreign etiquette is important for today's globetrotting business person.
   2) Failing to reciprocate business gifts is a bad etiquette.
   3) People should avoid gifts of a knife or handkerchief to person in Latin America.
   4) Knowing what to do and saying in the right places will help build trust and open lines of communication.
   5) If you have an university degree or any honor, put it on your business card.
   6) Business cards need not to be translated into Hindi as English is widely spoken within the business community.
   7) The Japanese places emphasis on status and hierarchy.
   8) During a meeting, place the business cards on the table in front of you in order people are seated.
   9) When the meeting is over, put the business cards in a business card case or portfolio.
   10) Business card etiquette is relaxing in the UK and involves little ceremony.
   11) It is not considered bad etiquette to keep cards in the pocket.
   12) Business cards might be kept clean and presentable.
   13) Do not feel obliged to hand out the business card to everyone you meet as it is not expected.
   14) The purpose of dining with business associates is not merely eat or drink.
   15) In some parts of the world, the main meal is at noon and in others the main meal is in the evening.
   16) In West, you will have your own plate of food.

Comprehensive Work

1. Pair Work: Analyze the following cases with your partner.

Case Study 1

A Grand Rapids, Michigan, export manager once entertained a group of valued Japanese customers. Knowing the Japanese propensity for gift-giving, the American placed a small, white boxed gift near each place setting at the dinner table. He had chosen a small Swiss penknife as his gift. After the group was seated, he insisted the guests open their presents. Each guest reluctantly opened his package and the American executive was greeted with a stony silence.

1) What mistakes did the American export manager make in gift-giving?
2) What do you think would be a better gift to the Japanese customers?

Case Study 2

After successfully opening a park in Tokyo, Disney decided to expand to the European market, opening Euro Disney just outside Paris in 1992. However, the standard model of Disney theme parks, long considered to be a recipe for guaranteed financial success, soon ran into trouble. Just as with the parks in the United States and Tokyo, all alcoholic beverages were banned. In addition, the park did not offer sufficient restaurant seating for European customers.

Disney was criticized strongly for sticking too closely to its homogeneous "It's a small world after all" philosophy. Euro Disney estimated that it would lose almost $350 million during its first year of operation.

1) What was wrong with Euro Disney's operations?
2) Disney must find ways to adapt their theme park model in a manner which preserves the best of Disney while more closely fitting the needs of the European market. What is your suggestion?

2. Pair Work: Talk with your partner about the following questions

Tom is a human resources manager of an international company. He is assigned to arrange a dinner party for the whole company. Since the employees are coming from all over the world, what cultural differences concerning dinner should he take into consideration? If you were him, how would you arrange this dinner party concerning when, where and what to eat?

3. Writing

Read menus from Western restaurants in your living place or in books and compare them with menus from Chinese restaurants. Write a short composition on what they tell about the cultures.

Text B   Business Card Etiquette

Pre-reading Activity

Work in pairs and role-play the following situation.

You are the manager of an American company. Now you meet your partner, the executive of a Japanese company at a dinner party. Your role play should include business card exchanging.

When doing business abroad, it is important to understand the local culture. Culture includes areas such as a country's norms, values, behaviors, food, architecture, fashion and art. However, one area of culture that is important for the international business person is etiquette.

Understanding business etiquette allows you to feel comfortable in your dealings with foreign friends, colleagues, customers or clients. Knowing what to do and say in the right places will help build trust and open lines of communication.

One aspect of etiquette that is of great importance internationally is the exchanging of business cards.

Unlike in North America or Europe where the business card has little meaning other than a convenient form of capturing essential personal details, in other parts of the world the business card has very different meanings.

For example, in Japan the business card is viewed as a representation of the owner. Therefore, proper business etiquette demands one treats the business card with respect and honor.

Below we have provided you with a few examples of international business card exchange etiquette that may help you on your business trips abroad.

General Business Card Etiquette Tips:
- Business cards are an internationally recognized means of presenting personal contact details, so ensure you have a plentiful supply.
- Demonstrating good business etiquette is merely a means of presenting yourself as best you can. Failure to adhere to foreign business etiquette does not always have disastrous consequences.
- When travelling abroad for business, it is advisable to have one side of your business card translated into the appropriate language.
- Business cards are generally exchanged at the beginning of or at the end of an initial meeting.
- Good business etiquette requires you to present the card so the recipient's language is face up.
- Make a point of studying any business card, commenting on it and clarifying information before putting it away.

Business Card Etiquette in China

Have one side of your business card translated into Chinese using simplified Chinese characters that are printed in gold ink since gold is an auspicious color. Ensure the translation is carried out into the appropriate Chinese dialect, i.e. Mandarin or Cantonese. Your business card should include your title. If your company is the oldest or largest in your country, that fact should be highlighted on your card. Hold the card in both hands when offering it. Never write on someone's card unless so directed.

Business Card Etiquette in India

If you have a university degree or any honor, put it on your business card. Always use the right hand to give and receive business cards. Business cards need not be translated into Hindi as English is widely spoken within the business community.

Business Card Etiquette in Japan

Business cards are exchanged with great ceremony. Invest in quality cards. Always keep your business cards in pristine condition. Treat the business card you receive as you would the person. Make sure your business card includes your title. The Japanese place emphasis on status and hierarchy. Business cards are always received with two hands but can be given with only one. During a meeting, place the business cards on the table in front of you in the order people are seated. When the meeting is over, put the business cards in a business card case or a portfolio.

Business Card Etiquette in the UK

Business card etiquette is relaxed in the UK and involves little ceremony. It is not considered bad etiquette to keep cards in a pocket. Business cards should be kept clean and presentable. Do not feel obliged to hand out a business card to everyone you meet as it is not expected.

Text C How Tipping Works

Pre-reading Activity

Are you top at tipping? Try this quick quiz!

In China, it is not customary to leave your money for the meal with the wait staff. Instead, you take the check up to the cashier. So what do you do about the tip?

A. Nothing. Tipping is not customary in China.
B. Leave a small amount by rounding the check up to the nearest 10 yuan.
C. It depends on whether you are in a Western-style restaurant or a Chinese-style restaurant. Since tipping is considered a foreign custom in China, one would pay tips at Western-style restaurants, but not at Chinese-style restaurants.
D. Tip 10% of the check.
E. Tip 20% of the check.

The correct answer is A. Tipping is not expected in China; wait staff, delivery people and cab drivers are all fully salaried professionals; giving them money would be an insult to their professions and dignities. One usually pays restaurant bills at a cash register at the front. So remember, no tip. Read the following text and you will find more about cross cultural tipping etiquette.

International Tipping Customs

Michael Lynn, an associate professor of market and consumer behavior at Center for Hospitality at Cornell University, researched the variations of tipping in different countries. Comparing the types of services that were tipped in each country with personality tests that had been given to people in those countries, he came to the conclusion that countries with more "extroverted" and "neurotic" people gave tips to the greatest number of services and also tipped the largest amounts. (The US was at the top of both of those categories, by the way.)

His theory is that "extroverts are outgoing, dominating, social people" and see tipping as an incentive for the waiter to give them extra attention. Neurotics are more prone to guilt and general anxiety, making them tip more because of their perceived difference in status between themselves and the server.

Aside from these facts, other cultures definitely see tipping differently. For example, in many European restaurants, 10 to 15 percent has already been added to the restaurant bill.

You can leave extra money or round up to the next currency amount (going from 27 to 30 Euros, for example) if the service was especially good, but it is not usually necessary. In South Africa and Mexico, you will be expected to tip almost everyone. In Australia, a 10 percent gratuity is usually only added to checks at fine dining establishments, but in New Zealand, tipping is virtually nonexistent in restaurants. And in Vietnam and Argentina, tipping is illegal in restaurants.

International Tipping Tips

Each country places a different value on service. Following these few simple rules from the *Washington Post* should keep you in servers' good graces and prevent any international faux pas:

- Familiarize Yourself

Guidebooks and many country—and city-specific websites list tipping protocol for regular services. Jot down a few you think you might use, like restaurant, taxi and hotel services. If you are uncertain whether a gratuity was added to a bill, ask.

- Know the Value of the Currency

Not understanding a country's monetary system can lead to over- or under-tipping.

- Be Nice

Even if the service is not great—or even good. Customs and language barriers are just a few of the circumstances that may prevent you from seeing the situation in its entirety.

Although it is difficult to establish definite rules for tipping or not tipping, generally service has been good or when service people go out of their way to do a favor, a tip is merited. Observing cultural differences in tipping can communicate nonverbally that you have researched the country and that you consider local customs to be important.

Book to Read

Morrison, Terri, Wayne A. Conaway and George A. Borden, Ph.D. *Kiss, Bow, or Shake Hands: How to Do Business in Sixty Countries*. Vincentown, NJ: Bob Adams, 1994.

- This is Amazon.com's best-selling business etiquette book. In a global economy, it is crucial for business people to be sensitive to cultural differences. This is an invaluable book for "doing well while doing good" in your intercultural relations, covering the protocols of appointments, business entertaining, greetings, forms of address, gestures, dress, and gifts in 60 of the nations you're most likely to be doing business with. The authors are very aware that no generalizations apply to all residents of a nation, and are careful not to stereotype or judge. This is an amazing book to any business traveler or any student of the diversity of human cultures.

Movie to Watch

My Big Fat Greek Wedding (2002) is one of the most successful independent productions of all time. The wallflower Toula Portokalos is 30, lives with her tradition conscious Greek family, works in her parents' restaurant and, to the dismay of her parents, she still has not married a Greek. During the film Toula detaches herself from her family: she completes a computer course, takes on another job and falls in love with a friendly teacher called Ian Miller. To the consternation of her family the man she chooses to marry is not a Greek, but instead a vegetarian American. The culture clash leads to all manner of funny incidents.

Unit 14
Cultural Differences in Business Negotiation

> Negotiation is a delicate business, made even more delicate by different cultural understandings.
> —— Andrew Rosenbaum
>
> Despite popular beliefs to the contrary, the single greatest barrier to business success is the one erected by culture.
> —— Edward T. Hall and Mildred Reed Hall

Unit Goals

- To learn what cross-cultural negotiation is
- To understand ways in which cultural differences can impact international business negotiations
- To understand negotiation strategies and guidelines in intercultural negotiations
- To learn useful words and expressions about cultural differences in business negotiation and improve language skills

Before You Read

Multicultural Negotiations Quiz

1. People from which country tend to be the most proficient negotiators?
   A. Germany.   B. England.
   C. The United States. D. Mexico.
2. People from which country are likely to take the longest to get down to negotiations?
   A. Canada.   B. The United States.
   C. Japan.   D. Mexico.

3. People from non-negotiating cultures are most likely to negotiate over:
   A. Jewelry.   B. Clothing.
   C. Food.   D. Car.
4. The first thing savvy negotiators should do at the start of the bargaining process is _____.
   A. to build rapport   B. to introduce yourself
   C. to do research   D. to get to the bottom line
5. The best way to build rapport in negotiations is to talk about _____.
   A. the item the parties are bargaining over
   B. the price of the item
   C. the terms of the purchase
   D. anything except the subject of the negotiation
6. The Japanese are least likely to say which word during negotiations?
   A. Yes.   B. No.
   C. Maybe.   D. Later.
7. For which group is a negotiating deadline likely to be the shortest?
   A. Mexicans.   B. Asians.
   C. Americans.   D. British.
8. In cross-cultural negotiations, the practice of continuing to bargain after a contract has been signed is _____.
   A. unethical   B. unthinkable
   C. standard practice D. rare
9. Giving strong eye contact during multicultural negotiations is _____.
   A. necessary   B. questionable
   C. unnecessary   D. common courtesy
10. The group that is mostly likely to stand or sit closest during negotiations is _____.
    A. American   B. Japanese
    C. British   D. Middle Eastern
11. The group that is most likely to be prompt for a negotiation session is _____.
    A. Japanese   B. Mexican
    C. German   D. American
12. The group that is most likely to be late for a negotiation session is _____.
    A. Japanese   B. Mexican
    C. German   D. American
13. In which culture should a gift be given before negotiations begin?
    A. Japanese.   B. Mexican.
    C. German.   D. American.
14. In which culture would negotiation issues most likely be taken in a step-by-step logical order?
    A. Middle Eastern.   B. Mexican.
    C. Chinese.   D. American.
15. In which culture would issues most likely be discussed simultaneously?
    A. Middle Eastern.   B. Mexican.
    C. Chinese.   D. American.

16. In which culture would data and information likely be the most important factor in negotiations?
    A. American.   B. German.
    C. South American.   D. Canadian.
17. In which culture would relationships likely be the most important factor in negotiations?
    A. American.   B. German.
    C. South American.   D. Canadian.
18. Which group would probably be the least animated during negotiations?
    A. Japanese.   B. German.
    C. Mexican.   D. American.
19. Which culture is most likely to use group decision-making during negotiations?
    A. Japanese.   B. German.
    C. Canadian.   D. American.
20. When negotiating with Asians you will learn the most about your opponents from _____.
    A. facial expressions   B. words spoken
    C. gestures made   D. what is not said

Start to Read

Text A Cross-cultural Negotiation

Cross-cultural negotiation is one of many specialized areas within the wider field of cross-cultural communications. By taking cross-cultural negotiation training, negotiators and sales personnel give themselves an advantage over competitors.

There is an argument that proposes that culture is inconsequential to cross-cultural negotiation. It maintains that as long as a proposal is financially attractive it will succeed. However, this is a naïve way of approaching international business.

Let us look at a brief example of how cross-cultural negotiation training can benefit the international business person:

There are two negotiators dealing with the same potential client in the Middle East. Both have identical proposals and packages. One ignores the importance of cross-cultural negotiation training believing the proposal will speak for itself. The other undertakes some cross-cultural training. He/She learns about the culture, values, beliefs, etiquette and approaches to business, meetings and negotiations. Nine times out of ten the latter will succeed over the rival. This is because 1) it is likely they would have endeared themselves more to the host  negotiation team and 2) they would be able to tailor their approach to the negotiations in a way that maximizes the potential of a positive outcome.

Cross-cultural negotiation is more than just how foreigners close deals. It involves looking at all factors that can influence the proceedings. By way of highlighting this, a few brief examples of topics covered in cross-cultural negotiation training shall be offered.

Eye Contact: In the US, the UK and much of northern Europe, strong, direct eye contact conveys confidence and sincerity. In South America it is a sign of trustworthiness. However, in some cultures such as the Japanese, prolonged eye contact is considered rude and is generally avoided.

Personal Space & Touch: In Europe and North America, business people will usually leave a certain amount of distance between themselves when interacting. Touching only takes place between friends. In South America or the Middle East, business people are tactile and like to get up close. In Japan or China, it is not uncommon for people to leave a gap of four feet when conversing. Touching only takes place between close friends and family members.

Time: Western societies are very "clock conscious." Time is money and punctuality is crucial. This is also the case in countries such as Japan or China where being late would be taken as an insult. However, in South America, southern Europe and the Middle East, being on time for a meeting does not carry the same sense of urgency.

Meeting & Greeting: Most international business people meet with a handshake. In some countries this is not appropriate between genders. Some may view a weak handshake as sign of weakness whereas others would perceive a firm handshake as aggressive. How should people be addressed? Is it by first name, surname or title? Is small talk part of the proceedings or not?

Gift-Giving: In Japan and China gift-giving is an integral part of business protocol. However, in the US or UK, it has negative connotations. Should one give lavish gifts? Are they always reciprocated? Should they be wrapped? Are there numbers or colors that should be avoided?

All the above in one way or another will impact on cross-cultural negotiation and can only be learned through cross-cultural training. Doing or saying the wrong thing at the wrong time, poor communication and cross-cultural misunderstandings can all have harmful consequences.

Cross-cultural negotiation training builds its foundations upon understanding etiquettes and approaches to business abroad before focusing on cross-cultural differences in negotiation styles and techniques.

There are three interconnected aspects that need to be considered before entering into cross-cultural negotiation.

The Basis of the Relationship: In much of Europe and North America, business is contractual in nature. Personal relationships are seen as unhealthy as they can cloud objectivity and lead to complications. In South America and much of Asia, business is personal. Partnerships will only be made with those they know, trust and feel comfortable with. It is, therefore, necessary to invest in relationship building before conducting business.

Information at Negotiations: Western business culture places emphasis on clearly presented and rationally argued business proposals using statistics and facts. Other business cultures rely on similar information but with differences. For example, visual and oral communicators such as the South Americans may prefer information presented through speech or using maps, graphs and charts.

Negotiation Styles: The way in which we approach negotiation differs across cultures. For example, in the Middle East, rather than approaching topics sequentially, negotiators may discuss issues simultaneously. South Americans can become quite vocal and animated. The Japanese will negotiate in teams and decisions will be based upon consensual agreement. In Asia, decisions are usually made by the most senior figure or head of a family. In China, negotiators are highly trained in the art of gaining concessions. In Germany, decisions can take a long time due to the need to analyze information and statistics in great depth. In the UK, pressure tactics and imposing deadlines are ways of closing deals whilst in Greece this would backfire.

Clearly there are many factors that need to be considered when approaching cross-cultural negotiation. Through cross-cultural negotiation training, business personnel are given the appropriate knowledge that can help them prepare their presentations and sales pitches effectively. By tailoring your behavior and the way you approach the negotiation you will succeed in maximizing your potential.

After You Read

Knowledge Focus

1. **Pair Work: Discuss the following questions with your partner.**
   1) How important is cross-cultural negotiation training?
   2) What are the factors that can influence the proceedings of international negotiation?
   3) What does "clock conscious" mean? How do Chinese and South Americans view time differently?
   4) When entering into cross-cultural negotiation, what are the three interconnected aspects to consider?
   5) Why do South Americans prefer using maps, graphs and charts when doing business?

2. **Solo Work: Tell whether and why the following statements are true or false according to the knowledge you learned and explain why.**
   1) Overcoming cultural barriers is relatively unimportant when negotiating. (   )
   2) A conscious endeavor to manage cultural differences is required if there is to be mutual understanding. (   )
   3) If a negotiation in Japan gets heated because of different objectives, avoid eye contact with your counterpart since it could be read as aggressive and disrespectful. (   )
   4) When visiting a potential business partner in the UK for the first time, do not bring a gift along as this could raise suspicion about your motives. (   )
   5) Developing a personal relationship with persons on the other side of negotiation is always recommended. (   )
   6) In Japan, it is strongly advisable to negotiate in a team rather than as an individual. (   )
   7) Germans usually prefer contracts to be simple and high-level, since they consider them a mere formality. (   )
   8) Greeks prefer using pressure tactics and imposing deadlines to close deals. (   )
   9) Cultures that emphasize relationships may negotiate differently from cultures that

emphasize results. ( )

10) Business negotiations between Asia and North America can be difficult due to language barriers. ( )

Language Focus

1. **Choose the right explanation (from a to j) to match the underlined words in the sentences (from 1 to 10). Put the right letter in the brackets.**

   1) There is an argument that proposes that culture is <u>inconsequential</u> to cross-cultural negotiation. ( )
   2) This is a <u>naïve</u> way of approaching international business. ( )
   3) The other <u>undertakes</u> some cross-cultural training. ( )
   4) It is likely they would have <u>endeared</u> themselves more to the host negotiation team. ( )
   5) They would be able to <u>tailor</u> their approach to the negotiations in a way that maximizes the potential of a positive outcome. ( )
   6) In South America or the Middle East, business people are <u>tactile</u> and like to get up close. ( )
   7) Some may view a weak handshake as sign of weakness whereas others would perceive a firm handshake as <u>aggressive</u>. ( )
   8) Should one give lavish gifts? Are they always <u>reciprocated</u>? ( )
   9) Personal relationships are seen as unhealthy as they can <u>cloud</u> objectivity and lead to complications. ( )
   10) In China, negotiators are highly trained in the art of gaining <u>concessions</u>. ( )

   a. made attractive or lovable
   b. lacking worth or importance
   c. make fit for a specific purpose
   d. very determined to succeed or get what you want
   e. marked by or showing unaffected simplicity and lack of guile or worldly experience
   f. make less visible or unclear
   g. the act of yielding
   h. given mutually or in return
   i. enters upon an activity or enterprise
   j. of or relating to or proceeding from the sense of touch

2. **Fill in the blanks with the proper form of the words in the brackets.**

   1) Misfortune tests the _____ (sincere) of friends.
   2) He has a well-earned reputation for absolute _____ (trust).
   3) They are not related by blood, but there was a(n) _____ (common) likeness between the two boys.
   4) Would you give me half an hour to _____ (conversation) with you?
   5) Rarely did she request help but this was a matter of _____ (urgent).
   6) Hollywood holds the _____ (connote) of romance and glittering success.
   7) I hope you will tackle the problem by yourself, for I have already had enough _____ (complicate) in my life.
   8) The judge had a reputation for complete _____ (objective).

9) A set of operations is performed _____ (sequence), each of which uses the output of the previous operation as input.
10) A _____ (consent) marriage does not always end happily.

3. **Find the appropriate prepositions or adverbs that collocate with the words in bold letters.**
   1) Her rich experience gave her an **advantage** _____ other applicants for the job.
   2) The events of that evening **speak** _____ themselves.
   3) The topic **focuses** _____ the crisis in these two countries.
   4) He came to the party, but did not really **enter** _____ the spirit of it.
   5) Excessive patriotism can **lead** _____ xenophobia.
   6) The advice to **invest** _____ those shares turned out to be a bum steer—their value has fallen steadily since I bought them.
   7) Charities **rely** _____ voluntary donations/contributions.
   8) Hard work is the name of the game if you want to **succeed** _____ business.

4. **Error Correction: Each of the following sentences has at least one grammatical error. Identify the errors and make corrections.**
   1) By taking cross-cultural negotiation training, negotiators and sales personnel give themselves advantage over competitors.
   2) It maintains that as long as a proposal is financially attractive it succeed.
   3) There are two negotiators deal with the same potential client in the Middle East.
   4) They would be able to tailor their approach to the negotiations in a way maximizes the potential of a positive outcome.
   5) In US, the UK and much of northern Europe, strong, direct eye contact conveys confidence and sincerity.
   6) Doing or saying the wrong thing at the wrong time, poor communication and cross-cultural misunderstandings can both have harmful consequences.
   7) Clearly there are many factors that need to be considered when approaches cross-cultural negotiation.
   8) Because Hiroshi read this as disrespect. The negotiation essentially ended days before their talks did.
   9) You will need to choose which the two classic negotiating styles you will adopt: Contentious or problem-solving.
   10) The contentious negotiator, a tough, demanding guy who makes few compromises, can be a great success being given the right conditions.
   11) It is obviously important to learn these negotiating rituals for a given culture, even if your foreign partner turns out to not require them.
   12) It also may become difficult for them to believe in the sincerity of the other side.
   13) It is at this stage, in which the actual issues go back and forth between participants, which your awareness of negotiating behavior typical to your potential partner's culture can be put to use.
   14) The great diversity of the world's cultures makes impossible for any negotiator to understand fully all the cultures that may be encountered.
   15) Although the written contract describes the relationship, but essence of the deal is the relationship itself.
   16) That you will not receive at a first meeting is a definite commitment or rejection.

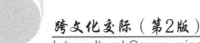

Comprehensive Work
1. **Pair Work: Analyze the following cases with your partner.**

Case Study 1

Once a US automobile parts manufacturer was shown on television trying to make a sale to some Japanese automobile firms. He was dressed in a boldly patterned cardigan sweater; his hosts were all in dark suits and white shirts. The TV camera caught a few of the hosts repeatedly looking at his sweater with something like alarm in their eyes, and looking away again. Finally it was reported that he failed to make even a single sale.

Do you think the sweater the US salesman wore was a factor in his failure to make a single sale? What was wrong with it?

If you had been there, how would you have reacted to the causally dressed salesman? Would you have decided not to buy his products just because of the impression his clothes had left on you?

Case Study 2

The marketing manager of a US knitwear firm was delighted with a multi-million-dollar order for men's underwear it received from a department store chain in Saudi Arabia. The jockey shorts were packaged in the usual way (three pairs to a package, with a picture of a male modeling the briefs) and sent off to the customer in Saudi Arabia. However, Saudi customs officials were shocked to see a near totally nude man on packages that would be displayed in plain sight of Saudi women and children. Consequently, to satisfy Saudi customs officials, the entire shipment of men's briefs had to be sent back to the United States for repackaging, costing the firm thousands of dollars.

What was wrong with the packages of men's underwear shipped to Saudi Arabia?

What do you think would be a proper way to package the underwear in order to be accepted by Saudi Arabians?

2. **Group Work**

The following statements are characteristics of US style of negotiation. Discuss with your group members: What cultural characteristics of American are they suggesting? What would be the statement for Chinese negotiators?

1) "I can handle this by myself."
2) "Please call me John."
3) "Pardon my Chinese."
4) "Let's go to the point."
5) "Speed up. What do you think?"
6) "Let's put our cards on the table."
7) "A deal is a deal."

Unit 14 Cultural Differences in Business Negotiation

_____
_____
_____
_____
_____
_____
_____

3. Writing

Text C listed "ten ways" that culture affects the style of negotiation. Choose one way in which there are cultural differences between China and the English-speaking countries. Study it further and then write a composition on it.

Read More

Text B   How to Steer Clear of Pitfalls in Cross-cultural Negotiation

Henry in Los Angeles and Hiroshi in Tokyo both like Armani suits, baseball, Mozart, and good Bordeaux. But Henry recently spoke for days with Hiroshi, his potential business partner, and yet the barriers between them were never broached — and the deal did not get inked.

The problem had to do with different conceptions of the negotiation process itself and misinterpretations of the other's behavior. For Henry, negotiation is about pushing through a deal. When Henry did not think their discussion was moving forward as quickly as he thought it should, his arguments became increasingly forceful. Because Hiroshi read this as disrespect, the negotiation essentially ended days before their talks did.

Although globalized communications and marketing have made the world smaller in many ways, deep differences between cultures remain. Despite similar tastes, Henry and Hiroshi each approach negotiation in a way heavily conditioned by his national culture. Because they sat down at the table without understanding the other's assumptions about the negotiation process, all they ended up with was an impasse.

Negotiation is always a delicate business, requiring determination and diplomacy in equal measure. But finessing a cross-cultural negotiation is a particular challenge. Here are some tips that can help you put together a deal with a foreign partner.

Understand Expectations

Your negotiating partner's expectations of the negotiation may well be very different from yours. Like you, he will want to succeed, but success may not mean the same thing to him and his co-nationals as it does to you.

Decision-making styles may be different, too. American managers usually make decisions by themselves, while Japanese managers tend to make decisions by consensus, a

179

practice that can add time to the negotiation process. Americans place a high value on flexibility, whereas once a Japanese manager has reached a decision, he believes it is shameful to change it, says Tokyo-based management consultant Mitsugu Iwashita, director of the Intercultural and Business Communication Center. Understanding these underlying attitudes helps you see what your potential partner's priorities are, and you can then adapt your strategy accordingly.

Establish Common Ground and Choose Your Style

Find anything that will allow your foreign colleague to share something with you. This can help you get past "people" problems—ego wars, saving face, and so on—which is a good tactic because these problems can crop up where you may least expect them.

Now the real work can begin. You will need to choose which of two classic negotiating styles you will adopt: Contentious or problem-solving. The contentious negotiator, a tough, demanding guy who makes few compromises, can be a great success given the right conditions. He either wins or loses, but never comes to a conditional agreement. The problem-solving negotiator takes a broader view, attempting to get as much as she can without handing out a deal breaker. She establishes common ground wherever she can find it and approaches negotiations on a step-by-step basis.

While one has to be careful about generalizing across cultures, experts agree that a problem-solving approach to cross-cultural negotiations is prudent. The problem-solving approach helps to avoid blunders, says Elaine Winters, co-author of *Cultural Issues in Business Communication* (2005). But there are limits to this approach. In many cultures, negotiation is ritualized, especially in its early stages. It is obviously important to learn these negotiating rituals for a given culture, even if your foreign partner turns out not to require them. Germans, for example, often need to spend a large part of the initial negotiations in number crunching. All the facts and figures must be agreed upon, and woe betide the negotiator who makes a mistake! However, this German trait is not really about number crunching; it is a confidence-building ritual in which two potential partners run through a series of routine checks just to display trustworthiness. So the problem-solving approach, which would try to find common ground quickly, could prove threatening for the ritual negotiators.

"When confronted with cultural differences in negotiating styles, we need to be aware of the potentially adverse effects of a flexible, mixed style," says Willem Mastenbroek, director of the Holland Consulting Group (Amsterdam) and professor of organizational culture and communication at the Free University of Amsterdam. "If it is not understood, people may perceive it as smooth and suave behavior and resent it. Because they are not able to counter it with equal flexibility, they may feel clumsy and awkward, in some way even inferior. It may also become difficult for  them to believe in the sincerity of the other side. They may see it as an effort to lure them into a game defined by established groups which will put them at a disadvantage."

Unit 14   Cultural Differences in Business Negotiation

Manage the Negotiation

Let's assume that you have passed successfully through the initial stages of the negotiation and that you have agreed upon common ground with your prospective partner. The game of tactics now broadens. It is at this stage, in which the actual issues go back and forth between participants, that your awareness of negotiating behavior typical to your potential partner's culture can be put to use.

Italian negotiators, for example, will often try to push through this stage quite quickly, repeatedly insisting on their terms to tire out their opponents. Knowing this, a foreign negotiator may find a good tactic is to display no great hurry to deal—change the subject, digress, etc.

On the other hand, Chinese negotiators usually make one offer after another at this point to test the limits of a possible deal. According to Winters, nonverbal communication in negotiations with a Chinese businessman can be quite important. He may say little in response to your questions, and expect you to garner what you need to know from his gestures and from the context of whatever he does say. More demonstrative Western cultures can find this conduct very difficult to work with, but the application of patience and deductive reasoning can take you a long way.

Most Europeans will not break off discussions unless they are deeply offended, but Asian negotiators are often happy to drop the project if they are uncomfortable with some aspect of the negotiations. If this happens, try to backtrack and fix the problem.

But in focusing on your potential partner's culture, do not lose sight of him as an individual. It is always best to learn as much as you can about his personality and communication style. "Personalize negotiation methods and approaches," Winters says. "Don't ignore culture (impossible anyway!), try to treat it as background; focus on the capabilities of the specific individuals at the table. This is frequently successful because a new, mutually agreed-upon culture is being created just for this effort."

Questions for Discussion or Reflection

1. What is wrong with the communication between Henry and Hiroshi?
2. What do we do to steer clear of pitfalls in cross-cultural negotiation?
3. To what extent can we say culture plays a decisive role in successfully doing business abroad?

Text C   The Top Ten Ways Culture Affects Negotiating Style

Negotiation practices differ from culture to culture and as such culture can influence "negotiating style" — the way persons from different cultures conduct themselves in negotiating sessions.

The great diversity of the world's cultures makes it impossible for any negotiator, no matter how skilled and experienced, to understand fully all the cultures that may be encountered. How then should an executive prepare to cope with culture in making deals in Singapore this week and Seoul the next? One approach is to identify important areas where cultural differences may arise during the negotiation process. The following "top ten" elements of negotiating behavior constitute a basic framework for identifying cultural differences that may arise during the negotiation process. Applying this framework in your international business negotiations may enable you to understand your counterpart better and to anticipate possible misunderstandings.

1. Negotiating Goal: Contract or Relationship?

Negotiators from different cultures may tend to view the purpose of a negotiation differently. For many American executives, the goal of a negotiation, first and foremost, is to arrive at a signed contract between the parties. Americans consider a signed contract as a definitive set of rights and duties that strictly binds the two sides and determines their interaction thereafter. Japanese, Chinese, and other cultural groups in Asia, it is said, often consider that the goal of a negotiation is not a signed contract, but the creation of a relationship between the two sides. Although the written contract describes the relationship, the essence of the deal is the relationship itself.

It is, therefore, important to determine how your counterparts view the purpose of your negotiation. If relationship negotiators sit on the other side of the table, merely convincing them of your ability to deliver on a low-cost contract may not be enough to land you the deal. You may also have to persuade them, from the very first meeting, that your two organizations have the potential to build a rewarding relationship over the long term. On the other hand, if the other side is basically a contract deal maker, trying to build a relationship may be a waste of time and energy.

2. Negotiating Attitude: Win-Lose or Win-Win?

Because of differences in culture, personality, or both, business persons appear to approach deal making with one of two basic attitudes: that a negotiation is either a process in which both can gain (win-win) or a struggle in which, of necessity, one side wins and the other side loses (win-lose). Win-win negotiators see deal making as a collaborative, problem-solving process; win-lose negotiators view it as confrontational. As you enter negotiations, it is important to know which type of negotiator is sitting across the table from you.

3. Personal Style: Informal or Formal?

Personal style concerns the way a negotiator talks to others, uses titles, dresses, speaks, and interacts with other persons. Culture strongly influences the personal style of negotiators. It has been observed, for example, that Germans have a more formal style than Americans. A negotiator with a formal style insists on addressing counterparts by their titles, avoids personal anecdotes, and refrains from questions touching on the private or family life of members of the other negotiating team. A negotiator with an informal style tries to start the discussion on a first-name basis, quickly seeks to develop a personal, friendly relationship with the other team, and may take off his jacket and roll up his sleeves when deal making begins in earnest. Each culture has its own formalities with their own special meanings. They are another means of communication among the persons sharing that culture, another form of adhesive that binds them together as a community. For an American, calling someone by the first name is an act of friendship and therefore a good thing. For a Japanese, the use of the first name at a first meeting is an act of disrespect and, therefore, bad.

Negotiators in foreign cultures must respect appropriate formalities. As a general rule, it is always safer to adopt a formal posture and move to an informal stance, if the situation warrants it, than to assume an informal style too quickly.

4. Communication: Direct or Indirect?

Methods of communication vary among cultures. Some emphasize direct and simple methods of communication; others rely heavily on indirect and complex methods. The latter may use circumlocutions, figurative forms of speech, facial expressions, gestures and other kinds of body language. In a culture that values directness, such as the American or the Israeli, you can expect to receive a clear and definite response to your proposals and questions. In cultures that rely on indirect communication, such as the Japanese, reaction to your proposals may be gained by interpreting seemingly vague comments, gestures, and other signs. What you will not receive at a first meeting is a definite commitment or rejection.

The confrontation of these styles of communication in the same negotiation can lead to friction. For example, the indirect ways Japanese negotiators express disapproval have often led foreign business executives to believe that their proposals were still under consideration when in fact the Japanese side had rejected them.

5. Sensitivity to Time: High or Low?

Discussions of national negotiating styles invariably treat a particular culture's attitudes toward time. It is said that Germans are always punctual, Latins are habitually late, Japanese negotiate slowly, and Americans are quick to make a deal.

6. Emotionalism: High or Low?

Accounts of negotiating behavior in other cultures almost always point to a particular group's tendency to act emotionally. According to the stereotype, Latin Americans show their emotions at the negotiating table, while the Japanese and many other Asians hide their feelings. Obviously, individual personality plays a role here. There are passive Latins and hot-headed Japanese. Nonetheless, various cultures have different rules as to the appropriateness and form of displaying emotions, and these rules are brought to the negotiating table as well. Latin Americans and the Spanish were the cultural groups that ranked themselves highest with respect to emotionalism in a clearly statistically significant fashion. Among Europeans, the Germans and English ranked as least emotional, while among Asians the Japanese held that position, but to a lesser degree.

7. Form of Agreement: General or Specific?

Whether a negotiator's goal is a contract or a relationship, the negotiated transaction in almost all cases will be encapsulated in some sort of written agreement. Cultural factors influence the form of the written agreement that the parties make. Generally, Americans prefer very detailed contracts that attempt to anticipate all possible circumstances and eventualities, no matter how unlikely. Why? Because the deal is the contract itself, and one must refer to the contract to handle new situations that may arise. Other cultures, such as the Chinese, prefer a contract in the form of general principles rather than detailed rules. Why? Because, it is claimed, that the essence of the deal is the relationship between the parties. If unexpected circumstances arise, the parties should look primarily to their relationship, not the contract, to solve the problem. So, in some cases, a Chinese negotiator may interpret the American drive to stipulate all contingencies as evidence of a lack of confidence in the stability of the underlying relationship.

8. Building an Agreement: Bottom Up or Top Down?

Related to the form of the agreement is the question of whether negotiating a business deal is an inductive or a deductive process. Does it start from an agreement on general principles and proceed to specific items, or does it begin with an agreement on specifics, such as price, delivery date, and product quality, the sum total of which becomes the contract? Different cultures tend to emphasize one approach over the other. Some observers believe that the French prefer to begin with agreement on general principles, while Americans tend to seek agreement first on specifics. For Americans, negotiating a deal is basically making a series of compromises and trade-offs on a long list of particulars. For the French, the essence is to agree on basic principles that will guide and indeed determine the negotiation process afterward. The agreed-upon general principles become the framework, the skeleton, upon which the contract is built.

9. Team Organization: One Leader or Group Consensus?

In any negotiation, it is important to know how the other side is organized, who has the authority to make commitments, and how decisions are made. Culture is one important factor that affects how executives organize themselves to negotiate a deal. Some cultures emphasize the individual while others stress the group. These values may influence the organization of each side in a negotiation.

One extreme is the negotiating team with a supreme leader who has complete authority to decide all matters. Many American teams tend to follow this approach. Other cultures, notably the Japanese and the Chinese, stress team negotiation and consensus decision making. When you negotiate with such a team, it may not be apparent who the leader is and who has the authority to commit the side. In the first type, the negotiating team is usually small; in the second it is often large. For example, in negotiations in China on a major deal, it would not be uncommon for the Americans to arrive at the table with three people and for the Chinese to show up with ten. Similarly, the one-leader team is usually prepared to make commitments more quickly than a negotiating team organized on the basis of consensus. As a result, the consensus type of organization usually takes more time to negotiate a deal. Despite the Japanese reputation for consensus arrangements, only 45 percent of the Japanese respondents claimed to prefer a negotiating team based on consensus. The Brazilians, the Chinese, and the Mexicans to a far greater degree than any other groups preferred one-person leadership, a reflection perhaps of the political traditions of those countries.

10. Risk Taking: High or Low?

Research supports the conclusion that certain cultures are more risk averse than others. In deal making, the negotiators' cultures can affect the willingness of one side to take risks — to divulge information, try new approaches, and tolerate uncertainties in a proposed course of action. The Japanese, with their emphasis on requiring large amount of information and their intricate group decision-making process, tend to be risk averse. Americans, French, British, and Indians by comparison, are risk takers.

Negotiating styles, like personalities, have a wide range of variation. The ten negotiating traits discussed above can help you better understand the negotiating styles and approaches of counterparts from other cultures. Equally important, they may help you determine how your own negotiating style appears to those same counterparts.

Summarize the negotiating style of Asian and the Western countries under the topics listed in Text C.

Topics	Asian Countries	Western Countries
Negotiating Goal		
Negotiating Attitude		
Personal Style		
Communication		
Sensitivity to Time		
Emotionalism		
Form of Agreement		
Building an Agreement		
Team Organization		
Risk Taking		

For Fun

Book to Read

Tan, Joo-Seng and Elizabeth NK Lim. *Strategies for Effective Cross-cultural Negotiation: The F.R.A.M.E. Approach*. Hong Kong: McGraw-Hill Education, 2004.

- This book is about strategic negotiation across cultures. It is written for negotiators and students of negotiation who seek to understand the principles and processes of cross-cultural negotiation and develop effective strategies for negotiating in different cultures.
- This book takes a completely different approach in the analysis of cross-border negotiations by examining the negotiations of US multinational companies in three major economies in Asia: China, Japan and India. Using a case study approach, the book presents an incisive analysis of the successes and failures in cross-cultural negotiations. Further, it provides valuable insights that will deepen negotiators' understanding of cross-cultural negotiations as well as strengthen negotiators' capability to deal with major issues in cross-cultural negotiations.

Movie to Watch

Gung Ho (1986) is an amusing culture clash comedy moive, released by Paramount Pictures, and starring Michael Keaton and Gedde Watanabe. This movie portrays the takeover of an American car plant by a Japanese corporation (although the title of the film is actually a Chinese expression for "work together").

　　A small-town labor leader convinces a Japanese auto manufacturer to take over his town's bankrupt auto plant. After the inevitable culture clashes, particularly over Japanese imposed work rules, the workers undertake a month-long "contest" to show that their individualistic American methods can surpass the best efforts of an auto plant in Japan. They succeed only after they embrace the communal approach of the Japanese. Central to the movie are American and Japanese cultural differences, particularly in management styles.

Unit 15
Developing Intercultural Competence

> Studying a second language without learning the culture is like learning how to drive a car by studying a driver's manual and never getting behind a steering wheel.
>
> —— K. J. Irving

Unit Goals

- To learn to adjust in a new culture more effectively and develop skills for culture reentry
- To explore the potential improvements that can be made to the intercultural competencies of the future
- To learn useful words and expressions about developing intercultural competence and improve language skills

Before You Read

Getting Along with the Chinese

Suppose you are studying in the United States. An American friend tells you he is about to study in Beijing for two years and wants you to give him some advice on how to get along well with Chinese people. Discuss with your partner and make a list of tips for him. State each as a piece of advice. Be prepared to share your list with your classmates.

Start to Read

Text A A Four-step Approach to Intercultural Communication Training

Perhaps a substantial way to conclude this book on intercultural communications is to give some helpful suggestions on how to combine the components of communication competence into a practical training approach. What is being presented here is a four-step approach based on the work of Brislin, including awareness, knowledge, motivations, and skills.

1. Raise Awareness

First of all, we should be aware of the importance of intercultural communication competence. Sue *et al.* identified four awareness competencies.

- Self-awareness

The first competency requires people to move from being culturally unaware to becoming aware of the way their own lives have been shaped by the culture into which they were born. This should also be accompanied by learning to respect and be sensitive toward culturally different others.

- Consciousness of One's Values and Biases and Their Effects

The second competency requires conscious awareness of one's own values and biases and how they affect the way one interacts with culturally different people. This can at least help people monitor their ethnocentrism.

- Necessity of Becoming Comfortable with Differences

It is neither possible nor healthy for people to adapt themselves to every value system in which they find themselves. People should not be afraid to recognize and admit that there are differences. In addition, they should feel comfortable with the awareness that they may not be able to behave according to these other values.

- Sensitivity to Circumstances

Being sensitive to circumstances implies that human beings are not infallible and that there may be certain cultural groups in which some people have a very hard time interacting. Instead of denying this difficulty, sometimes it is wiser to refer the client (or business partner) to someone else who is better able to serve the client.

2. Obtain Knowledge

Knowledge refers to the cognitive information you need to have about the people, the context, and the norms of appropriateness that operate in a specific culture. Without such knowledge, it is unlikely that you will interpret correctly the meanings of other people's messages, nor will you be able to select behaviors that are appropriate and that allow you to achieve your objectives. Consequently, you will not be able to determine what the appropriate and effective behaviors are in a particular context.

"Knowledge" here is divided into **culture-general** and **cultural-specific knowledge**. The former refers to specific theories or themes that are commonly encountered in intercultural interactions regardless of the cultures involved. It provides insights into the intercultural communication process abstractly and can therefore be a very powerful tool in making sense of cultural practices. The latter refers to customs, etiquettes, and rules that are specific to the various cultures. Such information is used to understand a particular culture. For example, businesspeople may need essential information about the cultural dynamics of doing business in a specific country. In addition, the knowledge of one's own cultural system will definitely help one to understand another culture.

3. Enhance Motivation

Motivation includes the overall set of emotional associations that people have as they anticipate and actually communicate interculturally. As with knowledge, different aspects of the emotional terrain contribute to the achievement of intercultural competence. Human emotional reactions include both feelings and intentions. The former refers to the emotional or affective states that you experience when communicating with someone from a different culture. Feelings involve your general sensitivity to other cultures and your attitudes towards the specific culture and individuals with whom you must interact. The latter refers to the goals, plans, objectives and desires that focus and guide your choices in a particular intercultural interaction. If your intentions are positive, accurate, and reciprocated by the people with whom you are interacting, your intercultural competences will likely be enhanced.

4. Master Skills

Finally, skills refer to how well the behaviors that are regarded as appropriate and effective are actually performed. Understanding the theories and concepts in intercultural communication does not automatically lead to culturally sensitive behaviors. People who are aware of the need to take swimming lessons, understand the basic ideas behind swimming, and have overcome emotional barriers  and are strongly motivated are still unable to swim. The prior steps are necessary, but they alone are insufficient to make competent swimmers. In the same way, people who are aware, emotionally prepared, and knowledgeable about intercultural issues are not necessarily competent communicators until they also have practiced the appropriate skills.

"Skills" can also be divided into **cultural general** and **cultural specific skills**. Cultural general skills, such as the ability to tolerate ambiguity, manage stress, establish realistic expectations, and demonstrate flexibility and empathy are helpful tools in all types of intercultural adjustment. Cultural specific skills cover a large area, which can be trained and developed through your everyday lives and business practices.

In short, intercultural communication competence requires sufficient awareness, knowledge, motivations, and skills. Each of these components alone is insufficient to achieve intercultural communication competence.

After You Read

Knowledge Focus

1. Pair Work: Discuss the following questions with your partner.

   1) What are the four components of four-step approach to intercultural communication

training?
2) What are the four awareness competencies mentioned in the text?
3) What is cultural-general knowledge? In what way is it different from cultural-specific knowledge?
4) What are the two kinds of motivation mentioned in the text?
5) What are the appropriate and effective skills in intercultural communication?

2. **Solo Work: Tell whether the following statements are true or false according to the knowledge you learned and explain why.**
1) One should respect cultural differences in intercultural communication. (　)
2) Being aware of the one's values and biases and their effects can help people monitor their ethnocentrism. (　)
3) Cultural-specific knowledge refers to specific theories or themes that are commonly encountered in intercultural interactions regardless of the cultures involved. (　)
4) Intercultural negotiation requires business people to be equipped with cultural-general knowledge — customs, etiquettes, and rules of a specific country. (　)
5) Motivation can be divided into cultural general and cultural specific motivation. (　)
6) One's intercultural competences can be enhanced if his/her intentions are positive, accurate, and reciprocated by the people with whom you are interacting. (　)
7) One can automatically become sensitive to culture by learning the theories and concepts in intercultural communication. (　)
8) Cultural specific skills can be trained and developed through everyday lives and business practices. (　)

Language Focus
1. **Choose the right explanation (from a to h) to match the underlined words in the sentences (from 1 to 8). Put the right letter in the brackets.**
1) Perhaps a substantial way to conclude this book on intercultural communications is to give some helpful suggestions on how to combine the components of communication competence into a practical training approach. (　)
2) The second competency requires conscious awareness of one's own values and biases and how they affect the way one interacts with culturally different people. (　)
3) This can at least help people monitor their ethnocentrism. (　)
4) It provides insights into the intercultural communication process abstractly and can therefore be a very powerful tool in making sense of cultural practices. (　)
5) Different aspects of the emotional terrain contribute to the achievement of intercultural competence. (　)
6) If your intentions are positive, accurate, and reciprocated by the people with whom you are interacting, your intercultural competences will likely be enhanced. (　)
7) Cultural general skills, such as the ability to tolerate ambiguity, manage stress, establish realistic expectations, and demonstrate flexibility and empathy are helpful tools in all types of intercultural adjustment. (　)
8) Being sensitive to circumstances implies that human beings are not infallible and that there may be certain cultural groups in which some people have a very hard time interacting. (　)
a. tendencies to be either for or against something or someone

b. belief in the superiority of one's own ethnic group
c. never wrong
d. large in size or value
e. the power of using your mind to understand something deeply
f. the ability to imagine and experience someone else's feelings
g. given or done in return
h. the area of land, and whether it is rough, smooth, easy or difficult to cross

2. **Fill in the blanks with the proper form of the words in the brackets.**
   1) Men are often more _____ (aware) of their feelings than women.
   2) How can we provide them with the _____ (motivate) to learn?
   3) We will not buy a car until the _____ (necessary) arises.
   4) It is unnecessary to worry about it because this is a(n) _____ (fallible) plan.
   5) He is full of good _____ (intend), but can do nothing to help.
   6) The food was _____ (sufficient) for our needs, so we have to find more resources.
   7) There were several _____ (ambiguous) in her statement.
   8) He is very _____ (knowledge) about plants.

3. **Find the appropriate prepositions or adverbs that collocate with the words in bold letters.**
   1) We cannot always **combine** work _____ pleasure.
   2) Their sudden attack made us more **aware** _____ the danger around us.
   3) She is determined to do **regardless** _____ all consequences.
   4) The door **communicates** _____ my room.
   5) He is too **sensitive** _____ criticism.
   6) For knowledge **involved** _____ computer, you can ask him.
   7) The testimony sheds more light on how former Commissioner **interacted** _____ her employees.
   8) For further particulars, please **refer** _____ Chapter Ten.

4. **Error Correction: Each of the following sentences has at least one grammatical error. Identify the errors and make corrections.**
   1) Perhaps a substantial way to conclude this book on intercultural communications is to give some helpful suggestion on how to combine the components of communication competence into a practical training approach.
   2) What is being presented here is a four-step approach basing on the work of Brislin, including awareness, knowledge, motivations, and skills.
   3) The first competency requires people should move from being culturally unaware to becoming aware of the way their own lives have been shaped by the culture into which they were born.
   4) It is neither possible nor healthy for people to adapt themselves to every value system which they find themselves.
   5) Instead of denying this difficulty, sometimes it is wiser to refer the client to someone else who is able better to serve the client.
   6) The former refers to the emotional or affective states that you experience when communicate with someone from a different culture.
   7) Without such knowledge, it is unlikely that you will interpret correctly the meanings of other people's messages, nor you will be able to select behaviors that are

appropriate.

8) The former refers to specific theories or themes that commonly encountered in intercultural interactions regardless of the cultures involved.
9) Finally, skills refer to how good the behaviors that are regarded as appropriate and effective are actually performed.
10) People who are aware of the need to take swimming lessons, understand the basic ideas behind swimming, and have overcome emotional barriers and are strongly motivated still unable to swim.
11) Cultural specific skills cover a large area can be trained and developed through your everyday lives and business practices.
12) Each of these components alone is insufficient to achieving intercultural communication competence.
13) The issue of stereotypes and generalizations have to be tackled within this context.
14) While the former can open the door to communication, and the latter will inevitably impose sanctions and barriers to effective intercultural exchanges.
15) This is commonly connected to the notion that everyone is an individual and can only be dealt with such as.
16) It does not only serve as a tool for communication but also a "system of representation" for perception and thinking.

Comprehensive Work

1. Pair Work: Analyze the following cases with your partner.

Case Study 1

At a 1970 summit meeting between U.S. President Richard Nixon and the Japanese Prime Minister Eisaku Sato, they discussed a growing problem concerning trade in textiles between Japan and the United States. Nixon, for domestic political reasons, put heavy pressure upon Sato to curtail Japan's proliferating textile exports to the United States. In response, Sato used a Japanese phrase which, loosely translated, means "I'll do my damnedest." All that Sato meant to convey was that, as they were on such good terms with each other, he would look into the problem and see if there was some way he could alleviate it without too many ugly repercussions. To Nixon, however, it sounded as though Sato had promised to remedy the situation.

During the next few weeks both were shocked at the consequences in their meeting. Nixon was infuriated to learn that the new policies he expected were not forthcoming, and he bitterly concluded that he had been double-crossed. On the other hand, Sato was upset to find that he had unwittingly triggered a new wave of hostility toward his country.

1) Why did Nixon think that he had been deceived by Sato?
2) What can we learn from this case about the differences between the Japanese and Americans in the way they normally communicate?

Case Study 2

A French woman who had just come to live in the United States said that she was really shocked by the way Americans behaved on the telephone. In some cases, when she attempted to converse with American acquaintances who answered her phone call, they would ask whom she wanted to speak with, and, without allowing her to continue, they would hand the phone over directly to the person she intended to speak with, as if they did not like chatting with her. On other occasions, she answered the phone, heard the voice of an acquaintance, and was surprised and hurt when the caller, instead of greeting and conversing with her, simply asked for somebody else. Apart from that, she sometimes felt a little annoyed because, unlike people in France, many American callers did not say anything to apologize for disturbing her.

1) Why did the French woman feel shocked and hurt by the way Americans behaved on the telephone?
2) What can you say about the habitual Chinese way of making telephone calls?

2. Group Work

Each of the following sentences contains some ethnocentric attitude. Edit the statements so that they are no longer ethnocentric.

- Fantonia (a fictitious country) is a superior country because it has produced the world's greatest literature.
- The Fantonian language is the best one for poetry.
- If everyone did things the Fantonian way, the world would be a better place.
- Non-Fantonians do everything the wrong way round.
- Fantonian has produced the greatest technology in the world.

3. Writing

Search the Internet and try to find out information about the two cities—Shanghai and Chicago. Compare these two cities. What differences can you think of? How should we look at cultural differences? Write a composition about your attitudes toward the differences.

Read More

Text B   Developing Intercultural Communication Competence

To identify the positive attributes applicable to individual intercultural communication and the extent to which a developed intercultural competence can help a practitioner, we have to look at the opposite of intercultural communication, mono-cultural communication.

Mono-cultural communication is based on common behavior, language and values. This means that the day-to-day interaction between members of the same culture is based on roughly common definitions. These similarities allow the members of the same cultural background to be able to predict the behavior of others and assume a common perception of reality. Mono-cultural communication therefore is based on similarities.

Intercultural communication does not allow for assumptions of similarity to be made that easily. If we define cultures by their difference of language, behavior, and values, these differences have to be recognized. Intercultural communication therefore, is based on differences.

The issue of stereotypes and generalizations has to be tackled within this context. It is often a matter of expediency to work with generalizations and stereotypes. More important factors are, whether the stereotypes are based on respect for the other culture (positive stereotypes) or by disrespect (negative stereotypes). While the former can open the door to communication, the latter will inevitably impose sanctions and barriers to effective intercultural exchanges.

A related aspect is the assimilationist approach to intercultural communication. This is commonly connected to the notion that everyone is an individual and can only be dealt with as such. It normally implies that the individual should change to enable monocultural communication and that the host society should avoid the dangers, pitfalls and the hard work required by intercultural communication.

What then are the attributes needed to establish effective and meaningful intercultural communication?

- Firstly, there is language. It does not only serve as a tool for communication but also as a "system of representation" for perception and thinking.
- Secondly, there is nonverbal behavior or communication. In some cultures the nonverbal way to express things is much more common and much more important than in many European cultures. Nonverbal communication can be something, as Hall defined, "in which most of the information is already in the person, while very little is in the (...) explicit transmitted part of the message." Therefore, the understanding of the "hidden" messages of nonverbal behavior in some cultures can be absolutely essential in dealing effectively with members from these backgrounds.
- Thirdly, communication style. There may be quite a difference between the ways an European might describe a problem and someone from an African background. Some cultures may go straight to the point whilst others may circle round the topic. The difference between a linear and a more contextual way of expressing things can cause anger, impatience and misunderstanding. This can be avoided or at least limited by some basic knowledge of different communication styles.
- Fourthly, values and assumptions. Kluckhohn and Strodtbeck have developed five dimensions of cultural assumptions: people's relationship to the environment, to each other, to activity, to time, and to the basic nature of human beings, operating either individualistically or collectively. Knowing that someone operates as an individual with an apprehension towards authoritarianism or operates as a member of a group, with an inherent subservience towards a superior, provides insight into how someone may adapt to a workplace or job in a different culture.

There are four underlying assumptions that ensure the success of individual intercultural communication:

1. The smaller the similarities between two cultures, the more problematic intercultural communication is.
2. Intercultural interaction offers the possibility of social change arising from new ideas and insights that will not always be immediately apparent.

3. Only if you operate as *partners* from different cultures, action on an equal basis will be ensured.
4. These plans for action will be more successful if a high degree of cultural awareness, i.e. of intercultural competence, is available.

Questions for Discussion or Reflection

1. In what way is intercultural communication different from mono-cultural communication?
2. What are the attributes needed to establish effective and meaningful intercultural communication?
3. What are the four underlying assumptions that ensure the success of individual intercultural communication?

Text C Cultural Awareness

People usually are not aware of their culture. The way that we interact and do things in our everyday lives seems "natural" to us. We are unaware of our culture because we are so close to it and know it so well. For most people, it is as if their learned behavior was biologically inherited. It is usually only when they come into contact with people from another culture that they become aware that their patterns of behavior are not universal.

It is impossible to be entirely objective when we observe another culture. Having been brought up within the context of a particular culture, we have been influenced and shaped by its values, even if we cannot articulate them. Although it should be one's goal to observe another culture with pure objectivity, this is very hard to do. We must remember that in comparing cultures, "different" does not mean "bad" or "inferior" — it just means "different." It is important to remember that although many moments of discomfort occur when we are interacting with people from other cultures, no one culture is inherently better or worse than any other. Each culture has its own set of values, norms, and ways of doing things that are considered "right" for it. That one culture's way of doing things is right for its people does not necessarily mean it is "right" for everybody, and herein lies the potential conflict in cross-cultural encounters.

As a point of reference, an initial step towards developing respect for cultural differences is to look for situations from your own life in which you would behave like a person from another culture. You can learn to appreciate and respect behaviors and values different from your own. Thinking about situations in your own life may help you understand that behaviors that seemingly differ are different only in terms of the type of situation in which you observe them, not in terms of their function. This will prevent you from prematurely valuing a behavior as negative and, more importantly, help you understand what the other person is actually trying to do. Respect is most effectively developed once you realize that most cultural differences are in yourself,

even if you have not yet recognized them. For example, you may think that certain ethnic groups are cold and distant. You never know what they are feeling or thinking. But, do you allow yourself to think about why you are warm and hospitable? In fact, the main cultural differences among nations lie in values, not just observable behavior. Once you understand the meaning of others' values, you will have a better grasp of their behavior. Becoming more aware of the influence of cultural values has many positive consequences. It leads to better understanding of ourselves and others. We become more tolerant and less defensive, and we can enjoy cultural differences as well as the similarities.

Questions for Discussion or Reflection

Discuss the following statements with your group members.
1. People usually are unaware of their culture until they come into contact with people from another culture.
2. In comparing cultures, "different" does not mean "bad" or "inferior."
3. Once you understand the meaning of others' values, you will have a better grasp of their behavior.
4. Developing respect for cultural differences is to look for situations from your own life in which you would behave like a person from another culture.

For Fun

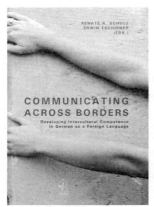

Book to Read

Schulz, Renate A. and Erwin Tschirner. eds. *Communicating across Borders: Developing Intercultural Competence in German as a Foreign Language*. Munich: Iudicium Verlag, 2008.

• This book is a compilation of selected papers presented at an international Expertenseminar on the topic of intercultural competence hosted jointly by the AATG and the Herder Institute of the University of Leipzig in June 2007. This joint effort attempts to define an important subdiscipline within German as a foreign language, indeed within foreign language teaching in general, by some of the leading experts on this topic from both sides of the Atlantic.

Movie to Watch

People are born with good hearts, but they grow up and learn prejudices. *Crash* (2004) is a movie that brings out bigotry and racial stereotypes. It is set in Los Angeles, a city with a cultural mix of every nationality. The story begins when several people are involved in a multi-car accident. From that point, we are taken back to the day before the crash, seeing the lives of several characters, and the problems each encounters during that day. An LAPD cop is trying to get medical help for his father, but he is having problems with a black HMO clerk who will not give his father permission to see another doctor. He in turn takes out his frustration on a black couple during a traffic stop. A socialite and District Attorney are carjacked at gunpoint by two black teenagers. Sandra takes out her anger on a Mexican locksmith who is changing the door locks to their home. Later that night, the locksmith is again robbed of his dignity by a Persian store-owner. Many of the characters switch from being bad person to hero in ways that may surprise you.

主要参考文献

- Chen, Guo-Ming, William J. Starosta. (2007)《跨文化交际学基础》[M]. 上海:上海外语教育出版社.
- Gudykunst, William B. (2007) *Cross-cultural and Intercultural Communication*. Shanghai: Shanghai Foreign Language Education Press.
- Samovar, Larry A., Richard E. Porter, Lisa A. Stefani. (2000) *Communication Between Cultures*(跨文化交际). Beijing: Foreign Language Teaching and Research Press.
- Samovar, Larry A., et al. (2007) *Intercultural Communication: A Reader*. Shanghai: Shanghai Foreign Language Education Press.
- Snow, Don 编著. (2004)《跨文化交际技巧——如何跟西方人打交道》(教师用书)[M]. 上海:上海外语教育出版社.
- Snow, Don 编著. (2004)《跨文化交际技巧——如何跟西方人打交道》(学生用书)[M]. 上海:上海外语教育出版社.
- Xi, Jinping. (2000) *Xi Jinping: The Governance of China* (Volume Ⅲ). Beijing: Foreign Languages Press.

- Business Card Etiquette: http://www.streetdirectory.com/travel_guide/545/business_and_finance/business_card_etiquette.html, accessed May 15, 2021.
- Communicating Across Cultures: http://www.culture-at-work.com/ex1xcincidents.html, accessed May 15, 2021.
- How Tipping Works: http://people.howstuffworks.com/tipping4.htm, accessed May 15, 2021.
- Journal of Intercultural Communication: http://www.immi.se/intercultural/, accessed May 15, 2021.

- 窦卫霖编著. (2007)《跨文化交际基础》[M]. 北京:对外经济贸易大学出版社.
- 顾曰国主编. (2000)《跨文化交际》[M]. 北京:外语教学与研究出版社.
- 何维湘,John Jamison,Peter H. Antoniou,Katherine Whitman 编著. (2004)《跨文化交际技巧》[M]. 广州:中山大学出版社.
- 胡超编著. (2006)《跨文化交际实用教程》[M]. 北京:外语教学与研究出版社.
- 胡文仲. (1999)《跨文化交际学概论》[M]. 北京:外语教学与研究出版社.
- 胡文仲主编. (1999)《跨文化交际面面观》[M]. 北京:外语教学与研究出版社.
- 林大津,谢朝群. (2005)《跨文化交际学:理论与实践》[M]. 福州:福建人民出版社.
- 刘凤霞编著. (2005)《跨文化交际教程》[M]. 北京:北京大学出版社.
- 史兴松. (2007)《跨文化语言社会化进程中跨文化交际能力的培养》[M]. 北京:对外经济贸易大学出版社.
- 宋莉主编. (2004)《跨文化交际导论》[M]. 哈尔滨:哈尔滨工业大学出版社.
- 王催春,朱冬碧,吕政主编. (2008)《跨文化交际》[M]. 北京:北京理工大学出版社.
- 文秋芳主编. (2005)《跨文化口语教程》[M]. 北京:外语教学与研究出版社.
- 邢建玉. (2007)《跨文化商务交流中的关系管理——中方商务代表团访英案例分析》[M]. 北京:对外经济贸易大学出版社.
- 许力生主编. (2004)《跨文化交际英语教程》[M]. 上海:上海外语教育出版社.
- 许力生主编. (2004)《跨文化交流入门》[M]. 杭州:浙江大学出版社.
- 许力生主编. (2008)《跨文化交际》(学生用书)[M]. 上海:上海外语教育出版社.

- 尹丕安主编.(2007)《跨文化交际——理论与实践》[M].西安:西北工业大学出版社.
- 余卫华主编.(2006)《跨文化研究读本》[M].武汉:武汉大学出版社.
- 张爱琳主编.(2008)《跨文化交际》[M].重庆:重庆大学出版社.
- 张红玲.(2007)《跨文化外语教学》[M].上海:上海外语教育出版社.

跨文化交际（第 2 版）

尊敬的老师：

　　您好！

　　本书练习题配有参考答案，请联系责任编辑索取。同时，为了方便您更好地使用本教材，获得最佳教学效果，我们特向使用该书作为教材的教师赠送本教材配套电子资料。如有需要，请完整填写"教师联系表"并加盖所在单位系（院）公章，免费向出版社索取。

北京大学出版社

------------------------✂------------------------

教 师 联 系 表

教材名称	跨文化交际（第 2 版）		
姓名：	性别：	职务：	职称：
E-mail：	联系电话：	邮政编码：	
供职学校：	所在院系：		（章）
学校地址：			
教学科目与年级：	班级人数：		
通信地址：			

　　填写完毕后，请将此表邮寄给我们，我们将为您免费寄送本教材配套资料，谢谢！

北京市海淀区成府路 205 号
北京大学出版社外语编辑部　吴宇森
邮政编码：100871
电子邮箱：wuyusen@pup.cn

外语编辑部电话：010-62759634
邮　购　部　电话：010-62534449
市场营销部电话：010-62750672